Tinkle Tinkle Little Star

Simon John G. Edgington

ISBN: 1508933723
ISBN-13: 978-1508933724

FOREWORD

I like reading autobiographies. Somewhat star struck and keen to find out about the journeys that celebrities and people in public have taken before reaching that status where by they become a household name to all of us, either Internationally or within the borders of their homeland.

With the exception of achieving that "Celebrity status", what they all seem to have in common with me is humble beginnings flavored with self doubt and inadequacies. Also I share with many, that fear of one of these days the entertainment police will surely knock on my door and declare to me "OK buddy; you have been found out! What on earth did you think you were doing? How on earth did you imagine you would get away with THIS!"

I have not reached the destination of Celebrity. (Yet! Quite honestly now like a dog chasing a car, I am not sure I would know what to do with it if I caught it!) I am not a household name, and for that reason when people have suggested that I write a book about my life's journey, I have constantly resisted. But then a very wise young lady pointed out to me, "Forget about the destination, life is about the journey, Everybody's journey is interesting, I would like to read about your journey as I am sure many others would too."

Well that got me thinking. Maybe there is some truth to that Mantra .. "Life should not be about the destination, but the journey." I began to ponder. How much would I have liked to be able to read my Paternal Grandfathers story? Wounded in the First World War. Married three times. All sisters! How much do I know about my Fathers journey, and now he is gone how much would I love to have that story. All of my relatives, friends, Brothers (and Sisters) in arms in the Entertainment world have stories worth sharing for all of those reasons.

This is my story, as I recollect it, from my perspective. My truth. My feelings. Honestly related. Yes, fading memory and poetic license may from time to time present inaccuracies. Being a romantic soul at heart, I tell my tale in a family friendly voice. However; out of respect (and gratitude), for the ladies who shared the more intimate aspect of my adolescent journey, I have kept them anonymous. Names have been changed to protect the guilty! Do not regard this to be a history textbook. Just a chronicle; of a time as seen through the eyes of this storyteller.

So Reader. If we are related, or somehow our paths have crossed to the extent that you feel you would like to know more about my life's journey, I hope I can share this with you in a way that is not too self indulgent as to make you yawn and gaze side on to this publication as you contemplate "I've still got a lot more pages to read than I have read!"

INTRODUCTION

2014, Torrevieja Spain, My House.

I have a houseguest this weekend. My 12-year-old Grandson, Daniel. He was looking forward to us hanging out together. I don't get home so much as my music takes me around the world. My timetable involves long periods away followed by maybe breaks at home of between 6 to eight weeks.

My, how he has grown since I last saw him ! Concerned about how Granddad was going to amuse an 12 year old for a weekend. I needn't have worried, its not so hard. Just add food!

Having grown up in a time of imagination, climbing trees, playing outside, exploring the occasional derelict building, I really know nothing neither care for Wii games, Sony Play Stations, and other various electronic amusements. I always argued to my own kids if they spent the same amount of effort learning proper computer skills, or like me learning to play a musical instrument, it might prove more profitable in life than getting to level five in Doom or Grand Theft Auto.

It was a message I believed in but somehow failed to get across to my kids. So imagine my delight when in the generation after, Daniel showed an interest in my piano.

I asked him, "Would you like me to show you where it all started for me? If you like I can show you the very first thing I taught myself to play on the piano "

The beginning of my musical journey on piano was St Louis Blues. A twelve bar blues featuring three chords was the start of a career that has employed me for over 35 years and counting. It has sent me around the globe and enabled me to visit all the countries I could only dream of visiting. And fair to say a number of destinations that I didn't particularly care to go to. But even those experiences were part of an overall fulfilling life's journey.

I thought back to 18 year old Simon on his mothers newly acquired piano. St Louis Blues was a good first exercise for me. I remember what was hard to do. Holding my left hand in a claw shape to play the every other note forming the C, F, G, Chords which I learnt years earlier on guitar. Without embellishment, I showed Daniel the chords and the right hand melody. He was determined and it was a joy to see him practice.

I have never taught. I didn't care for my school teachers maybe with the exception of Mr. John my music teacher. But I have always believed in the art of entertainment to grab someone's attention. So I attempted to entertain Daniel and try to encourage his enthusiasm.

"This song was the start of my career, " I explained. "Whatever career you choose to pursue, you need to apply the same discipline and staying power as it takes to learn a song on the piano. Every new skill or tune is like Money In The Bank! So as you attempt this simple exercise, which will get easier with practice and perseverance, I want you to recite these words when you make a mistake. If you error in the chord of C, you must say 'DO YOU WANT FRIES WITH THAT?' If it is the F chord that is giving you difficulty then say ' WELCOME TO THE CALL CENTRE, HOW MAY I BE OF ASSISTANCE? " He was both encouraged by the challenge and amused by the penalty which did have a poignant message. Not to be disrespectful to those serving fries at McDonalds, many students do as a means to an end and support their studies. But I would venture a guess that they all see that as incentive to succeed in their ultimate goals, rather than an alternative career option. As for the call Centre reference. What can I say, it made both Daniel and me laugh!

Well on that weekend, I was very encouraged that he wanted me to give him some pointers to take home with him to practice on the Keyboard I gave him some time ago. To begin with the piano playing was taking its time and showing marked improvement, but his Indian accent .... Just Brilliant!

So my mother's purchase of a piano was the start of my career on the keyboard, it wasn't my first instrument. My first instrument was a cardboard guitar and my first public performance was on my 11th birthday in the assembly hall of Ley Hill Junior School Four Oaks Sutton Coldfield. But my dream of being an entertainer goes back a lot further than that even !

DEDICATION

Frederick Thomas Edgington

For My Grandfather

Frederick Thomas Edgington

1894 – 1988

Born in the 19th Century.

He gave us our name.

And for my Grandson

Daniel Lee Edgington Navarro

Born 2001

One Hundred and seven years later

Who carries our name forward

Into the 21st Century !

Foreword

Introduction

Dedication

ACKNOWLEDGMENTS

Thank you for the many of you who have prompted me to tell this story. No one more surprised than me, that so many of you want to read it! Thank you to my friends, in particular Magdalena Lachowicz, a fellow Entertainer and Sharon Rutland for reading my text, providing valuable feedback, inspiration and encouragement. Special thanks for my Brother Adam Tomas Burton. His design genius; for cover and help with photographs.

1 EARLY MEMORIES 77. PARK ROAD

I was born in Warrington Cheshire in the early fifties. Britain was well recovering from the Second World War. By the time I had arrived, there was considerable modernization, Queen Elizabeth ll was recently crowned, we had a Modern National Health Service, and Electricity. It was a comfortable moment I think to time my arrival.

I have no recollection of Warrington; I don't think we were there for long. Both my parents were from Four Oaks Sutton Coldfield, in the leafy county of Warwickshire. The first house I recall is 77 Park Road Sutton Coldfield. This was, and remains today a small two up two down quaint Terrace house with a bay window overlooking a modest front garden hedged with a small wooden latched gate, right bang next to the Town entrance of Sutton Park.

My Father Warwick, was then working for Black and Decker in Birmingham selling power tools among other things. Our house was handy for the train to Birmingham. We just turned left up the station path under the tunnel. The tunnel was a great treat for a youngster to try out his lungs. A long arched brick construction, which reverberated the sounds of Morris minor exhaust sounds as they passed through and the whoops, hollers and screams of a young boy. My first echo chamber!

At some time during our time in Number 77, Dad changed jobs, and was able to pursue his passion as a photographer, working for a Kodak Eastman Dealers. Leonard Ellis's. He was later to tell me tales of Wedding Photograph Sessions and also presenting films using a huge Projector set up with a loudspeaker system. The advantage of this line of work was that he was provided with a Bedford van to drive around in or sometimes Mr. Ellis would make his car available for the family to use. A legacy of my father's keenness of photography is a large collection of slides. Taken mainly on family holidays. We were able to view them on a contraption that he won in a photograph competition. It had a screen and a large bright light. You loaded the slides into the carriage at the top and push the handle and the slide would be presented in front of the light and shine onto the small screen at the front of this contraption. As I type this on my laptop today, eyes glued to a similar screen, I wonder at how technology has progressed since then!

Warwick Greatrex Edgington My Father

My Mother Marie; a beautiful lady. She was schooled for some time in Horton, a residential catholic convent school. Then she became a student at Sutton Art College. She was the oldest of two girls, her sister Christine ten years her junior. My parents Married in Sutton Coldfield and Honeymooned at the Lodge in Arthog on the Welsh coast. I have photos of my father posing pipe in mouth and my mother looking like a Hollywood starlet glamorously posing with cigarette in hand. How times / fashions change!

Marie Therese Philomena Hope My Mother

Being so close to the entrance to Sutton Park was a great place to live. In 1957 The Queen came to Sutton Park for the International Scout Jamboree. My father captured pictures of the motorcade as the procession literally drove right past our front door. The street was covered in bunting and the crowd was out in force all dressed in their Sunday best to welcome our new Queen. Was I upstairs in the bay window waving my Union Jack as the car drove by? I would like to say I was, but maybe I was just four years old then and it is Dads slide photo's that have produced those memories. But I do remember well that magical moment on a small bike, training wheels removed when my father running behind me clutching the back of my saddle released his grip and I was like a bird in first flight. I learnt to ride my bike! What a big boy now!

But I am getting ahead of myself! I was three when my Sister Sally arrived. Don't think I quite knew what to do about this. I was used to all the attention. Who was this intruder into my comfortable world? I think throughout our childhood Sally and I shared a sibling rivalry, I know as kids we used to squabble lots. Thankfully, we were to become best friends in adulthood.

One of my most prevalent memories of our time at 77 was every week had a Gangan day. This was my Mothers mother, my Gangan as we all called her. Well my father actually called her the Queen Mother and My mum and her younger sister Christine both called her Mummy. Her real name was Leonora Ethel Hope. Photographs of her youth revealed that she was quite a beauty in her day. She originated from London and had been a dancer in her teens. For a lady by this time in her fifties, she still had an elegant well-proportioned figure. She was always immaculate in her turn out, and wore horn-rimmed spectacles. She was very proper, perhaps to the extent of snobbery. Keeping up appearances was important to her. Quite a force to reckon with about the jewelry quarter which Hockley was referred as. She was a director of Samuel Hope Ltd manufacturing jewelers in Vyce street Birmingham, not too far from Winson Green Prison.

Leonora's Husband, my grandfather, a large rotund gentleman, Dennis helped form the Catholic Church in near Mere Green. During the war he was an Air raid warden. His profession was that of manufacturing Jeweler. He carried on the family business from his father. My Mother always told me about what a wonderful man he was. Sadly I never knew him. He died in his forties of a cerebral hemorrhage, before I was born.

Leonora Ethel Hope "Gangan"

So Leonora, or Gangan to me, became the remaining Hope of Samuel Hope Ltd. Every Thursday, she would take the train to Birmingham, followed by I am guessing a taxi from New Street Station to the jewelry quarter to do her director things which more will be mentioned of later. The point of me mentioning any of this now reader is every Thursday she would take the same train home, from Birmingham New Street presumably after some shopping and Lunch at Rackham's Department Store and alight at Sutton Station. Walk under the tunnel down towards Park Road and number 77.

Young Simon would be waiting eagerly in the window. Gazing expectantly through the gateway. Standing on the large windowsill so that he could see over the garden hedge. Ready to wave a greeting every Thursday to Dad's Queen Mother as he did when the Queen came to visit.

I loved my Gangan; she features quite prominently in my early years. The first memory however has to be these visits. We would sit in the lounge in the bay window, decorated with the most dreadful curtains (Reference the slides) and she would teach me the days of the week. Friday, Saturday,

Sunday, Monday, Tuesday, Wednesday, Gangan Day!

Gangan's House was "Chadsway" a detached four-bedroom house on the Lichfield Road just north of the village Mere Green. Number 405. Chadsway is the venue of most of my childhood memories. We had three homes during my childhood, but Chadsway was always a constant.

When you turned into a small driveway across a grass verge separating the house from the pavement, you were presented with a house with a garage built into the building on the left, a front door with a wooden surround with the word "Chadsway" emblazoned in black above the door. To the right of the front door, a large bay window looking into the dining room where many a Christmas feast, Sunday Lunch, and family dinners would be enjoyed.

Apparently I was told on enquiring that Chad or St Chad as the Catholics refer to him was once navigating his way along the A38 as indeed Lichfield Rd once was before being renamed the A5127 in the 70's Hence "Chadsway"

So we can presumably safely say without contradiction. Chad was definitely here!

Of course alternatively Chad could have travelled to Birmingham the way my Gangan did. By train. After all, Butlers Lane Halt is just around the corner. Down the road; linking Lichfield Road with Clarence Road. What on earth was it called? Of course Butlers lane! I wonder if it was so named because that was where all the butlers to these fine houses on Lichfield Road lived?

The Garden at Chadsway was a joy for a young child and his younger sister to play in. The back of the house opened onto a huge patio with steps leading down to a path either side framing a beautiful lawn. The path would continue down past the flowerbed at the foot of the lawn and enter an apple orchid. What a wonderful playground for us kids while the adults did adult things and talked adult talk. I used to move the stones on the steps that would reveal colonies of ants that I would harass quite ruthlessly. Ladybirds in abundance would be there to find. Count the spots, count the spots. In the summer we had to beware of wasps. I got stung, What a shock! You don't mess with them! Even to this day I am very uncomfortable around wasps, much to my families amusement.

The Garden at "Chadsway"

My Fathers parents Fredrick Thomas Edgington and my father's stepmother Dorothy had a house at the Mere Green end of Little Sutton Lane. It was a beautiful detached home similar in size to Chadsway and similarly, with a well husbanded garden. The main difference being my grandfather, Grandy as he became known to all the family was a keen gardener, carpenter before the term Do It Yourself was voiced. Grandy worked as a sales rep for Buck and Hickman tool wholesalers. His job involved visiting Ironmongers in his area and demonstrating the latest in house hold tools. Consequently he owned a large inventory of tools and was a most skilled craftsman. A slight dapper man; always the English gentleman.

He married late for his era. Probably due to adolescence, interrupted by the First World War. He served in the South Staffordshire Regiment; I only know that because later on he gave me his campaign medals of which he had many. He also gave me a metal cigarette case, emblazoned with the South Staffordshire Badge. This had a huge dent in it, the story goes caused by a bullet bouncing off his breast pocket. Saving his life. Ironic to think that in this instance smoking not only saved Fredrick Thomas Edgington's life, but also the line of Edgingtons to follow him!

Frederick Thomas Edgington "Grandy" and Dorothy

He was stretchered out of the trench that was the end of his war. He never spoke to anyone about his war. Being the gentleman he was, it was made very clear that that was something that had to be done, but it was most distasteful a thing to relive. There was many who shared that attitude post first and second war. It was never mentioned in School history lessons in my day. I guess the wounds needed time to heal first.

At the age of four and a half, I was packed off to school. My first school was private. Keys School Sutton Coldfield. I have very little memory of this school. I remember it was an old mansion type building. I recall break time when we were all given a putrid warm bottle of milk that had been left in crates outside in the sun. It was a third of a pint, and in those days all school children had free milk. It came with Tony Benn and the National Health Service and the Labour Government.

About this time things were a foot for a change. My parents had managed to put a deposit on a brand new house in Four Oaks on a brand new Cul De Sac development in Crockford drive. Number 23. It meant a change of school, the new house was only a short walk from Chadsway so I was delighted that I would be living near to my Gangan! Our house must have been one of the first to be completed. We would take excursions up there to visit the work in progress. It was very exciting to see a building site. Lots of dumper trucks, trenches, ladders, partly built walls, what a fantastic play ground for a young kid. No such thing as health and safety back in those days a hard hat was nowhere to be seen. Builders would wear a trilby or a cloth cap. Most likely with a pencil stuck behind his ear. I remember asking one of the builders what was in his sandwich. "Kippers Legs" he replied. One should be careful about what one says to young children, I have believed Kippers have legs ever since!

I guess it was my Grandmothers influence with the Catholic Church that had some bearing on the decision to send now 5-year-old Simon to St Josephs Catholic School. I was introduced to the head master one day, and told that this was going to be something really special. So the days of 77 Park Road were drawing to an end. We were moving to Mere Green, and I was to leave Keys School and its disgusting milk bottles and attend St Josephs.

2 CHADSWAY, CROCKFORD DRIVE, SCHOOL.

The family were all very excited. We were moving to our brand new house. Crockford drive was still a building site. A T shaped Cul De sac, number 23 was situated at the end of the left of the T's cross. Still muddy from construction works on the incomplete houses, Crockford drive was a veritable adventure playground for the kids on the drive.

I soon met some friends, mostly a bit older than me. The older kids would show me dens they made among the piles of cement bags and sand. Old scraps of wood planking used to form a roof. Goodness knows what the builders must have thought when they came to work the next day and found some creatures had nested in amongst their work place.

The builders were friendly. As builders are. Where there is a kid, there's a Mum. Where there is a Mum, and you are friendly to her little darlings, there is the prospect of a plentiful flow of tea and biscuits!

So it was off to St Josephs Catholic School I went. The teachers were Nuns, I remember before I went to St Josephs one day the family went to my Mums old convent School Hornton for a visit. The nuns there were pleased to see my mother and her young children. We had tea and biscuits with them, and they all talked about how much they love little Val Doonigan on the TV and asked me how much was I looking forward to going to the catholic school. I shyly replied, "Oh yes very much Sister" before returning to my chocolate digestive.

On the journey home my mother remarked on how lovely and friendly the nuns had been during our visit. So much friendlier than when she was actually at school there. I was to discover the exact same. St Josephs was a tyranny, and the Nuns were tyrants. Instilling a fear of God, Hell and damnation into the souls of parents little darlings. Corporal punishment was conducted at every school assembly in front of the whole school. Children were beaten across the hand with a long cane for reasons that I could not fathom.

The school building was of a prefabricated construction. It comprised of a long corridor with classrooms leading off its length on both sides. It was a miserable place to be. I honestly cannot recall how long I was there, but I was scared, I was learning nothing and eventually my parents took me out of there and put me in Mere Green Infants School.

This was a nice village school. I can remember Christmas there. Even Santa Clause visited that school. We all congregated in the hall, excitedly speculating on how Santa would arrive. Somebody suggested helicopter, so we were all listening intently for the sounds of the rotor blades. This was a huge magical treat, so much nicer than the evil Nuns at St Josephs and their stories of Satan and Hell. Eventually Santa arrived. I was quite puzzled by the fact, even at an early age that such a totally international icon such as Santa Clause or Saint Nicolas should have such a broad Birmingham accent. It was quite uncanny how similar his voice was to the old school caretaker in fact!

Somebody mentioned to me that I should make sure I wear clean underpants when it's PE Physical Education Day. Because all the children just wear their pants and vests for PE. So in the cloakroom I wasn't really paying any attention to the other kids getting ready. Being shy, I didn't want to take my shorts off in front of strangers so I hid in one of the toilet cubicles until all the boys went through the door into the hall. Then I sneaked out gingerly and through the door into the hall hoping that nobody would pay any attention to me. That plan couldn't have got a more opposite result. What I hadn't realized was not only was I about to draw attention to myself, I was about to create an anecdote for everybody to recite for the remainder of my school career.

Everybody noticed me. Everybody was laughing at this small boy in his Ladybird Underpants. All the boys were still wearing their shorts. Only the girls did PE in their Blue School Knickers!

I have always been smaller than average. Even as an Infant School Pupil I was smaller than my classmates, despite the fact that my Gangan called me a big boy now because I was going to school.

Playtime was the time of interaction. I suppose the playground or schoolyard was actually quite small, but to a five or six year old, it was enormous. Situated so that the main buildings at either end surrounded it, a whitewashed wall on one side and classroom huts on the other side.

There was one boy who was perhaps as much bigger than the rest as I was smaller. He discovered quite early on that he could rule the roost in the school playground.

Christopher Temple was the class bully. I was new to the class, and at playtime I hadn't yet made any new school friends. I would occupy my little corner of the playground and watch the kids playing. I noticed another lad who was quite small too. In fact to be honest, he was a bit smaller than me! I watched him playing with his mates, and he seemed to have a lot of mates. Then I watched Christopher and his crony's move in on him. He started pushing his way amongst them and they all laughed at him and ran away.

I suppose I was getting a bit close now as I watched this spectacle. Because as Christopher, turned to find alternative prey, his eyes caught mine. Within a flash he was in front of me slowly rotating his fists contemplating his move. I was going to die! I was frozen to the spot in fear like a deer being stalked by a lion. If I ran, instinct told me I would just provide good sport and still be pursued and captured, if I raised my puny hands I would be beaten so I just stood there unable to move apart from the now uncontrollable trembling.

My heart was beating like a drum I could do nothing but await my fate. The school bell sounded and my nemesis took flight. Raincoat blazing behind him only held on by its hood he wore it like a cape and disappeared with his arms spread like wings as he hooted the sound of Rolls Royce Merlin Engine. My nemesis had turned into a Spitfire. Empty arms trailing like wings. Wing tips decorated with flapping woolen mittens tied together by a length of elastic threaded up one sleeve and down the other. Oh no! First Nuns in habits and now I am being bullied by a rain coated boxing Spitfire.

Christopher Temple was no doubt the very first Transformer.

I went home in tears. I didn't like school I wept. "I hate school!" Eventually my mother got the reason out of me and she must have mentioned it to my father because he came and gave me some advice. "Bullies are just cowards" he said "It's really quite simple, all you have to do is find the biggest one and just punch him on the nose ………. Hard!"

Well that was it. I was sorted.

The next day we had painting. We had wooden easels that sat on our desks. These held the paper upright. The paints came in powder. The idea was you wet your brush in the Robinsons jam Jar containing water, then dip the wet brush in the paint powder, then paint your picture.

To this day reader I have to declare this is a skill that I have never mastered. If you put too much water on the brush, then as soon as you touch your paper you get a nice result for a millisecond and then the paint will run down the page. I was looking at everyone else's efforts; they were doing well compared to me. Houses with chimneys with smoke and trees. Lovely efforts. All I could produce was colored rain pouring down a window! Until, I made an exciting discovery.

If you got the water / Paint ratio just right and held your brush upright and flicked it backwards and forwards towards the paper, you got some really cool spotty effects. Mix the colors about and the result was a very pleasing abstract spotty scene. The more I did this the spottier my page became. This was good, much better than those houses and trees the other kids were painting.

In fact I looked at my masterpiece and decided to glance at theirs for comparison now that I was getting the hang of this.

Surprisingly my neighbors painting were now containing spotty features too. Flipping copycats I thought. But they were not looking pleased. It turned out that my flicking paint technique not only landed spots on my painting. Spots landed on everyone else's painting too. When I flicked backwards, just as much paint left my brush as when I flicked forwards so I too was completely spotty from head to toe. As was the desk, the floor and the ceiling immediately above me. The teacher stepped in to stop me much to the amusement of the class.

Robert Brown was the boy next to me. As tall as Christopher Temple, my nemesis but not as bulky. All the kids were laughing at me, I remembered my dad's advice so here we go, I punched poor Robert hard, right in the nose.

I was confused, and I guess so was he. He stood there with a puzzled look, tears welling in his eyes and not unlike my paint running down the page a trickle of red ran down from poor Roberts nostril. I made his nose bleed. Sorry Dad, but how was that supposed to make me feel better?

Play time again. I walked out towards the railing leading towards the playground. Two boys were waiting by the entrance. One was the small boy I had noticed the day before. The other was Robert Brown. I walked towards them then tried to avoid them by dodging under the railing. But they were too quick for me and had me cornered. Oh no school sucks, but it doesn't matter any more because now I am definitely going to die.

The small boy said to me "My mum says it's not nice to hit each other and we need you to say you are sorry for hitting my friend Robert "

I was sorry. I think I cried and I said sorry and that is the story of how Robert Brown and John Chawner his little buddy from that moment on became my best friends through school. Christopher Temple too. He quickly grew out of that phase and turned out to be a great kid in the end.

I read Janet and John and Chicken Licken books at that school. I think I was behind with my reading skills, because myself and one or two others would go to a class room way up in the attic of the main school and have extra reading tuition. I read and read about Janet and John and how the sky was falling on Chicken Licken's head.

I cannot recall how this was diagnosed, but apparently I had flat feet. To correct this every Tuesday afternoon my mother would collect me from school and we would take the Midland Red Bus to Sutton from Mere Green. During that time, it was my time with Mum. I loved our Tuesday afternoons. We would get off the bus at the Upper Parade. Sometimes we visited the Tudor Rose Gents Barbers, I would get a Roman Haircut ! Which made me feel very special. Then we would visit the bike shop. My Christmas or Birthday? Present was to be a Dawes Dapper Bicycle and mum was paying 5 shillings a week towards it. I would see my bike gleaming in the window. 24inch wheels, So much more grown up than the little bike I had learned to ride on in Sutton park which I was still having to ride around Crockford Drive.

Then it was off to Paterson's Café on Sutton Parade for a Horlicks and a large white iced bun for lunch. We had called in on WH Smiths for a She Magazine for Mum and a Beazer Comic for me. I would save my Beazer for the waiting room at the Cottage Hospital where I went to have these foot exercises. I would be waiting to go impatiently whilst Mum smoked a Kensitas Cigarette.

She never really smoked properly. She would sit elegantly drinking her Horlicks and holding the cigarette stylishly between her index and middle finger like a Hollywood poster. I have never in my life experienced any body that could somehow have an entire cigarette burn down to a long piece of ash without ever falling away. "Can we go now Mummy?" "Yes darling, as soon as I've finished my cigarette!" She never inhaled, she would just smack her lips and a secondary cloud of smoke by her mouth would augment the smoke billowing from the burnt ash and drift off into the atmosphere that was Patterson's Café.

My foot clinic regime comprised of picking up marbles with my toes, and walking along an inverted wooden PE Bench intended to encourage my big toe to act independently to the rest. Curiously, my big toe is shorter than the one next to it. This seemed to create a lot of interest in the therapist. I have never since heard of such therapy. I really cannot say what it was about. I was unhappy because I had to wear Clarkes Shoes instead of baseball boots like the other kids in School. But, to this day; if I drop a towel in the bathroom. I can pick it up with my toes!

Life was good in Four Oaks. After School on a Monday we would walk up to Gangan's at Chadsway for tea. She had a TV and on Monday night we could watch Popeye.

TV was very much in its infancy. There was only one Channel to watch. BBC. Eventually Independent Television was born and Leonora Hope needed to buy a television with a channel selector switch. Ever the centre of society and hostess with the mostess well when it came to choice of TV programs, she acquired a brand new modern TV so that on a Saturday afternoon Jean Bertioli and other neighbors could come round and have afternoon tea and professional wrestling on ATV!

So the old BBC only TV which was a huge wooden cabinet, with a small cathode ray tube screen was passed on to us at Crockford Drive.

It was a magnificent piece of modern technology in so many ways. Did I say wooden cabinet? Well on first appearance that is exactly what it looked like. It would have done Chippendale proud! But in actual fact is was molded out of Bakelite a new material of the 20th century. It was being seen more and more as a wooden substitute because it could be molded to any shape.

What was interesting about modern materials, they enter the market, mimicking their predecessor and then as their own properties become recognized then design concepts develop with the new material in mind. What ever happened to Bakelite? Well in one word Plastic! One of Bakelite's drawbacks was it was quite brittle. It would crack like china! Bakelite is still used for electrical circuits, motor distributer caps because of its insulating properties, but I guess when the invention of other plastics soon followed, Bakelite products were to be relegated to museums.

The black and white screen was small and took about long enough to turn on and warm up that you found yourself checking the wall behind it to see if the thing was plugged in to the socket. Then one would gaze through the vent grills in the hardboard back of the cabinet to see if any of the valves were glowing with their red luminosity. Then low and behold a humming would occur in the loudspeaker and the screen would illuminate with its rather dull grainy picture.

A portable aerial sat on top of the cabinet. Sometimes it was necessary to move it about to get the optimum quality picture, which to be honest was never really that good.

All of this despite the fact, that within falling distance of our house in Crockford drive, there was the Sutton Coldfield Television Mast. With an aerial so close we should surely have had color. But no, those days were still a long way off.

Then when you turned the television set off, we would watch the picture disappear into the centre of the screen where a bright dot would sit for what seemed an eternity, gradually fading to nothing.

I remember Watch with Mother too. Bill and Ben the flower Pot Men, Muffin The Mule, Tales of the River bank and something with a puppet

Spotty Dog. Ooooooh and lets not forget Andy Pandy.

But Television was never the huge entertainment during my early childhood. The greatest toy that a child could amuse itself with back then was imagination. And we all had that in abundance.

Long before the builders put the fences up in our back gardens in Crockford drive, Grandy came a long smoothed out the rough ground with a rake, gathering all the large stones and putting them into a builders wheel barrow then I can remember him pacing up and down the smooth ground scattering grass seeds in our garden. Some of the owners opted for laying turf. This was more expensive and with a little patience seeding produced a similar result.

Grandy was always elegantly dressed. I can remember even as he was pacing up and down the new lawn scattering seeds he was dressed in a tweed suit with waistcoat and a bow tie. The only concession to the manual labour, which he was carrying out, was a pair of green Wellington Boots!

It was also more exciting, getting up every day and seeing the grass slowly growing turning our brown garden green.

I had a swing in the garden. It was my favorite place. That swing seat wasn't just a swing seat. It was an airplane cockpit. I would soar into the sky, high high as high as the top of the Television mast. I wondered at that mast and what the view must be like up there. My swing seat took me there. Then I would twist round, winding the chains tight until it would turn no more, then spin fast as the seat unwound itself.

The swing was anchored to the ground by four large u shaped tent pegs. It was more than firm enough for me. However my friend Colin Trigg who lived in the big house at the top of the T of Crockford drive flew my swing beyond the envelope one day.

Colin was quite a bit older and bigger than me. He had an older brother Robert and a younger sister Bonnie who was in my class at school.

23 Crockford Drive (Revisited 2012.) Notice the TV mast in the background.

Colin started swinging on my swing determined to put it through its paces. To begin with he got a healthy to and fro going and he would then jump off, momentarily propelling himself skyward and landing in a run on his feet. MMmmm Must try that out myself I thought, quite impressed. Then he got back on and started swinging higher and higher. The swing started to make noises of protest that I had never heard it make before. What was he trying to do, was he really trying to loop the loop on my plane? His seemed to be going beyond parallel with the ground I really felt any time he would swing over the top.

The swings protests seemed to get louder and I could see the base straining and rocking against the tent pegs holding it to the ground. Eventually it happened, this horse was going to have no more of it, this plane was going in, this game was about to end. Messily!

In one final swing the hind legs of the ride kicked away its anchors and bucked into the air like a stallion it ejected its rider forward so that poor Colin landed face first into the newly sown grass. The top of the swing flipped forward to the ground landing squarely across the back of his shins. The seat remained airborne a little longer twisting and chains rattling a death cry before angrily slapping him I thought quite unnecessarily across the back of his head.

For a moment silence prevailed. It was a very very short moment, then a cry. No, a scream erupted from Colin. "Mummy !!!!!! "He yelped "Mummy !!!!!" Within a millisecond he had untangled himself from the wreckage and took flight for home. "Mummy " I could hear as he ran back to his mum.

The days at Mere Green Infants School were drawing to an end. Now after the summer Holidays, John Chawner, Robert Brown, Christopher Temple Bonnie Trigg many others and my self were to move to our next school. Ley Hill Juniors School.

Some changes had occurred in Dads life too. He had a friend called Roy Suttle, Roy's son Steven was in my class. Roy owned a second hand shop / café in Willenhall. He drove a Commer van with sliding doors and Dad would sometimes help him at weekends deliver furniture or pick it up from his shop. Sometimes I got to tag along, which was great fun for me because I got to play shop. In the shop.

This was not Roy's full time job. Roy's full time job was a Life Insurance sales man for the Manufacturers Life Insurance Company of Toronto Canada (Manulife) I don't think he was a very successful sales man with Manulife, he was a successful second hand salesman / café proprietor however.

My father showed an interest in Manulife. He rather thought he could turn his hand to that sort of thing. Roy set him up with an interview.

It was a change in fortune for my father, and all of the family. He took to selling Life Insurance like a bird takes to the wing. Before his mode of transport would be Grandy's car or Ellis's Kodak van, now he was able to buy a car for the family.

One of our neighbors mentioned that he had a car for sale that the family had grown out of. It was a convertible Morris Minor. What fun.

This summer holiday, we had arranged with one of Dads colleagues at Manulife to hire a holiday home in Anglesey the small island just off Bangor North Wales. Assad Obied was his name. He was supposedly a Lebanese

Sheik who not only sold Life Insurance for Manulife but also worked as a TV extra on shows such as Danger Man starring Patrick McGowan. What was it about Manulife that everybody who worked there had a second job?

Sally and me and our Morris Minor

We had a nice two weeks at Anglesey. The house we rented belonged to a fireman. He was building another house next door that would eventually become the family home, but for the time being, he and his family had converted the double garage into a temporary home. Strange. A fireman; who worked as a builder too. I wondered if he also sold Life Insurance for Manulife.

Towards the end of the holiday we met another family from Sutton Coldfield. The Jones's. Mr. Jones was a schoolteacher. Mr. Jones it turned out wasn't any old schoolteacher. It turned out that he was the Deputy Head at Ley Hill School, where I was due to start next term time.

My father became friendly with Mr. Jones. My father was a friendly man, a funny man who always reminded me of the actor David Jason. I rather suspect that I was not the only person to suggest that to him. Because when I did in much later life, he annoyingly snapped that he had never been able to stand that irritating man!

But when we suggested David Jason, it was never intended in a Del Boy way, which my father was never like and I understand why such a comparison would sting, more as a Granville in his early days and I think in his later years Jack Frost. I have great affection for David Jason because of this.

The reason why it appears that Manulife salesmen have other jobs is that selling life insurance for a living is very difficult. You have to exploit all of your contacts in life, and if you pride yourself with honesty and integrity as my Father did, to do that with a clear conscience you have to be able to believe in your product.

Dad believed in his product, and didn't need to have a second job because he became very successful at underwriting life insurance. When Roy Suttle first came into our lives, we were adorned with marketing paraphernalia from Manulife. There were two main give a ways. The Calendar flip over Telephone Index and the large Globe Poster of Earth with a monthly calendar attached below. Emblazoned in large letters was "Presented by Roy Suttle Life underwriter"

My father never really discussed his job with me. He just went out to work in the morning and came home at night. But his presence became evident everywhere I went. If we had to go visit Dr. Malim in his surgery, there on the wall in the waiting room was a Manufactures life Insurance company World Map Calendar on the wall Presented By Warwick Edgington. When we entered the surgery, there on Doctor Malim's Desk was the Calendar Telephone Directory in pride of place.

The corner shop in Hill Village road just a short walk from Crockford Drive where occasionally Mum would stop and treat me to a Sherbet Fountain, Milky way or packet of Rollo's. As the shopkeeper put thru pence in the till there beside the "A Mars a day helps you work rest and play" poster was the Manulife World Calendar poster presented by Warwick Edgington Life Underwriter.

Then if you went into the dining room at Chadsway, Just inside the door was a large oak chest. On it sat a peculiar wooden Buddha holding a crocodile, both the Buddha and the crocodile sported teeth made of ivory. Next to this sat a miniature wooden chest of drawers full of assorted buttons. On the right of the chest sat Gangan's Telephone and beside that,

the inevitable Manulife Calendar phone directory presented by ......?
You've guessed it!

What a brilliant marketing tool this must have been for my father. Because every year end; he would visit his clients with their new calendar for the next year. How much repeat business and referrals to new clients must he have generated with those calendars.

Mr. Jones was never my teacher at Ley Hill. He was in Class 1 for fourth year pupils. I was in Class 2 Mrs. Wheetly's class in my fourth year at Ley Hill, but when I had occasion to run an errand for Mrs. Wheatly, which involved me asking for some chalk or whatever from Mr. Jones. There on the wall behind his desk was the old faithful Warwick Edgington World Calendar.

3 SUPER HERO'S

Eventually the houses were all completed, and one by one they became inhabited by new families. Colin Trig and his brother Robert asked me if I would like to join them at the Saturday Matinee at the Empress Cinema in Sutton Town Centre.

We would go on the bus. From Lichfield Rd, just opposite Chadsway, we could catch the Midland Red 112 to Sutton Town Centre right by the Empress Cinema. It cost 3d Thru pence return. Six pence or Nine pence; to get into the Cinema. Dad said he wanted me to get the nine penny ticket and go upstairs in the circle, away from all the rough kids ???. In fact everybody's dad said the same thing, so he was only repeating what he had heard.

Well we set off on our adventure, went down the footpath at the side of the White Lion and came out in a pub car park on Lichfield Road right next to the bus stop.

Most of the Midland Red Buses, running to and through Mere Green Village were double decker's. I was familiar with the 112 because it was the single decker service that ran between Birmingham and Lichfield via Sutton Coldfield. We speculated on why only this bus was a single decker. Maybe there were some low bridges to negotiate near Lichfield, we didn't really know. To us kids, it just was!

Well Thru pence; for the bus. I think we paid a penny half penny (Pronounced Haipney) each way, don't recall return tickets. We would get on the bus and pay our money to the conductor. All excited about our adventure to Sutton. We passed through Mere Green Village and down to Four Oaks Methodist church by Four Oaks Railway Station on down Lichfield road towards Sutton. As we came into the town the first thing I saw as I gazed out of the steamy window of the bus was Bishop Vesey Grammar School. I knew this building because it had been pointed out to me before. "That's where my Dad went to school!" I exclaimed. Then a bit further on was Sutton Art College "And that's where my Mum went to learn art." We went on past the Royal Hotel on the right turned down the hill to Sutton Parade and the Empress Cinema.

There were loads of Kids lining up by the marble stairs of the Empress Cinema. A very dapper looking gentleman, dressed in a dark suit and waistcoat stood by the entrance. He had heavily Brill Creamed hair combed over in attempt to disguise a rapidly receding fringe and sported a dapper pencil moustache. I learnt he was the Cinema manager.

As we lined up to enter the cinema, another bus drew up. A 102, Double Decker from Mere Green. Off jumped John Chawner and Robert Brown and they came to join us.

"Hello" said John "Where are you going to sit in the cinema. " " I got to go upstairs in the circle my Dad says." Was my reply. " All our parents say that!" Says John. " But none of us do. It's much more fun downstairs at the front. We all sit together and instead of nine pence to get in, it's only sixpence, which give us thru pence to spend on crisps! "

So we all paid our sixpence entrance and got a packet of Potato Puffs. Oh the fun of eating Potato Puffs in the dark. Every now and then a kid would go "Eurrrrrew!" With Potato Puffs you had to be very careful in the dark not to eat the blue crisp. That was the little bag of salt! As the bags were emptied, we all took turns blowing them up and slapping our hands together in attempt to make the loudest pop, much to the irritation of the cinema manager.

I loved the Saturday morning matinee. Eventually the curtain would rise and we all had to sing the song as the dot bounced over the words projected on the screen.

"We are the boys and girls well know as, Minors of the A B C

And every Saturday we all line up,

To see the films we like and shout aloud with Glee.

We like to laugh and have a sing song,

Just a happy crowd are we,

We're all palls together, we're Minors of the

A.B.C. !"

Then the films would start. There would be some short travel film, followed by a Warner Brothers Cartoon like Bugs Bunny, But then what we all came to see. The weekly Cliff Hanger, which would be either Dan Dare or my personal favorite Batman!

I have a strong recollection of a story line in one Dan Dare Episode that really struck me as amusing. Bare in mind that this was written a good decade before space travel being a reality. The cliffhanger was that the Space ship was disintegrating, falling apart. The following week it was revealed that some entity was eating all the wood in the spacecraft causing the windows to fall out! Ha ha Wood in a spacecraft!

The Batman episodes, were way before the TV show featuring Adam West. These were filmed in the fifties. The week before Batman would have been left in a terrible dilemma that was surely going to be the end of him. The conversation at school was always filled with speculation of how could he possibly escape. But some how by the next Saturday, incredibly escape he always did!

The whole cinema would erupt when the Batman show started. Kids would cheer when their hero gets up just before the train runs him over, or the building explodes and gets after the bad guy, only to find him self in a similar predicament at the end of that episode.

Kids would pour out of the cinema wearing their raincoats like capes, leaping down the marble steps and stampeding across the parade to the bus stop home.

I know I mentioned that I always wanted to be an entertainer. I am now reminded how that was not my first ambition. I was to become an entertainer only if my first ambition was to fall on stony ground.

But my first ambition was to become a super hero!

4 FRIENDS SUTTON PARK

I haven't spoken much about the great diversity of friends my childhood seemed to provide me with.

My first friend and oldest and most consistent even to this day is Philippa. Quite small with Blondie gingery hair, Brown eyes and very very cuddly. Philippa was there to cuddle up to me in my cot when I was very small. If Mum were taking me out to Patterson's café or to Chadsway in my Silver Cross Pram, Philippa would always want to come too.

Philippa had a friend who sometimes used to share our adventures. He was dark in complexion with black tight curled hair. He always wore the same brightly coloured waistcoat and trousers. His name was Golly.

Philippa was my Teddy Bear and Golly was her Gollywog constant companion.

You might be disturbed by the name of Philippa's friend. Well it was an age of innocence and none of the political correctness of today. Some are of the view that we are in more enlightened times now, but our Golly was quite happy.

In fact he told me once at teatime. "If Robinsons Jam could offer Robinson Gollywog Badges as collectable gifts to kids, well frankly Si John" Like my Dad, he always called me Si John "Who am I to complain?" Who indeed?

He particularly liked jam on his sandwiches at teatime. He was a good Golly, not at all like those naughty ones that Enid Blyton wrote about!

Eventually they collected a few other friends. There was a little dog that used to like to hide in little folds of my bedclothes, and quite a few others who must have long gone their separate ways.

Sister Sally had a Cindy Doll. And a Raccoon called Racky So called I believe because Gangan bought her at Rackham's. I was quite jealous that Sindy had all these wonderful accessories that you could buy for her. One birthday I went with Sally to the toyshop to spend her birthday money on treats for Sindy. I think Sally would have preferred to buy the wardrobe, but big brother was having none of it. Sindy definitely needed the Car I insisted to her. Sindy got her car!

If I had been born 10 or 15 years later, I guess I would have had Action Man or GI Joe to play with, but that was yet to happen. So, the cast, of all my imaginary adventures were Philippa Golly and Friends.

Then there were kids of my parents friends. Tony Hofton was a school friend of my father. Julie Clarke was a school friend of Mums. They married and their children Mark and Nicola came along pretty much in perfect sequence to Sally and me.

The Hofton's lived in Wilde Green. One train stop from Sutton Coldfield. 66 Eastern Road. Mark was my best friend. I was born on the 23rd June, Mark just a few days later on the 27th It was quite important to me that I was the oldest! We played together whenever we visited and had sleepovers. And Nicky and Sally would play their girly games.

Because of the different districts of Sutton Coldfield we lived in, we never went to school together and of course we had our own circle of school friends.

Another family who we would see occasionally was the Wheeldons. Bill and Wynne were my Mum and Dads friends. Their daughter Jean was my playmate. She was a girl, but it was all right because she was a bit of a Tom Boy. Eventually this family moved away to Leeds and our visits became less and less.

One thing that has always given me great pleasure even in adulthood was bringing a diverse collection of friends together and enjoying the interaction that then ensured.

The first time this happened was a Birthday Party for Mark and myself at the Faraway Tree in Sutton Park. The Faraway tree (Named after Enid Blyton's Book) is in a secret location called the enchanted wood near Four Oaks entrance of Sutton Park. Near Mayors Arbor. I would have to take you there!

The theme of the party was Cowboys against Indians. I was the cowboy side Mark's side was the Indians. As it turned out every body came as cowboys except John Chawner who had just got a new Indian Chief Feathered Head dress and a bow and arrow set.

So all the cowboys where firing off cap pistols around the wood and John was picking us off one by one with his rubber sucker pointed arrows. If only Paint Ball had been around in those days I would have spotted that Indian again, the way that I did in painting class!

The enchanted wood and the Faraway tree as we called it, was the families favorite spot for many a summers picnic in Sutton Park. I remember one such Sunday I had a Catapult Rocket toy. You would fire it into the air using its catapult and watch it sore skywards, then on reaching maximum height, it would deploy a parachute that would bring it safely down to earth.

Me on scooter in the Enchanted Wood

My Dad had a go. It went really high. Much higher than I could ever make it go. It shot up into the sky above the trees getting smaller and smaller to our view. Then once at optimum height, out popped the parachute. Well it must have caught a slight breeze. Imagine my dismay when as it floated down to tree level, it caught up in the top of the Faraway tree.

The only way to quell the tears of the inconsolable small Si John was the solution offered by Gangan.

"Well Warwick, you sent it up there, you are just going to have to climb up and get it down!"

The Faraway Tree was a large Oak tree. Not very much foliage low down, but once you negotiate the first 12 feet or so a pretty easy climb. I can only assume my father was more scared of the mother in law than he was of falling out of the tree to certain death, because fair play to him, we all saw him get up there retrieve the rocket and them both return to earth unscathed.

Every time I return to the Faraway Tree, I marvel at how my Dad managed that. Lots of climbable trees, in the enchanted wood. But not many ever attempted the Faraway tree!

There was a boating lake in Sutton park too. You could row in a family size boat, or there was a little kiddie's pen with Paddleboats. Blackroot Lake. Then there was Bracebridge Lake with a wooden walk with little plank bridges. Eventually you emerge at the other end of the lake where there was a popular swimming area. Back at the entrance was Bracebridge Café, where families would sit after a bracing walk and enjoy a cup of tea or hot chocolate.

In the summer, Sutton Coldfield would hold its Carnival. All the procession would end at Meadow Platt just inside the Town Gate near number 77. There would be clowns and motorcycle display teams. I saw my first live band at Sutton carnival. The Swinging Blue Jeans. Had just released their hit record The Hippy Hippy Shake!

Sometimes Billy Smarts Circus would come to the park. I loved the spectacle of the circus. We would go and visit the animals in the cages. Big Cats. Lions, Tigers.

We watched them erect the Big Top working the elephants to pull the ropes that drag the canvas over its frame.

This was magical to me. When the circus left, all that remained was a circle of brown grass where the ring had once been. We would play on this circle of grass, reliving the spectacle that had briefly been there. I would be the ringmaster, then the lion tamer and finally the clown.

Sutton Park was great for winter pursuits too. When my parents were kids during the war. First sign of snow and everyone would make for Holly Knoll. This was a hillock just beyond the Meadow Platt inside Park Road Entrance. Great, for sledging. My mother told me that when she and Christine were kids, her father would tie the sledge to the back of the car and tow them to the foot of Holly Knoll. (Surely not from Chadsway!!!) As a kid she and some friends got their picture in the Sutton Coldfield News in their wooly hats and mittens at the bottom of the slope. "Evacuees enjoying the snow!" was the caption. Gangan was not amused at the inaccuracy of the press. Something's never change.

Of cause sledging was a winter pastime my parents were eager to indoctrinate their kids to. Yes we had great fun slipping and sliding when the snow came to Holly Knoll.

Dad built me a snowman in the back garden of number 23. He was quite splendid. We rolled one chunk of snow into the body then placed a smaller one for his head.

Lumps of coal, for buttons and eyes. He stole a carrot from the pantry for a nose. Then he topped it off with one of Grandy's old trilby hats sporting a feather and he lent it one of his pipes.

Every morning when I woke up I would look out to see more snow had fallen and my friend the snowman was there, lording it all over his domain.

Eventually the thaw came and I was tinged with sadness to watch daily how he was becoming smaller until all was left was some pieces of coal in the soggy grass.

5 CHADSWAY, THEATRE, SAMUEL HOPE

We are now into the beginning of the sixties. Grandy has retired and sold up his house in little Sutton lane and He and Dorothy bought a cottage in Eastborn. Sussex. Near to Dorothy's family.

During the Holidays, we loaded up the Morris Minor and travelled down to stay with him. Dorothy's Brother Greatrex Newman is the proprietor of a Music Hall company called the Fol Da Rolls. I have often been told about this. Apparently coincidently, my Gangan was a dancer with them in her early days.

The Fol Da Rolls was a vaudeville company who toured music halls. I was quite impressed to learn that Leslie Crowther who was one of my favorites on the TV show Crackerjack hosted by Eamonn Andrews, was originally a Fol Da Roll.

Dad wanted to take us kids to see the show. Grandy didn't want to go. "I don't see the point of it! " He protested. "Its all very silly, grown men loosing their trousers for laughs." It's funny how I remember his words so clearly, yet I don't recall a single thing about the show. The theatre I do recall. Like the empress cinema, there is something about the magic of theatre that attracts me.

The glamour of the auditorium, the magic behind the curtain. There is a calling, an excitement, an anticipation of the spectacle that always draws me.

My Uncle Lloyd. Aunty Christine's husband gave me a Toy Theatre. It wasn't new, it was a hand me down. Maybe it belonged to him. I loved that toy.

It was about fifteen inches wide. It had a fire curtain and a normal curtain. There was a stage and you had cut out cardboard figures that had long sticks attached side ways so you could animate these figures from the wings. It had an array of foot lights which were flashlight bulbs connected to a battery and a switch. I would play with this theatre for hours and put shows on for the family.

Holiday times were also a time when Gangan would take us with her on her Thursday jaunts to the Jewelry Quarter. Sometimes we would meet her friend Ellie Brenninkmeijer family for lunch in Rackham's. Ellie's husband Conrad was Dutch and owned another department store in Birmingham. Conrad it turned out, is the C in C&A ! The kids in our family always looked forward to the Christmas presents from the Brenninkmeijer family.

It was a real treat to visit Samuel Hopes. We were treated like royalty. We were taken on a tour of the manufacturing Jewelers. Vyce Street comprised of a row of terraces. Typically of the Jewelry Quarter, a company would set up in one of these small terrace houses and as they expanded they would come to occupy neighboring properties. I think Samuel Hopes was in several of these houses before it relocated to new purpose built premises in nearby Warstone lane later in the sixties.

We would be greeted by reception and Gangan would go through to the manager's office. Leonard Cooney was the chief executive. They would have their weekly chat then I would be taken a tour of the factory. Narrow stairways and small rooms, as you would expect in a terrace. Wooden benches, with gas burners for each craftsman. What I remember most was a vacuum tube system. I am assuming when a product was finished it would be placed into one of these pods and whoosh it would be sucked up the tube to the next stage.

All I know is the craftsman would write a note and send it off. A moment later the pod would shoot back and I would be invited to open it. It contained some shiny penny coins for me! What fun.

After Samuel Hope it would be time for shopping. Sometimes we walked by the Birmingham Science Museum. We would look around at the wondrous exhibits. I loved the Spitfire and the Hawker Hurricane they had.

But Rackham's Department Store sticks in my mind. A huge modern building, with different departments on every floor. Men's Fashions, Ladies Fashions, Shoes, Furniture, Electrical Goods and Kitchen Ware. The Lift operator would take us to our floor announcing the departments of each floor. "Third Floor Haberdashery and ladies Under Garments " We would ascend to the top floor where the toy department was cleverly located and the restaurant. Lunchtime. There would always be a fashion show with models demonstrating the new styles of ladies fashion on sale. Gangan seemed to know all of the models personally, they would be doing their chic model cat walk posses and she would stop them mid stride and proudly introduced her grandchildren to each and every one of them.

Before catching the 112 back to Chadsway, some times she would treat us to the Birmingham News Theatre. This was a bit of an old fleapit cinema even by my young standards that showed Pathe News by day and adult films by night. Not that I was aware of that at the time. For my world was one of pure childhood innocence.

In addition to the Pathe News, which normally showed Queen Elizabeth and Prince Phillip on tour of some distant part of our commonwealth, there were cartoons. Disney Warner Mickey Daffy and Bugs with a smidgeon of Goofy, Wiley coyote and "Bib Bib" Road runner all wound up with Porky Pig stammering "Th Th Th That's all folks"

So sometimes it was the 112 Midland Red Home and sometimes the train from New Street Station. We would get home to Chadsway in time for tea.

Chadsway garden I have mentioned. But the house itself holds many memories of growing up. Chadsway was a veritable playground for an imaginative kid. The staircase became the 112 Midland Red Bus. Philippa, Not like the kids of today.

Golly Racky and Sally would be my passengers sat in rows on each stair. Sometimes Aunty Christine and her daughter, my cousin Tamzin would hitch a ride too!

The dinning room was our shop and the small chest of drawers sitting on top of the trunk was the cash register. The buttons in the draws was our money.

There was a Bagatelle game. This was an early pin pall game. A wooden base, with a channel on the right hand side. There you placed a ball bearing. With a stick you would propel the ball bearing onto the wooden table that was angled at a slant. Set in the table were various traps made from panel pins with scores written on them. As the ball descended from the top it would bounce of pins and hopefully come to rest at a point redeeming a high score.

I spent ages peering out of the dining room window listening for cars. Traffic was scarce back in those days. You would hear a car before you actually saw it pass the window. I got quite good at recognizing different cars by their sounds. The Morris Minor had a very distinctive exhaust sound. There were a lot of them on the road back then. I could always tell when one was coming. Other cars had their instantly recognizable sounds too. The VW Beetle too had a very familiar sound.

But, the best feature. The very very best feature of the whole of Chadsway was the doorway leading from the lounge to the back garden. It was a single door in a slight bay. It had a pelmet and a double curtain that opened and closed on the tug of one of the two chords hanging down.

This was our lift door in Rackham's "Third floor Ladies garments and Haberdashery" I would announce to my shoppers as they stepped off the lift.

On a Saturday afternoon however, that curtain became something else. It would become our theatre! Because we knew on every Saturday Afternoon we would have a captive audience. On Saturday afternoon, that curtain and doorway became our stage. Gangan Aunty Lena Jean Bertioli would all be sat around the TV like Harry Enfield's " OoOh Young Man Ladies" awaiting their weekly treat. Professional Wrestling. They all were sat there waiting to oogle Little Mick McManus the man they love to hate, and Jackie Pallo in their black speedos and leotards.

Well Me Philippa Golly Racky and Sally had a captive audience. We would clown around opening curtains, singing nursery rhymes and basically going "Dd dar !!!!!" to our audience who politely applauded us until it was time for us to be quiet, now Kent Waldon was to announce the first bout, and Mick McManus and Jackie Palo would turn, come out of "The Blue Corner" or the "Red Corner" not that it mattered on a small Black and White Television set, and the screen would erupt in an frenzy of manly grunts, fore arm smashes, and clothes lines off the ropes. Inevitably, Mick McManus would turn his opponent over for the Boston Crab, much to the delight of the Studio Audience and the three old ladies sat on the edges of their seats in "Chadsway Arena", and it would be all over.

This was show business and we loved it!

6 LEY HILL, OUR FAMILY POP STAR.

First year in Ley Hill junior school was pretty uneventful. Ley Hill was a modern building two stories high with two staircases each leading to two upstairs classrooms. So eight class rooms in total. At the rear of the building was a quadrangle with a garden area enclosed by wired glass panes. Down the one side were toilets and cloakrooms. The opposite corridor housed offices, and Mr. Cheshire the headmaster's Office These corridors led to the school assembly hall.

There was an enormous playing field at the rear of the school, laid out with goal posts. As modern an innovative as this school was, it soon became apparent that there were not enough classrooms. To rectify this, two classroom huts were erected in the playing field looking out onto the tarmac playground. Our first year was spent in one of these huts.

We had sum books that had a list of Arithmetic questions. The book was called "Eight a Day" And at the beginning of the day we had to do these simple times table sums.

It was all based around learning our multiplication tables. It was more a parrot fashion rhyming way of learning arithmetic, but it was perhaps one of the most useful things I ever learnt in school.

In later generations this was to become frowned upon as a teaching method. As a result my kids don't have a clue when it comes to times tables. But myself and I am sure many others of my generation, would strongly beg to differ. This was without doubt one of the most useful math skills I took away from school, and we learnt it, assisted by our "Eight a day " Books, in the first year at juniors!

Around about this time we had something very exciting happening. Within the family we have a "Pop Star" and he was to appear on the early evening news program with his band, performing his latest hit !

Gangan's sister May Hamber lived in a council house in Billaricay. In fact to be more precise, she lives in two council houses in Billaricay on account of the fact that she had TEN children!

First Year Ley Hill Juniors. First Row I'm in the middle right, Bonnie Trigg far left, John Chawner far right.

We had been down there before at Christmas when I was very young, and also whilst we were living in Park Road, May's youngest daughter Mary did come stay with us for a while. She also attended Riland Bedford High School briefly during her stay, the High School I was later to go to.

The Pop Star was Mary's brother David Hamber and his band was called the Embers.

So we all watched excitedly as David fronted his band singing his new record from the Decca Label "I've found Carol "

" I met a pretty little girl yesterday

such a little pretty girl yesterday,

now I'm walking in the five dollar crowd

because I've found Carol ....

She's the one that they write the songs about

She's the one that I can't live without

Every where I go I shout

I've found Carol ………

Carol is the love like, I guess she's the one

Looks like it's a million dollar prize that I won

Because I

And repeat "

Well the words were something like that. My Aunty Christine already had the record; it cost her 6/8d from Frosts Chemist in Sutton which also had a record and sheet music section.

So we watched David on TV basking in the reflective glory that one of our family was famous.

Now visits to Chadsway got to be more fun. Aunty Christine would let me play her records and I would stand behind the Curtain in the living room whilst the intro played on the 45 on Gangan's radio gram, pull the sash chord and come out on stage. Tonight Mathew little Si John is David Hamber, and Philippa and Golly were the Embers.

I even recall one visit to Roy Suttle's second hand shop café where he had a jukebox installed for the teenagers. There you pressed 58A after inserting a penny, actually Roy unlocked the coin mechanism so I could just flick a lever. Excitedly we would watch a vertical ring of 45's rotate until the selected record was top most, then an arm would pull it out of the ring, twist it horizontal then place it on the turn table to play. The record selected, yes you guessed it. David and the Embers "I found Carol" Select 58B and the reverse side would play "Please Bring My Little Girl Home"

I think my Dad and Roy may have lived to regret unlocking the coin mechanism because I played that record of my Family Hero so much.

Aunty Christine

In the end Roy gave me that record, and a lot of other discarded tunes from the jukebox when they were replaced by the next selections from the hit parade. These 45's had to have their middles removed for juke boxes which meant unless you had an adaptor, which I eventually got, you had to be very careful how you placed them on the turntable. If they were slightly off centre, it would produce some very unusual note bending sounds!

I remember sitting on the 112 bus in Gangan's hallway, Yes folks it was really the stairs. Aunty Christine was negotiating the small kitchen steps in a mini skirt trying to put the hallway Christmas Decorations up. I told her I wanted a guitar for Christmas. "That's quite difficult" she said she'd tried and found she was OK with the right hand strumming, but the left hand bit was very fiddly. I said " That's OK, I'll just do the right hand bit then."

Mark Hofton and his family were spending Christmas with us and my main present was to be shared between my Dad and me. A Scalextric; Racing Car Set.

It was set up in the small spare bedroom at Chadsway and the two families descended on Gangan's for the opening of the presents and Christmas Turkey.

Well I was quite excited about having a Scalextric for Christmas, but not as excited it would turn out as my Dad and Mark's Dad Uncle Tony. They seemed to get quite competitive and Mum was called in to protest on my behalf that perhaps Mark and I would like to have a go.

They begrudgingly handed over the hand controls to us and started to coach us on the finer points of being a race driver. Of course our early attempts resulted in the cars spinning off at the first corner amid a lot of eye rolling by our expert fathers.

I guess most of the present budget that year went on Dad and Tony's Scalextric, because when I unwrapped the guitar shaped present that I was most excited about, it turned out to be a toy one. Plastic with nylon strings that refused to stay in tune. Learning to play was going to have to wait, But I was happy, it was a good tool for me to practice my Pop Star moves on nevertheless.

So time to sit down in the Dining Room for our feast. The room looked splendid. The large Dining Room Table had a mechanism to expand it even more by sliding out the two ends and two extra leaves hinged up from below to enable more place settings.

Each setting had the best silver ware place mats and of course Christmas Crackers. Conversation quite understandably turned to motor racing. More significantly Scalextric Racing. Jibes were made, by our fathers over how bad Mark and I were at it. Perhaps the game was a bit too old for us.

Both of our mothers came to our defense not without a good deal of eye rolling and tutting emerging from their direction. One or both perhaps suggested. "If you two hadn't been hogging the damn thing all morning and given the poor kids a proper go, they might have stood a chance!" To which Gangan added "Warwick, the only reason why you and Tony were any good today, was when you two came round to set it up two days ago, you were up there playing on it for three hours. Honestly I couldn't get rid of them! " More tutting and eye rolling came from Gangan and our two mothers whilst they commented on how they had become Scalextric Widows!

Second Year at Ley Hill differed to the First Year in so much that our class had now moved into the main school building. I had proudly taken delivery of my Dawes Dapper 24 inch bike and I was told by my father, that if I passed my Cycling Proficiency Test, I could ride my bike to School. The School arranged the course with some local police volunteers. It was actually Jackie Hickmot's Dad who was a sergeant in Sutton Police Station. It was basically High Way Code stuff and when we passed we were presented with a badge that we could display on our handlebars.

I would park my bike in the back of the cycle shed in the middle on it's own kickstand. That way I could look out of the classroom window and admire it. In my mind, it was the best one there!

There was an extra question in our morning math's book. This year we were studying from "Nine a Day" !

The next year was different apart from "Ten A Day" being the morning Math's book. Mum was expecting her 3rd child.

So I recall pushing my Dawes Dapper up the final slope of Hill Village Road, before I could mount it once more and cycle the final few hundred yards up Crockford drive when Mrs. Trig Bonnie and Carl's mother saw me and enquired. "How is your Mum Simon? Has she had the Baby yet" "Not yet" I replied, and quoted knowledgably, what every one was now saying in answer to that question " But it should be any time now!"

And indeed it was. I got home, put my bike in the garage, went in through the kitchen door and there was Gangan. "Come upstairs and meet your baby brother " I rushed upstairs, and there was Mum and Nurse Jones the midwife. Mum was sat up in bed with my baby brother Adam Tomas Edgington in her arms. It was May 8th 1963.

Dad needed a new car. The Morris Minor convertible had served its purpose. I remember waiting for him to come home in the Black Worsley

1500 he'd acquired. I was excited because it was the same as the police cars they had at Sutton Coldfield. Eventually he came up Crockford drive with a proud grin from ear to ear. On Sunday he set to, to polish it. I could see my reflection in the bodywork it was so shiny.

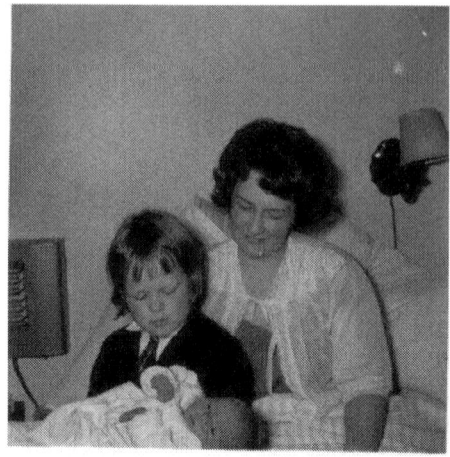

Sally says hello to Adam for the first time

I had a new car once myself. When we were in 77 Park road, I had a Bright Red Shiny Peddle Car for my Birthday. It was my pride and joy. Well all the kids in Crockford drive were building go carts or soap boxes. They comprised of planks of wood and pram wheels.

Well now that I had a baby brother come along, there was no way that I was going to get the wheels of Mum's silver cross pram any time soon.

So Dad and a neighbor, set about removing the wheels from my old pedal car and constructing for me a soap box go cart.

This was great fun, Carl had already discovered some good hills for us to play on. It's quite hard to comprehend now how far afield we went in search of suitable roads to propel ourselves down. All the kids did this, it was great fun, and it was safe in those days.

There was hardly any traffic on the estates. It was very rare that we had to wait for a passing car. How times have changed.

I had many go carts. The ingredients were simple. Find an old pram and remove the axle and wheels. Get some planks of wood. Plenty of those about on the building site. Some Nails and heavy duty U shaped staples with which to attach the axles to the frame. The rear axle would be held on to the main chassis plank by two heavy nuts Bolts and washers. The front axle by one single Bolt Nut and Washer. This would allow you to steer with the front axle turning on that Bolt. We learnt early on the value of a second lock nut on that bolt to prevent the whole assembly working itself apart. Steering control was by a clothes line tied to each side of the front axle.

John Chawner was building one at his place too. He was lucky, leading off Darnel Hurst Road was a great hill down Clarendon Road. Ideal for Go Carts. One day at school he asked me if I could come look at it. He was having trouble getting the steering to work and his cart kept crashing into the curb, on Clarendon Road. When I got to his place, it was immediately obvious to me what the problem was. "John?" I asked. "Why have you got two bolts holding on your front axle" "You TOLD me I had to have two bolts on the front axle for safety! " He protested. "No John" I replied patiently. " I told you one Bolt with TWO NUTS " "That makes sense " John's Dad Roy replied" "I thought it was funny when you insisted we used two bolts ! " Well he should know. He worked for Fords !

If I wasn't go karting, at weekends I would ride my bike to Darnel Hurst Road to see John Chawner. John's Mum Hazel was a fabulous funny lady. She stood about 4ft 11 so us ten year olds were nearly as tall as her. When we first met she said. "Oh I know all about you Simon. Aren't you the one that went into PE class in your Knickers?" Thanks John! His Dad Roy was a nice man who worked for Ford in Birmingham. John had an older brother Stephen too. They were all the most fabulous family and were to become my best friends for life.

John and I would ride our bikes up to the Dugdale estate and call on Robert Brown, or we would go down the Worcester lane to the bottom beyond the houses where it became countryside. Unbeknown to us at the time, this part of Four Oaks was to become one of our favourite locations in future years when our chose transport would change from Bicycles to Scooters and our interests firstly became elicit smoking then with Ford Cortina's or Anglia's, the interests were Girls!

Another memory of that time was whilst watching one of my favorite TV shows, perhaps during Blue Peter where Valery Singleton was showing how to make something or other using Paper Mache and a fairy liquid bottle, something very strange happened.

The program was cut and the BBC announcer came on with a news flash. President John F Kennedy had been shot. It was a Friday November 22nd 1963.

John Kennedy was very popular in Britain. Even a young ten year old such as myself was aware of that. We'd keenly watched him win the election, and it was a matter of great shock to everyone, to learn he had been assassinated.

My Dads Step Mother Dorothy had not been enjoying the best of health. I can remember being on the landing of Crockford Drive and my father just receiving the news that she had died. We had no telephone I am assuming he got the news via Telegram. He immediately set off to Eastbourne to console my Grandfather and assist him with the arrangements.

Grandy sold up in Eastbourne and returned to Shropshire to stay for at time with my father's sister Pam's family. They had a beautiful Mansion Called Dorrington Grove Near Church Stretton in Shropshire. Pam's husband Maurice was a banking executive. Dorrington Grove was a lovely home with stables and huge lawns and gardens. Grandy would have plenty to do there.

With the arrival of Adam and the prospect of visits from Grandy, our family was starting to outgrow number 23 Crockford drive. Talk was on of a move.

My fathers Best Man and fellow Old Vesian (Ex Pupils of Bishop Vesey

Grammar school) John Slater followed in his fathers footsteps and joined the family business of Slater Dann and sons, Auctioneers and Estate Agents Sutton Coldfield.

John told my father about a house on Lichfield Road that was an opportunity not to me missed.

7 HOLLY LODGE

217 Lichfield Road, Four Oaks. "Holly Lodge" Perhaps so named after the well established Holly Bush marking the boundary between the lawned front garden and pavement of the A38.

Holly Lodge (Revisited 2012)

You entered the drive and followed the path to the left to the front door, passing a huge living room bay window. The front door had a vestibule which opened onto a good sized hall way. On the opposite side of the ample living room was a second large room, with a passageway leading to the back of the house and a doorway into the garden. "Perfect !" Dad announced. "This can be my office!"

We went back into the hallway and climbed the stairs. The Banister at the bottom sported a large wooden ball. The kind of thing, I thought could probably do a young boy some damage if he decided to slide down the stairs! Dad grabbed it to follow us upstairs and it came off in his hand. "There's something to fix right there! " He exclaimed.

At the top of the stairs above the lounge, there was the master bedroom. A connecting door led to a small nursery room at the rear of the house. "Perfect for Adam Tommykins." Dad pronounced, I think he was already well sold on the place. Next to that was the bathroom, then a separate toilet and yet another large bedroom. "Mine! " I laid my claim.

Two more bedrooms, at the front of the house, making five in all. Sally can have the smaller one, and we have a guest room for when Grandy comes to stay.

Back downstairs now to explore the rear of the house. Through a hallway door we entered a passage way with coat hangers with a cupboard at one end and a doorway into the Morning Room.

This was a large room with a pantry at one end and a huge fire place containing an Aga cooker. Run on coal, not only did this have two impressive ovens and two large hobs, it also provided hot water for the whole house.

Suspended from the ceiling, was a large laundry rack, which came down by means of a pulley system. "Ideal for drying Adams Nappies" Mum exclaimed.

Above the door way to the front corridor was fitted a box affair with an array of little 1 inch square windows. All labelled. Front Door, Living Room, Dining Room, Hall, Bedroom 1, Bedroom 2, Bedroom 3, Bedroom 4, Bedroom 5. On closer examination we were to discover, every room either had a push button by the fireplace, or a cord hanging from the ceiling with a bell push on the end of it.

Well, Sally and I immediately set to explore this feature. When the button was pressed, a bell would ring and the flag in the little window of the box would wave and indicate from what room the maid was to be summoned to. We didn't have a maid of course, but boy we were going to have some fun with that!

The morning room led into a small kitchen with a gas cooker and sink. From there the door led out to an enclosed passageway containing a downstairs toilet and two rather large coal bunkers.

An outside door led into the back garden. The Garden had a huge lawn, with a highly climbable tree then a vegetable garden to the rear of that. A very old garden shed at the back fence that overlooked an embankment leading down to the railway track.

There was also a large detached garage with doors at front and rear. The garage had an inspection pit. The rear doors opened onto a drained bay area where presumably one could hose down and wash ones car.

We all fell in love with the house. Dad for his office space where at last he too could hang one of his Manulife World Map Calendars, Mum for her Nappy Drying Solution and me for my great new room and Button pressing gadget!

Holly Lodge is situated half way between Mere Green Village and Four Oaks Station. Over the road was a bus stop and shops at the Clarence Road junction. Clarence road takes you to Mere Green Road from there it was about the same distance to John's house as Crockford drive. No problem on my bike!

So we moved into Holly Lodge. I don't recall any of the dramas of moving house, or selling up Crockford drive, I just remember us getting there!

I also remember that much to my distaste, it was to become my responsibility to keep the Aga stove topped up with coal in the morning and keep the coal scuttle full for Mum before setting off to school.

Woe betided me if I allowed the thing to go out. In fact it seemed to me, Woe betided me if it went out on its own. It was still somehow my fault!

Well the new house was a lot bigger than 23 Crockford drive. We needed furniture and who better to help us with that, other than Café / Second hand furniture shop owner Roy Suttle!

Dad managed to acquire a beautiful leather topped desk for his office, with large draws for storing Manulife Calendars presumably.

We got beds for the bedrooms and a fantastic set of army style bunk beds for my room. Great for when Mark Hofton came to stay, or school friends for sleepovers.

One of my best surprises was when Dad came home from Roy's one day with an old valve radio. "We have a radio in the Morning room that Mummy gave us!" Mum protested to him. "I thought Si John would like this for his room " Dad explained!

Would I !!!

Well my career as a Superhero inspired by Saturday Morning Cinema wasn't going that well. I had already tried to emulate Batman by putting my fist through a glass window at a derelict house. I felt like a real hero when the glass shattered. Until I saw the blood oozing from a deep cut on my thumb. Then all of a sudden, I felt very faint as shock set in.

Steven Suttle used to lecture me on the Merits of Superman against Batman. We would discuss this at length whilst strolling around the playing field at Ley Hill. It was quite obvious little Si John was going to be too small to be a Super Hero, and have Lois Lane fall in love with him.

So Pop star it is.

Cliff Richard was about to release his next Movie and hurray! At last I was going to be allowed to go see it. In spite of all my Saturday Morning matinee friends being allowed to go, Mum said I was too young to see his first film when it came out. The Young Ones, in 1961.

Now with my radio in my room, I could listen to the Light Program by day. The Goon show, Jimmy Clitheroe, but the BBC would not play any of that awful Pop Music and Rock and Roll. So by Night I would be able to tune into Medium Wave 208 Radio Luxemburg.

Radio Luxemburg was the only way that Pop fans in England could hear Rock and Roll, Elvis Presley, Bill Hayley and the Comets on the radio.

We all used to listen intently time and again to learn the most sort after lyrics to these tunes.

What a thrill when I would ring the bell in my room run to the landing and shout down "Mum David Hamber is on Radio Luxemburg again!"

This station used to be the main means to promote major record labels in the UK. Later on in 1964, Radio Caroline would follow. A pirate radio station operated from a ship. Eventually much later in September 1967, the BBC were to relent at the instruction of the government and launch BBC Radio 1.

Grandy came to stay. Quite soon after we settled in. For some reason, he didn't sleep in the guest bedroom. Maybe we hadn't yet completed furnishing it. So Dad dismantled my bunk beds and made them into two separate single beds in my room. Grandy stayed in my room with me.

One night as we were just getting to bed, he enquired of me. "So Simon what do you think you would like to do for a living if you pass your 11 plus?" The attitude in educational circles was at the end of the fourth year in primary school. You had a test. The eleven plus. If you passed, you would be accepted into Grammar School. If you didn't, well it just didn't bare thinking about.

Really?

Your future determined at the age of eleven ?????

So I pondered on my reply. Did you need to pass your eleven plus to be Superman or Batman. Most likely but I was afraid I might sound ridiculous saying I wanted to be a super hero. So I went with what I had pretty well decided.

"I want to be a Pop Star!"

"Oh I don't think that is a very good idea Simon." He replied. "You see these Pop Star people, well they are not really very intelligent you know, are they?" I was quite puzzled by his response. After all, cousin David was a Pop star and everyone else in the family seemed very proud of him.

"And tell me Simon," He continued to enquire." What do you think you will do for a living if you don't pass your eleven plus?"

Well I hadn't really considered anything in terms of the eleven plus having any bearing on my future employment. I was quite vexed that my Grandy wasn't too impressed with my answers so far, so I thought I better try to do better.

"Oh I expect I will just go and work for the family business. Samuel Hope!"

Well I can only guess that the following day, a concerned Grandy must have related our conversation to my father. He was annoyed with me and told me in no uncertain terms that working anywhere especially somewhere like the family business would be dependent on my passing my eleven plus! So I better buck up my ideas and work harder at school.

Grandy stayed a while at Holly Lodge. Once more he set a task at the garden. He dug up large stones and with them constructed a patio wall and flower bed in front of the path by the Morning room window. Still dressed as the county gentleman he was. Sports jacket leather elbow patches, waste coat bowtie and the trusty Wellington boots.

In time, that was to become a glorious garden view to welcome us, whilst we ate our cornflakes in the morning before setting off to school.

I loved Holly Lodge. It was to be the house of many changes in my life.

The only thing I can remember about the two years left at Ley hill was now we could all do up to our 12 times table and Mrs Wheatley our form teacher for those two years taught us about William Shakespeare's 4th Century and building a replica of his birthplace out of cardboard and paper Mache.

This was a skill that I embraced whole heartedly. For if I could make Shakespeare Birthplace out of cardboard and paper Mache I could surely make an electric guitar!

The Beatles were beginning to hit the big time. I remember going to visit Mark Hofton in Wilde Green. He had a copy of the Radio Times and the cover photo was that famous album cover "With The Beatles" Mark was so excited about this pop sensation. He knew all their names. I was quite ashamed that me the future pop star in the room didn't.

It was a big deal, the Beatles had somehow broken through the discrimination of a very snooty BBC run by people who shared my Grandy's attitude to these Rock and Roll beatnik types ! Brian Epstein, the Beatles manager had somehow succeeded in promoting their clean-cut image, which was going to get their foot in the door of the BBC and change popular music forever.

I remember sobbing uncontrollably one night after being told I couldn't watch them on TV because it was way passed my bedtime. I crept out on to the landing and gingerly negotiated the creaky stairs of Holly Lodge so that I could at the very least eavesdrop on the dulcet sounds of Paul McCartney emerging from the TV set in the living room.

This is what I wanted. This mattered to 11-year-old Si John.

8 FIRST PUBLIC PERFORMANCE JUNE 23RD 1964

My Beatle Haircut, Cardboard/Paper Mache Guitar, Bean Pole Mike Stand and Cotton Reel Microphone.

John Chawner was well impressed with Holly Lodge. We went out into the garden John immediately started doing handsprings and Cartwheels on the lawn. I tried to emulate him but my feeble attempts just caused amusement with my Dad.

We had to plan our Gig. We asked Mr Cheshire the Headmaster if we could do a concert in assembly. We had been working hard at school building our cardboard guitars. Mrs Wheatley, so impressed by my cardboard Shakespeare Birthplace told us if we bought some cardboard egg boxes in we could make them in class.

We cut out the shapes for the front and the back. Then we cut strips, and rolled them around the front and back to make the sides, stuck with scotch tape. Then we covered the whole body in paper Mache. We took them home when they were dry so we could rehearse in my "new" garden shed. We rolled up some more card board and attached this as the neck. Then we painted them.

John made a Paul McCartney violin bass. I wanted to be Paul McCartney! But John was adamant. We practiced our moves. I seem to recall we had Brian Green on Vox continental Organ Too. This just comprised of an egg box.

So the big day was looming. It was to be my 11th Birthday. I had asked for my Birthday Present for the album "With The Beatles" which at that point I hadn't even heard.

The plan was I would get up, open my Birthday Present, and rush to school with it for assembly.

"With the Beatles" was to be the sound track of my first concert. The stage consisted of an array of eight one metre square box sections that stood about half a metre or 2 feet high. I had a bean stick jammed between two of these sections to make it upright. This was my mike stand, and scotch taped to the top of it was a cotton reel. This was my microphone.

Gradually the school started to assemble in the hall. Mrs Wheatley opened the lid of the School gramophone, selected 33 1/3, RPM on the speed control and stood by for her cue.

Mr Cheshire stood in front of the stage and addressed the school. "Well we have a something of a treat for you today" and he turned to me and John on our guitars and Brian Green on cardboard box. "Take it away boys" I nodded at Mrs Wheatley and a needle crackled away on the turntable before the first song sprung our concert to life.

"It wont be long Yeah Yeah Yeah

It wont be long Yeah Yeah Yeah

Till I belong to you ...."

This was the first time I'd ever actually heard this song, but it didn't stop me and John gyrating with our pop star moves, whilst Brian pounded on his egg box which by now I think he decided was a drum.

I have no recollection of what kind of reaction was coming back from our audience, if indeed there was any reaction at all. School assemblies were always renowned for less than enthusiastic audiences. It didn't matter at all to us, John and me were having a good time being John and Paul, and by now Brian had decided he was Ringo.

I figured that we would perform the whole first side of the album, and if our audience wanted more, then Mrs Wheatley could simply flip over to the other side.

Well that was what I thought, but at the end of the first song, the record was stopped, Mr Cheshire thanked us for our efforts and invited us to join the rest of the school in the hall, so he could lead the whole school with the hymn "All things Bright and Beautiful" accompanied by Mrs Wheatley on Piano

My first taste of an audience was over. I have to be honest and confess the anticipation was a lot longer lived than the actual event. As in so many aspects of life that were to come.

9 CAMPING HOLIDAYS

I have many memories of living in Holly Lodge. Our family was growing up. Adam was fun but I would get told off for sometimes being too rough with him.

In fact Mum was very protective of us kids and that sometimes caused Dad anguish. I think he was of the belief that if we fell and bumped our heads, that was all part of growing up. But Mum was always there to say "There there" maybe sometimes a bit too much.

I guess us kids, being kids may have noticed this. If we wanted sympathy, to be mothered, Mum was there.

My Dad tried, he was a good man but I think my mother and possibly my Gangan were a force he was no match for. So he provided for us and we were well looked after.

One Christmas at the Ford garage in Sutton Town Centre across the road from the Empress Cinema, Santa Clause was appearing. We all piled into the Worsley 1500 to see Santa. Peter Howe was the manager there and the Manulife Calendar hanging on the wall of his office revealed that he and Dad knew each other from before. I think Santa must have spent his down time having elocution lessons. For he seemed a lot better spoken in keeping with his international status than those infant school days. Well I cannot remember what Santa gave me that visit, but I do remember Dad came away with a New Ford Zodiac.

Oh Yes ! No longer driving around in TV's Dixon of Dock Green's Wolsey. Now we were in Z Cars ! We were all happy with this car. Bigger, and great for holidays.

Another friend of Dads was Bob Miller. He was the proprietor of the Miller School of Motoring. He was a keen camper, and one weekend we all went off to the countryside to stay in his big army tent.

Well that was that for us. We had been camping before with the Hofton

Family. We had a holiday in Newquay in Wales one year. It was the weekend of the regatta.

Flash back to Camping in Newquay Mark Hofton, Me and our sisters

At the end of the day, there was a ladies canoe race across Newquay harbour. They had two ladies enter and they needed a third. Somehow, Mum was persuaded to enter. Well the other two canoeists set off in earnest across the harbour entrance. I think it was Mums first time in a canoe and she couldn't quite figure out how to prevent it from spinning round in circles! Eventually she started to make headway across the harbour mouth. By the time Mum reached the finish, much to the amusement of the large cheering crowd. The other two contestants had exited the water and enjoyed a cigarette. First prize was 30 Shillings, Second Prize was a pound, Mum was third and she won 10 shillings. The two families dined out on fish and chips that night on her winnings!

So now after the weekend camping with Bob Miller, Dad decided we should buy a tent and a trailer for camping holidays. This we did and our camping fun was to begin.

He bought a huge continental tent with three separate internal bedrooms. Just for practice we pitched it on the back lawn at Holly Lodge. John Chawner came over and we camped out side that night. We had torches that we would shine on our faces from below our chins and try to scare each other with ghost stories.

Grandy had recently moved into a small cottage in Little Stretton called

"The Ancient House" It was a lovely small oak cottage with a garage and a small garden. Grandy's Garage was an Aladdin's cave of work benches lathes and drawers so filled with every tool imaginable that a hardware shop would be hard pressed to equal its stock inventory.

Sally and I would spend hours there playing shop!

We must have sometimes stayed there because I remember across the road was the small church and we would awake on a Sunday Morning to the chimes of the bell.

But most of the time we would stay in a field along a small lane and over a ford. The stream ran along the bottom of the field. We would pitch our tent. Mum would light the camping Gaz cooker; I would take the water carrier down to the brook and fill it with cold fresh stream water. Further down stream, we would empty our portable toilet.

It was a lovely spot to camp in the country. There were trees to climb and hills strewn with heather. We would climb to the top and roll down through the heather, or play hide and seek, aki aki 123 or cricket rounder's. Sally made friends with a local girl who allowed us to ride her horse. Poor Sally fell off. This put her off riding, so Dad got on the horse to show her it was all right. And promptly fell off himself! Even he saw the irony and joined in the laughter at his misfortune.

In the Summer Holidays, our camping excursions took us further afield. We discovered a lovely camp site between Combe Martin and Ilfracombe in Devon. That became our holiday destination. The Farmer named John Barton would hang hurricane lamps from the trees. In the evening you would see him set off with a tribe of the camps children each holding a lantern. These trees were great fun in the day too. They had rope swings hanging from their large branches.

Next to the camp site, was Watermouth Cave Caravan site. This had a lovely cove beach, a café caves to explore and plenty of rocks to climb.

Sally and I soon joined the procession of children following John Barton with the Hurricane lamps.

One year Bob Miller and his family came too. This was great for me because he gave me a driving lesson in the field in his Mini. Dad wouldn't allow me to drive his Zodiac. But in the end John Barton allowed me drive his Ferguson Tractor around the site, empting the dustbins into the trailer. I loved camping there so I could drive the tractor.

After our first camping Holiday in Devon it was going to be time to change schools. Before we broke up for the summer, it was time to discover our fates. Had we passed the 11 plus?

10, THE BIG SCHOOL

I cannot remember how we discovered the results of the 11 plus. I can remember the exam. I felt that I had done alright.

I hadn't.

So there was a day when we all were in Mrs Wheatly's class discovering who passed and who didn't.

Our friend Gary Cottrell passed. He lived near Brian Green in Clarendon Road close to John Chawner. They had known each other forever. Brian and John had failed. Gary cried that he was going to have to be separated from his best friends. How cruel for friends to be separated at such a young age.

But I was relieved that I was still to have John Chawner, Brian Green, Robert Brown and many others from Mrs Wheatley's class in School with me. Where were they going to send us. We hoped Arthur Terry School. It was new and we had visited it. It was close to Chadsway perfect!

For some geographical reason we discovered Arthur Terry would not be our School. We were to be sent to Horror of Horrors Riland Bedford High School in Sutton Coldfield! We had heard horror stories about this school. The only consolation was my best friends were going there too.

I remember us being invited to an open day at Riland Bedford. It was a huge formidable array of buildings housing the Boys school. Next to this was a similar mirror image array of buildings housing the girls school.

What I recall most of all of the open day was the Chemistry Lab. There was a boy some how blowing bubbles with an attachment to a gas Bunsen burner. The gas bubble would float sky wards and another boy held a flame to it and whoosh it would erupt into a fire ball !

"This could be fun!" I decided. That was the first and last time I was to see anything approaching fun in the chemistry lab.

Nigel Blacklock was the son of a friend of my mothers. He was already attending Riland Bedford and I became friendly with him. He told me the school really wasn't that bad. Another reason why I got on well with Nigel, he played the guitar.

So eventually our first day at Riland Bedford came along. All the Mere Green kids had to wait at the Mere Green bus stop for the school bus to pick us up. Brian Green told us it was just a regular Midland Red bus. He knew because his Dad was a mechanic at the depot in Sutton Coldfield

Well we waited at the bus stop. There were a lot of older kids there too. It was a culture shock for us now First Years. We had just left a school where we were the big kids, and now we felt so small. The bus arrived, a double decker all the big kids went upstairs and sat at the back. Could I smell smoking?

Us First Years piled in downstairs. There was an Indian bus conductor. "You boys upstairs, please stop smoking!" he begged. It fell on deaf ears.

John Robert Brian and me, we just huddled together wondering what the hell was to become of us.

We all had uniforms and school caps. It was a school rule punishable by cane that you wore your school cap at all times in public. We all wore our caps.

Some of the bigger kids had their caps rolled up in their blazer pockets. As we got off the bus, they would flip our caps off our heads sending us into blind panic that we would surely get caned. Sometimes one bully would simply remove a small boys cap and put it on his own head. "I got my cap on today Sir" he would announce, with his own cap still rolled up in his pocket, whilst the poor First Year was left trembling with fear.

Then we arrived in the School Yard. We all had to line up and the teacher would tell us what House we were to be in. Red, Yellow, Blue, Green. Then, our form teacher led us off to our classroom.

Our form teacher was also our English Teacher. Mr May.

I think, this was about the time in my journey, I was awoken to the reality of what a totally sheltered life I had been living.

My values were instilled into me by first my Grand parents and by their influence towards my parents, then by them.

This is not a story like so many stories of hard times, quite the opposite we were raised in relative middle class comfort. My Father was a little more in touch with reality than my mother. He had to work outside the protective bubble, which was our family unit. He had to remove his Edgington Hope cloak and exist in the real world.

My Grandparents (Leonora (Gangan) on my mother's side and Tom (Grandy) on my fathers side were well spoken with accents worthy of a Buckingham Palace garden party. In 1960,s Sutton Coldfield, the local accent was soft with a slight suggestion of Birmingham about it. This was strongly discouraged in my family.

If I ever presented a tinge of Brummy in my speech, I would be immediately ridiculed and made to feel stupid by my family. All the adults in my family could immediately adopt a strong Brummy accent, which was considered gormless, stupid, and at it's very best comical. "Dow yow rur---lay want tow by one of thowes orrrful poipal what talk loik thisss ?" I would be asked. I didn't any longer.

(TRANSLATION "Do you really want to be one of those awful people who talk like this?")

Like the story, of the builders kipper legs. You really have to be careful about what you say to kids.

It may be wrong of me, but to this day, I am at best amused by strong dialects, but mostly find them an abomination of the English Spoken word. Likewise, with badly, written English.

I have great difficulty over coming my early programming of this during childhood, to the extent that it is a struggle for me, to take anyone with a strong accent seriously.

I would venture to say that this was not a good thing for my parents to have instilled in me. I believe, being overruled was frustrating my father, whenever he attempted to introduce a bit of reality into us kids lives. We would just retreat away from him into the protective bubble that was our Mother and Gangan. It was easier!

So now here I was in the first year of Riland Bedford. For a child used to his protective bubble. It was hell on earth!

I hated it. I hated the noise. My preprogramed disdain for strong regional dialect left me bewildered by the way everybody spoke. With the exception, of a number of the teachers who were Welsh. I was straining to understand what was being said. The Welsh accent, I liked. I found it musical in its delivery and I felt comfort by the fact that I understood them.

One day Nigel Blacklock and his mates found me on the stairs leading up to the Library. "Time for your initiation Edgington!" I looked at Nigel, I thought he was going to look out for me. He kind of shrugged; clearly he wasn't going to loose faith with his peers.

They lifted me over the balcony and hung me by one leg. There I was dangling upside down over the first flight of stairs. "Help! Help!" I screamed much to the amusement of these third years. Mr James the Science teacher came into view, at last I would be saved. "What the bloody hell is all the noise about Edgington? " He yelled at me with a strong Welsh accent. " Get down from there before I send you to the headmaster for the cane!"

Well the third year boys hauled me back over the bannister and by the time Mr James climbed the stairs they were gone. Just leaving me in a sobbing heap on the floor. I was miserable at school.

There was a rumour that another initiation for first years was having your head flushed down the toilet. Oh why hadn't I passed my eleven-plus? I became very introverted as a first year. I was totally unprepared for this dose of reality. John Chawner gave me some advice. Plainly he was a lot more street wise than me. "Don't show them you are angry." He explained as we were walking down the cloakroom corridor. "Be friendly to them, and have a laugh and a joke with them and they will be fine with you."

Just then some older lads from the Dugdale estate who knew John turned up. "Hey Chawner you know what happens here don't you?" They asked him. "Yes lads I do, ha ha. Come on then, Lets get it over with. " John went into the boys toilets, entered a cubical grabbed hold of the chain, and flushed his own head down the toilet. They all erupted in laughter. John turned to them with a now soaking wet head of hair smelling of some kind of toilet cleaning product and said with a grin. "Well I'm glad we got that over and done with lads!"

John was initiated, respected and because he was funny, he was never to be bullied again. And, because I was one of his best mates, neither was I.

John was our saviour, bravely accepting his watery crucifixion so that we, his disciples would live on in peace.

What I was to find out many years later from Hazel, John's lovely mother. That night John had come home sobbing his heart out because his head got flushed down the Lu. When I heard that, it just filled me with even more respect and love for my friend.

One Saturday I decided to take a walk up to Chadsway to visit Gangan. As I got close to the house, I noticed a Commer Mini Bus parked in the driveway. To my amazement I noticed through the window. Guitar Cases, Amplifiers, Drum cases, Speakers. On one of the cases "The Embers" was emblazoned in big-stencilled letters. My God he's here!

I came into the kitchen via the back gate and there was David Hamber talking to my Aunty Christine. "Hi Simon, this is our cousin David" I knew who he was. David was very friendly to me, and he took me into the lounge and introduced me to the other members of the band. In my mind I was in the presence of the family Royalty. These guys were doing what I had been dreaming of. I soaked in the experience like a sponge. David was wearing these high leather boots with THE EMBERS emblazoned on the side. It was so cool to a small boy to encounter his dream. Yet I couldn't help noticing. Disappointingly normal. which was a bit of an anti climax. I don't really know what I was expecting. Should our hero's somehow project some kind of grand presence? Well the genie definitely comes out of the bottle on stage. But, off stage? They were after all, just regular people. Even to this day, I can be bewitched by talent and the glamour on stage, and taken aback by the shear normality of the same person. Off.

11 SAINT JOHN AMBULANCE

Shy ness descended on me during first year. There was little going on there that I wanted to participate in. I was rubbish at sport that seemed to be a subject very close to the hearts of the school fraternity.

One day, Mr Llewellyn the PE teacher, caught John Chawner doing hand springs down the corridor. "You boy !!!!! get in my Gym !" he was ordered. That was to become the start of a very successful gymnastic career for John throughout his time at Riland Bedford.

I started to make friends with some other classmates. Roy Hammond sat next to me in some classes. Another shy boy, whose cheeks would light up bright red if ever he was addressed in class.

Roy was a real electronics enthusiast. He would have these gadgets that he would keep in his pocket. A wooden base with pins stuck on it and various electronic components soldered to the pins, then normally a battery and a small flashlight bulb. Connecting the battery would turn on the light and make it perform in some way as a result of the circuitry attached.

Roy's gadgets were always a lot more memorable than the classes we were attending. Each day the same gadget would make the light dance in a different way. Oh how I admired this genius. Was there no limit to this ability?

I wonder what he went on to be in adult life. Sadly we have lost touch, but it would come as no surprise to me to learn that a career in some kind of electronics was to become his destiny.

Another boy I sat next to in a class was John Titmus. It was John that was going to help me discover an interest that I could engage myself in. Also, John Titmus, was instrumental in my first real step to launching my music career. Literally!

I hated the regime that was Riland Bedford High School for Boys. Classes were noisy; I had real difficulty concentrating above the din. As a result of this my interests focused on activities outside of school time.

One day John Chawner said to me. "Brian Green's neighbour Cliff Griffin, you know Cliff he's the prefect on the school bus every day. Well he is going to take us to St John Ambulance tonight. Do you want to come?"

Apparently if you were a Cadet you could get into cinemas free. I thought to myself, "I like the sound of that!"

The Saint John ambulance Brigade had a hut in Duke Street at the top of Sutton Town not far from the cottage hospital. Cadet night would be at 7 O Clock every Monday..

So we took the bus into town around 6.30 after tea and followed Cliff Griffin to the hut. It was a long white wooden building, with an Old Ambulance parked outside emblazoned with the Saint John Ambulance Brigade motive which is a Maltese Cross.

We got there early, and we were the only ones there. Slowly a few others arrived. Richard Benton also a classmate joined us.

So we were all talking outside the hut and examining these uniforms that Cliff and now a few others were wearing.

Black school trousers and surprisingly shiny, Black shoes. The shirt was grey with epilates and a white lanyard finished off with a black tie. A Black Beret sporting the Saint John Badge was tucked into the right epilate.

Across the shoulder was a white strap that held a white bag on the waist. "What's in the bag? " We asked Cliff.

He opened the bag to reveal a plastic sealed bag full of dressings and triangular bandages. This was the St John ambulance first aid kit that all cadets would carry. Also in the bag was a well-read copy of the Saint John's Ambulance Brigade First Aid Manual.

Just then a green Austin A40 car arrived and turned into the space next to the old ambulance. I noticed John Titmus sitting in the passenger seat. The driver of the car was in uniform too, but his was Black and could be mistaken for a Police Officer uniform.

This man got out of the car. Put on a cap, which finished off the look of authority, and walked to the door to unlock the hut.

Frank Titmus opened the door, flicked a switch and the strip lights bought the hut to life. "Berets on lads ready for parade!" he ordered.

"Corporal Griffin! get the company on parade and show these new lads how to stand to attention." Frank instructed Cliff.

With this I noticed that Cliff's sleeve sported corporal stripes. He lined us all up in a row tallest to the right, shortest to the left. That put John Chawner and me at the far left.

He then drilled us in standing to attention and standing at ease, which we picked up very quickly. We learned to dress the parade to the right, which would involve us extending our right arm to the right to effect an arms length position to the person next to us. "Parade, Parade AtenSHUN!" And we would enthusiastically click our heals together and bring our arms to our sides. "Parade, Stand at ease and we would stand legs apart with our hands linked behind our backs.

Once satisfied with our performance, Cliff bought the parade to attention, executed a very impressive left turn, marched up to Mr Titmus and saluted in a military long way up short way down fashion, and announced. "Parade all present and correct and ready for inspection sir!"

Superintendent Frank Titmus returned the salute and said, "Thank you corporal, you may join the rank"

With this Corporal Cliff Griffin executed a series of military turns and joined the rank at the end of the far right.

Mr Titmus, as we came to know him, started to inspect the ranks. His uniform was turned out immaculately. It became apparent very early on that this was a matter of great importance to him. He had an array of medal ribbons on his chest and carried an authority in his stance. He was not a tall man but he exuded respect.

I liked this!

All of the discipline and order and respect that was lacking in that awful school was here. There was no chaos; this was going to be a big part of my growth and journey into adulthood.

Another thing happened on that first visit to The Saint John Ambulance Hut. A Reporter for the Sutton Coldfield News showed up with a large camera. Corporal Cliff and some of the other lads had won a trophy at a First Aid Competition in Birmingham. We all had to pose around the trophy. The following Friday the family eagerly looked at the photo in the Sutton News. There was young Si John in the Paper!! "I would be so proud to see you win some trophies too." My Dad said. Me too I thought. Me Too!

With this, I could manage the unpleasantness, which was school. I guess we all look for validation. I was not athletic; John Chawner didn't come to Saint John Ambulance ever again. He had Gym Club at school and he was doing very well with that.

With Saint John Ambulance Brigade Cadets and the influence that was Frank Titmus, little Si John found something that was to fire up his enthusiasm. Something that was character building and something that he was to become actually quite good at.

Every Monday evening after Parade, we would then be tutored in First Aid. Eventually we all got our uniforms and Mr Titmus would insist that we turned out looking immaculate with shiny shoes.

For some reason, our uniform shirts came from a batch of different material to the others we had seen. Instead of a smooth cotton style with a stiff collar. Our new shirts appeared to be more woollen in appearance. They were warmer than the cotton shirts, but it had to be said, they were not so smart, and if you didn't wear a vest underneath, your chest and back became almost as itchy as your collar!

One Monday at school John Titmus got all the cadets together and said "When you come to the weekly divisional meeting tonight, No Uniform!" He was being very secretive, and insisted that we have to wait and see.

So we showed up at the hut wondering what was going on. When we walked in there was a drum set and guitars at the end of the hut and some older lads hanging around.

When every body got settled, these four lads started playing. Wow this was fantastic. The lead guitarist was banging out the intro to Chuck Berry's Roll Over Beethoven. Well in actual fact it was Chuck Berry's intro to every song he recorded, and any guitarist in that day who could play that was OK by me!

I loved that night. It was perhaps one of the first times I had been near actual Live Music being played. Apart perhaps from that time the Swinging Blue Jeans played at Sutton Carnival. The event, the occurrence, the energy that is live music has all my life been a great privilege to witness. Non-live music just has never done it for me.

It turned out that these boys, all seventeen years old had formed a band and needed somewhere to play to an audience. The singer guitarist was John Titmus's Cousin and Frank had agreed to forego one Monday Division Night to give us a treat, and the band a gig.

So this got me talking to John Titmus about music. I told him that I had been disappointed years ago when I thought I was getting a real guitar and it turned out to be a plastic toy. How I got a Scalextric set that has basically lived in its box under my bed ever since.

"I've always wanted a Scalextric!" John exclaimed. "I had a guitar for Christmas that is just hanging on my wall. Do you want to swap?"

Did I?

12 FIRST GUITAR, AT LAST!

Well I rushed home excited. John had to ask his mother if it was ok for him to swap his guitar for my Scalextric. Oh how I hoped this would be OK.

I spoke to my Mum and she said if I was sure that's what I wanted to do, that was fine by her "Better ask his lordship if its alright with him" Dad was in the living room watching TV. He seemed to spend a lot of time in there on his own. "Simon wants to know if he can swap the Scalextric for a guitar, I said ok if he really wanted to." Was Mum's preamble. "Well it sounds like it is all sorted out between you" Dad replied. "Shall we get the Scalextric down from under your bed, Si John and check it's OK? Ask your friend when you want to make the swap"

Well next day at school was good news day. John's Mum was happy for him to swap the guitar. We arranged that my Dad would take me to John's house that evening so we could do the swap.

I could hardly wait to see my new guitar. John bought it down from the bedroom. It was a beautiful acoustic guitar with a cut away body and sound holes not shaped like the typical F sound hole. The finish was a deep starburst, which showed up the wood, grain magnificently, what a truly wonderful instrument this was, and it was to become my most prized possession.

There was a string missing, and the remaining strings; it appeared had seen better days.

My Dad met Frank Titmus, who was quite delighted when he was presented with the Scalextric box and as a final relish, A Manulife world map calendar for himself and one for any friend he might like to share with. Also the flip telephone index.

Dad had made a new friend too. Another line; in contacts for his client base too. So he was happy.

Well once home, I had to pose about in my dressing table mirror with my first real guitar. I needed a strap, and some strings, but I was in my element.

For an eleven-year-old boy, the guitar body was very large, which helped to make me look even smaller.

Little Si John could see how his dreams of stardom were on their way to coming true!

My father could see my enthusiasm. It was a nice feeling to be connected by this. High School was not an area where I was excelling. I know my friend Mark Hofton who lived on the other side of Sutton and now attended Boldmere School, was giving his Dad, Tony a lot more to be proud of academically.

I was not thick by any means, but finding my path through Riland Bedford High School For Boys was proving to be a difficult one. Dad was pleased that I found an interest in St John Ambulance, and always knew that I loved music.

I am the eldest of three kids. My mother, who I have loved all my life, was very protective of us children. When I was playing with my sister Sally, nearer my age but a girl. I was not allowed to be rough. If that was difficult, playing with baby Adam was really not worth the trouble. He would cry, I would get scolded; I wanted to be more involved. But I was becoming aware of how mollycoddled we had all become. Other parents it seemed would encourage a little rough and tumble.

I think my father spent a lot of relaxing time on his own too. He wasn't used to this degree of mollycoddling either. He seemed more relaxed playing with other people's kids. They were being raised to be more resilient than us.

I can remember one time when my father became furious with me. Like I said before. One has to be careful what one says to kids. It sticks. Remember the kipper's legs?

After squabbling with sister Sally. My father yelled "Simon!" Simon not Si John this MUST be serious!" You never, ever hit girls!"

That stuck!

High School is an era in ones life of significant change. I was growing apart from my brother and sister who were still children. I was becoming a big boy. High School was a reality check, no mothers mollycoddling going on there, quite the opposite.

I was starting to feel a bond with my father. It was a nice feeling.

The next evening Dad came home with a gift for me that he bought from work. Norfolk House on Small brook ring way, Birmingham which houses Manulife, also had a music shop.

I think Dad enjoyed finding a level where we could connect too. He enthusiastically handed me a bag containing a set of Cathedral Guitar Strings, a set of pitch pipes for tuning and a copy of the book that was to launch many generations of guitar heroes. "Burt Weedon's Play in a day"

In side the front cover of my copy Dad wrote with his fountain pen in his immaculate hand writing scroll. "To Si John, Practice and Persevere. Love Dad x."

This was the best present ever! "On Saturday, I'll take you into Birmingham, if we take your guitar, we can get a case for it. You don't want it getting scratched do you?"

Saturday. We drove in the Ford Zodiac up the A38 through Gravelly Hill, Aston High Street (No Spaghetti Junction back then) to the city centre. Norfolk House. Dad had his own personal parking space in Norfolk house. He proudly turned the Zodiac into the bay marked Warwick G. Edgington. Manulife. (G, for Greatrex). Being a Saturday however, Dad's car was the only one parked there. Making us both feel quite exclusive!

Gingerly I carried my guitar up the stairs, being very careful not to bang my prized possession on the railings, to the foyer level and exited Norfolk House onto Small brook Ring way. I recognised New Street Station from journeys with Gangan into the city centre, and there too was the Birmingham News Theatre where she had taken us to watch Pathe News and cartoons.

Just a few doors up from Norfolk House entrance was a double fronted shop window display that made my heart leap a beat.

The first window was ablaze with colours. Rows of Electric Guitars. Red Blue Wooden Starburst, sporting pick-ups and tremolo arms. Behind the guitars was a bank of Vox amplifiers. Microphone stands, column speakers. Everything I wanted in my world.

The second window displayed music books and Brass and wind instruments. Wow this was a shop that I could live in.

We entered the shop and the proprietor who was attending to some young men interested in a guitar, looked up and acknowledged my dad. When he finished with the other lads he came over to us. "Hellow Warwick ." he greeted in a healthy Birmingham accent. "How noice tur soy yow again sow soon"

(TRANSLATION "Hello Warwick, How nice to see you again so soon.")

We showed him my guitar and he found a soft case with a zip opening that fitted. I also saw a rotary display with a selection of guitar straps hanging from it. "Well Si John, you are going to need to choose one of those too I suppose." Dad said.

To be treated by my Dad was so nice. I had a grin on my face from ear to ear as he handed over the cash in the shop, and I couldn't help noticing the Warwick Edgington name emblazoned on the Manulife globe calendar on the wall of the music shop next to a pile of Burt Weedon's Play in a day books and a poster of Acker Bilk in his bowler hat.

13 TAMING OF THE WICKED MUSIC TEACHER

My new guitar was to spend very, very little time in its case! My guitar was my constant companion. I remember very little about actual homework. I know I had it, and I would always do it for fear of the cane if it didn't get done. Or detention, which would mean you, would miss the school bus after school. Then you would have to fork out a penny-halfpenny to get the regular bus home.

So I would get homework out of the way in my bedroom. Unless it was something I could do rushing on the bus to school. There was always a bunch of us comparing notes at the back of the bus.

Homework done I could open my Burt Wheedon book and dream about becoming a pop star.

Burt teaches you to tune your guitar and then goes on to practicing chords. The first ones specifically; C and G seventh.

Struggling between these two chords seemed impossibility. My untrained fingers would move in what seemed an unnatural way. "Practice and Persevere Si John, Practice and Persevere, you know you want this!" Grooves would cut into my fingertips, I would continue until my fingers were sore and cramped. I would then have to stop, feeling quite dejected. It was like hitting a brick wall.

The next day during English at school, I could feel my fingers fidgeting. I held a ruler in my left hand and adopted the chord shapes on it.

When I got home I picked up the guitar and hey presto like magic. I had it. Faster and faster I could change from one chord to another. Also I noticed it was no longer painful. My fingertips were beginning to develop calluses, hard pads of skin, which made handling the strings much better.

One of the teachers, it turned out was giving guitar lessons after school. He was a Welsh guy called Mr Jones (Oddly). So I asked him when I could come. "Well boyo," he replied "I am doing a lesson tomorrow night, if you bring your guitar into my classroom, I will lock it in the stock room for you. I wouldn't trust the Tea leafs (Thieves) in this place to leave it alone in the cloak rooms!" Quite right, I thought.

I was getting on well with Burt Wheedons exercises, but "She'll be coming round the mountain when she comes" wasn't really the musical genre that I had in mind. I was hoping to learn some Beatles.

So the next day, Dad dropped me off at school on his way to work. I got out of the Zodiac under the gaze of my schoolmates who were just alighting the Midland Red Number 2.

Armed with my huge guitar in its bag I entered the school gates and preceded down the corridor to Mr Jones classroom. "Bloody Hell boyo that thing is twice your size!" he exclaimed "Is that a case or a bloody cof---fin ?" He teased Welshly.

I put my guitar case in his stock room. There was another guitar case, and a number of other nylon strung guitars that looked like they had seen better days. Mine was the best, I proudly convinced myself.

At the end of the school day I rushed eagerly to the music room. A few other lads were already in there tuning their instruments to an old upright piano.

"Well today boys, I am going to show you C and G7" He announced and proceeded to strum and sing "Hang down your head Tom Dooley" Well to be honest his choice of music was even less inspiring than the Bert Weedon's genre.

But what was good about these lessons was it got me a new circle of guitar playing friends. The hardest chord to learn is F. Either as a 4 string or six string chord for an eleven-year-old hand. But with the aid of the Practice and Persevere Mantra, written by my father on the inside of Burt's Play in a day. I eventually scaled yet another of the brick walls that all guitar players have to endure.

My new Friend Warren who was in Nigel Blacklock's year proved to be a much more effective teacher than dear old Mr Jones.

Warren and I would sit opposite each other. We must have been quite a sight. Him adult size now with his small Spanish nylon guitar and me barely visible behind my large bodied acoustic.

He taught me to play rhythm and twelve bar blues, I would strum away to his lead playing songs like "Green Onions" Jimmy Hendrix "Hey Joe" and the "House of the rising sun"

These would be the tunes that future guitar tutor books would include.

Now armed with an arsenal of chords, I could play lots of songs that I would listen to on Radio Luxemburg. John Chawner had a Philips Reel to Reel Tape recorder and he would record many of these tunes. I have just got to get one of those, I decided.

John used his tape recorder more for reading out scripts from the Goon Show. He and his brother Steve were both very good at silly voices. As was their Mother, Darling Hazel.

I was finding my identity a bit more in School. Often bringing my guitar in. Mr Jones was not a permanent teacher there and he moved on.

Our permanent Music Teacher was Mr Peter Day. He was a very fine Pianist and Organist. The school stage had a magnificent pipe organ that had recently been restored. John and I became sopranos in the choir.

I remember well one day in class, Mr Day asked if any one played a musical instrument. Being shy I wasn't the first boy to have his hand fly sky wards. Another lad exclaimed, "I have a mouth organ Sir" "Oh do you? And do you read music?" Mr Day leered at him. "No Sir" "Then how can you call yourself a musician if you don't even read music" Mr Days tirade was so brutal that you could feel all musical enthusiasm drain from this small boy. Along with any desire, in me, to announce to this twat that he was actually in the presence of a future pop star.

I seriously doubt that boy ever picked up his mouth organ again. David Hamber our family Pop Star didn't read music, but he was making more money and visiting more places around the world than Mr Frigging Stick up his ass, Peter Day.

Mr Day was all about the classics. We were singing Handel, and our school choir got to perform in Birmingham Cathedral on more than one occasion.

John and I and another boy Anthony were the sopranos. Anthony had been singing Soprano all his life. He had a much more powerful voice than John and Me. That was until on one fateful recital, his voice let out an unexpected squeak followed by a croak and a tuneless grunt as a boy sopranos voice does before transition down the score to the Tenor Stave.

Anthony was so distraught by his voice betraying him so spectacularly when it broke in front of such a large congregation that was the last of his singing at Riland Bedford.

Mr Day was a music snob. He was capable of sucking the joy out of music. Which was no mean feat. We had to endure endless lessons of classical Music history, when all we really wanted to do was listen to the Beatles.

But one memorable music lesson did warm us to him somewhat.

John Chawner was fast getting a reputation for mimicry. He would mimic the teachers much to all of our amusement. One day he had to run an errand that resulted in him visiting the staff room. Well it turned into an ambush.

Apparently his mimicry had not gone by unnoticed by the teachers. "Chawner" Mr James, The Science teacher from Wales said, "It has come to my attention that you do a pretty good impersonation of me laddie. Well come on then boyo lets be 'avin it. " John was cornered and he could see no way out of it.

With a little resignation he realised that he had little choice other than to do as he was told. He started with his impression of Mr James lighting his Bunsen burner and setting fire to his lab coat cursing in a strong Welsh accent. Well there was uproar. All the teachers were belly laughing with tears in their eyes. "Wow Chawner you got him to a T there" One of the others announced. " I tell you what. Do me!" one by one they all commanded. John was in his element; he had found a new audience for his well-rehearsed mimicry. Feeling the love from his new crowd he stepped his performance up a gear as he ridiculed one teacher after the other. There was so much hilarity coming down from the staff room, that the headmaster had to come up from his office below to see what the commotion was. All were laughing except for the very serious music teacher Peter Day.

Well next music class. Peter Day wanted to lecture us on the importance of the conductor in an orchestra. With a batten in hand, he demonstrated how to direct 3 to the bar and four to the bar. Showing how the movement of the baton can direct tempo and feeling in a piece of music.

He then got some of us up to conduct him as he played a piece on the piano, following the direction of the boy conducting. It was all very serious until he made the mistake of summoning John Chawner to the baton.

Well John took to the baton like a natural. He soon got the hang of the control that he had over his pianist. He also had observed Mr Day enough to mimic some of his characteristics. One being pushing his glasses back on his nose every time he looked up from the piano. So that got the appreciation of the class, who started to giggle. He waved the baton in a flourish of movements that sent the music piece from a small tinkle to a roaring crescendo. Altering tempo along the way. The look of concentration on Peter Day's face was a site to be seen, when he looked back up at the piano and quickly pushed his glasses back on his nose, the class erupted. John turned on the class displaying the Peter Day frown he uses to get order in class. A mannerism that John; must have practiced at home in his mirror. Then as a coup de grace. He mimicked the pushing the glasses back on his nose using the hand holding the baton and comically poking his eye. The whole class just fell about laughing.

And the music stopped.

John turned back towards the piano. There was Mr Day silent. His shoulders were heaving up and down like a Mike Yarwood impersonation of Eduard Heath. And he had tears pouring down his face. Then he began to laugh. Uncontrollably.

With this John stood to attention, and conductor like tapped the baton rapidly 4 times on the top of the piano. As one would; to gain order from an orchestra.

Well that was too much for Peter Day. Already lost in his laughter, he appeared to then loose control of his legs, he slipped off the stool into a heap on the floor behind the piano, now out of sight of the class and all we could hear was him weeping, howling then giggling.

Peter Day was a crap schoolteacher, arrogant. Like most of the teachers at this school, I really don't think he liked kids at all.

But, John Chawner tamed him for us.

14 GIRLS

Julia Sims was my first girlfriend. I met her in Junior school. She was a very pretty little creature who lived in a bungalow in Midgley Drive very close to Holly Lodge. I would ride my bike over to see her, and was always invited to her birthday parties.

Once we started at Riland Bedford Boys School we became separated from all female company. Occasionally on St John Ambulance, the girls division would accompany us, and we would practice putting the girls arms in slings and splints on their legs. Frank Titmus would explain that carrying out first aid examinations, looking for injuries, diagnosing the problem was a perfectly proper and natural thing to do.

Well for us lads rapidly approaching the dawn of puberty and adolescence, we were discovering how quite by accident our chosen activities were presenting us with very acceptable ways of copping a feel.

John Titmus would explain how Jane's titty rubbed itself against the back of his hand as he adjusted her arm sling. We would snigger to ourselves and exaggerate our experiences in an attempt to achieve one up man ship.

By this time Cliff Griffin had left Riland Bedford to go to teacher training college, He had also moved from the Cadets to the regular St John Ambulance brigade. John Titmus Myself Dickie Benton and David Hughes had stepped up to become the new competing first aid team in our division. We were beginning to see some success too.

I remember Diane was my opposite number in the girl team. We were at an age when we didn't really know what we were supposed to do about girls. I remember arranging to go on a date with Diane. We went ten pin bowling, and I think we were both so shy, neither of us spoke through the whole experience. Needless to say that was a painful one off.

During the summer holidays, we loaded the tent up and went back down to Devon. Dad would stay for a week, then travel home alone to work and then come back and have the final week with us.

I had my guitar, and sometimes I would take it to Watermouth Caves next to the campsite and sit in the café with the kids from the caravan site. That is where I met Susan Sadler. She was from Five Oaks, which has a match made in heaven as I was from Four Oaks. I would impress her with my guitar playing and singing my song that I wrote for her.

"I've got a fever, that only she can cure

I just can't leave her, gotta stay near......."

Sadly that was over at the end of her two-week holiday. We swapped addresses and did exchange letters for quite some time, fantasising over when we would see each other again. I imagined her getting off the train in Snow Hill Station Birmingham. She would run to my arms in a slow motion like way and we would embrace and share our first kiss. We never did.

Second year came and went at Riland Bedford. The most notable difference in the second year was a change of Music Teacher. Malcombe John was the new guy. What a nice man he was. Much more in touch with us kids than his predecessor. He organised a production of Gilbert and Sullivan's Pirates of Penzance. As second years we were not included in the actual play, but music Classes involved the whole school singing from this gem of musical comedy theatre. We were promised that we would be in the following years production.

By this time I was making regular trips to the St John Ambulance Birmingham Headquarters for advanced first aid practice and drill training. We were starting to gather trophies for the team and getting recognition in the Sutton Coldfield News; much to the satisfaction of my father. It was a proud moment for me when Frank Titmus pulled up outside Holly Lodge with a boot full of the cups and trophies that we had won. It was my turn to hold them for a week. My father and I proudly arranged them on the mantle piece in the living room.

We would load up the Bedford Van belonging to Jerry one of the kids fathers and drive to Corris in Mid Wales. St John, Birmingham owned a cottage there. Frank would take us on marches around the beautiful valleys that is mid Wales all around Cader Idris the large mountain near Dolgellau. On one weekend, the girls division accompanied us. It was all good fun around the campfire stuff. And of course, I had my guitar. I enjoyed the times in Mid Wales.

On one occasion George Blackburn, one of the other superintendents took us hill climbing at the back of the cottage. We climbed so high the building was a mere speck. The view down the valley was just spectacular. Green speckled with sheens of white reflections of the clouds on the lake water.

As we climbed back down we heard a scream. "Help us! Please somebody help!" was the very distressed female cry. It sounded like it was coming from around the front of the cottage.

Hastily we ran down the hill as fast as our legs would carry us.

When we got to the front of the cottage there was a scene of total carnage. The girl's bodies laying everywhere and the van stopped awkwardly against a dry stonewall.

At the wheel of the van was Frank Titmus, plainly unconscious with a deathly white complexion. Jerry, the other adult with us was holding a cine camera. "Come on lads." He shouted. "You should know what to do by now, get in there and do your stuff!"

The whole scenario was a mock up of an accident. Supposedly the van driver Frank had suffered a heart attack and ploughed into this group of hikers. The lady in charge of the girls was a medical make up artist, and she had skilfully "Injured" these girls in ways that we had to diagnose and treat.

Once back in Sutton, we eagerly awaited the arrival of the Cine film footage back from Boots, so that we could watch, analyse and laugh at our performance.

It was a very useful exercise in First Aid. We were taught to prioritise our casualties. Remove the casualty from the danger. Breathing Bleeding Fractures. Frank in the van could only be put in the recovery position.

One girl had brilliant plasticine swellings on her fore arm with bits of bone sticking out. Another was covered in a menu of baked beans and bits of tomato signifying vomit. But the best bit of the cine film, which we played over time and time again was when John Titmus goes to raise a girls leg to control the bleeding. It came off in his hand ! The look on his face was a true picture.

They had cleverly put the girl on top of a dry stone wall, tucked her leg under her, hidden by more stones. Then they placed a false leg below her knee and made up the knee joint with a bloody injury.

We had other activities with Saint John's Ambulance that kept us out of the house. In addition to the Monday Night Divisional meetings, Tuesday night was a social night for handicapped people at a public hall next to the Midland Red Depot. It was our job to assist them in and out of their vehicles. Help with tea making and distribution and sometimes provide some entertainment.

On one occasion there was a gymnastic display. I was very proud to see that the star of the display was my best friend John Chawner. We both surprised to see each other there. Our two separate interests found the same venue one night.

If there was a particular movie showing that we wanted to see. We could just put on our St John Ambulance Uniform and we could sit at the back of the Empress or Odeon Cinemas for free. I remember the first time I did that watching "It's A Mad Mad World" at the Odeon. Starring Phil Silvers and Terry Thomas.

One time we manned the Ambulance at a football match at the Aston Villa Ground. As I walked around the edge of the pitch as we do I heard "Oi Edgy, How the fuck did you get out there?" I turned to the stand and there were some of my classmates out to watch the game. I am not remotely interested in Football, but I did enjoy the irony that my privilege was the envy of my classmates and yet it totally passed me by.

Another duty that was fun on a warm weekend day, was hanging out in the St John first aid hut just by the town entrance to Sutton Park. Sometimes a crew manning the ambulance would accompany us. Most of the time it was giving plasters to kids who had scraped a knee.

My guitar playing was becoming so much of a passion to me that it inspired my father to buy himself a banjo. He bought a tutor. The chords on a banjo seemed a little simpler than on guitar. But the best thing about this was it was a point of connection between my father and me. It has to be said. He wasn't good, he had difficulty strumming in time and it gave me a feeling of superiority to be able to pass my expertise back to him.

" ME" Plunky plunky plunk "AND MY" Plunky plunky plunk "SHA" Plunky plunky plunk "DOW" Plunky plunky plunk he would perform from his tutor book.

Thankfully when we set off for our next annual holiday he didn't feel the need to include the banjo in the trailer.

This time we pointed the Zodiac beyond Devon as we ventured into Cornwall. Crackington Haven Bay to be precise. A beautiful bay a high cliff on one side. The sea would come cascading up the beach with surfboard waves. You could smell the salt and seaweed in the air and feel the wind born sand, as it pummelled your face. Seagulls and breaking waves competed with each other for sound effect. Opposite the cliff side of the beach, lay a green fenced meadow. The sign on the gateway afforded us our greeting. "CAMPING SITE TENTS AND CARAVANS WELCOME." That will do us we decided and pitched our tent.

15 FIRST CRUSH

Holiday time in Crackington Haven. I have to admit that by now I was starting to get a bit too grown up for holidays with my Little Brother and Sister.

I was at the age where I was still a child, but becoming an adult. I was easing into, that period of adolescence. When you have the luxury of playing the grown, up or the child, depending on, which is more convenient for the circumstance. As yet a newcomer to this phenomenon, and it's conventions. By watching my peers, I would soon learn the finer points of comfortable transit through the teenage years.

The Saint John Ambulance Brigade was instilling discipline and responsibility in me. I was rapidly starting to resent the mollycoddling from my mother. I wanted to be treated more like a grown up than like my little brother and sister.

I was beginning to understand my fathers irritation, when watching how cocooned we had become by this maternal blanket.

I was trying to break away from childhood.

The lady that ran the campsite lived in a beautiful touring caravan. She came over to welcome us and introduce herself. Her Name was Diane McQueen and she was there for the summer with her family.

"You'll be seeing a lot of us about the camp." She had a son Ian who was about my brother Adams age and two daughters. Susan. Who was about a year younger than me then Alison. A couple of years, older than me.

One day they all came to our tent so we could get to know them. Alison (Ali), was like me a bit too aloof to be playing with the kids, after all she was 15. So she decided to sun bathe.

"Could somebody put some lotion on my back"

She asked. "I cannot right now Darling" her mother said "I'm smoking this cigarette and I got this cup of tea in my hand. Simon, be a dear and put some sun cream on Ali's back."

I was very embarrassed; my Dad grinned and picked up his camera. "Go on Si John. She wont bite will you Ali?" he urged.

So I proceeded to rub sun cream onto Ali's back. "mmm that's nice, you have a knack for this don't you." She purred with a Cornish accent.

I liked touching Ali, she moved her back in response to my palms and I started to feel a stirring sensation in my loins. I believe I was developing a crush on this little Cornish girl, whilst discovering, it's actually quite nice, to touch girls.

I lay in bed that night, thinking about Ali. Was she too grown up for me? She was fifteen and I was thirteen. That is a huge age difference at our time of life.

Ali McQueen My First Crush.

Yet she was so nice. I liked her accent, and detected some teenage rebellion inside her. I should take some pointers from her so that I would be treated more like a grown up. Ali McQueen seemed to have it all sorted out. In fairness, she was two years ahead in her adolescent journey. I wondered if I would get to touch her again. That was nice.

The next day I walked down to the beach. It was a beautiful warm summers day, the sea was glistening and the high tide was up. Waves were nibbling at the shingle stones, which clicked together in protest of being moved by the retreating wave. Some sprigs of seaweed lay across the stones along with some pieces of driftwood. The Seagulls were out in force once more hunting out the occasional crabs in the rock pools.

What a lovely romantic location for Ali and I to share our first kiss, I fantasised. We could walk along the seashore, hand in hand, splashing our feet as each new wave comes in and out. Then we could go sit on that rock together and daydream about how wonderful our life together will be.

I'd made up my mind; I was going to get to know Ali better. When I saw her next. What would I say? I asked myself. What would John Chawner do at a time like this? He would smile with his cheeky grin and say something funny. That's what I would need to do. Act cool and smile. I had a smile on my face, just thinking about it. Life was going to be good.

To celebrate my sea air induced euphoria, I decided to treat myself to a Mars Bar. I unwrapped it and started to eat it. It was a bit soft from the sun so I decided to finish it quickly; before it's soggy chocolate disgraced me.

I remembered in the corner shop in Hill village Road with the sign on the wall next to Dad's Manulife Calendar "A Mars a day helps you work rest and play." I feasted on the chocolate caramel treat and threw its wrapper in a nearby litterbin. It was when my mouth was full to bursting with Mars Bar who should I see coming the other way towards me? The object of my desires. Ali!

I tried my best to finish the Mars bar by the time she got to me but it just wasn't going to happen. "Hello Luver, What you been doing today?" The girl of my dreams asked with her musical Cornish drawl. I struggled to swallow the remains of my Mars bar so that I could reply and our life together could begin. But I just started to choke. "Oh my God luver, yesterday you did my back, now I suppose oi beddar return the favour!" With this she slapped me squarely on the back and the grass beneath me became speckled with chewed up Mars Bar. "Feelin bedder now moi luvver ? " My saviour enquired. What was it I was supposed to do John? Oh yes. Smile.

Ali was presented with a chocolate stained toothy smile. Not the first impression I had planned creating on the beach. Nice one Si John. Could my humiliation have been more complete?

It turned out that the McQueen family lived in Launceston. Diane's father was a solicitor. He owned the camp Site and some other land in Crackington Haven. Diane was divorced but she had a partner who was manager of a Ford dealership in Launceston. Eventually he came to Crackington and we were all to meet him.

John Hall-Say was a nice jovial man. But it was no contest to see between Diane and John, which one of them wore the trousers. In fact John wasn't even number two in the pecking order of that particular family dynamic. Diane's two daughters made sure of that!

Our family and the McQueen – Hall-Say's got on famously together to the extent that on our way home we were invited to go stay with them all in Launceston.

Meanwhile, I was trying, and failing to convince Ali that I was a worthy contender as boyfriend. The girls were becoming bored with Crackington Haven and they would find ways to misbehave to amuse themselves.

One thing that we all joined in on, involved the public toilets. There was a signpost that identified the ladies and Gents entrance. We would wait for someone to go in there, and then turn the sign round. After retiring to a safe distance, we would observe the pandemonium to follow. It was very naughty but hey we were teenagers and that was about as much anarchy we could come up with in Crackington Haven.

So on the way back to Sutton, we stopped at Trekensa, which was Cornish for End House or something. We all stayed at the McQueens home. I went for a walk with Ali and Susan into town. We found a playground and Ali sat on a swing and shocked me. She pulled out of her pocket a packet of Ten Players Number Six. "Do you want one? " she asked "I don't smoke." I replied. "Neither do I! Disgusting 'abbit innet." Susan put in. "You don't smoke?" Ali exclaimed. "I thought all the grown ups in our families smoked."

Good point! They do don't they.

"Take a drag out of mine, and I might kiss you." Ali teased, blowing a perfectly practiced, Smoke Ring.

Well it was now or never, I thought. Obviously time for me to step up, be a man. I took the fag from Ali's hand and puffed on it like I'd seen my mum. "Not like that you got to inhale so it comes back out your nose and mouth." She snatched back the fag, and skilfully demonstrated. So I took another puff this time breathing in a little. Well my head went into an immediate spin and I felt nauseated and began to cough. Ali was laughing, "I only said I might give you a kiss. You are going to have to do better than that my lover!"

Plainly, this being grown up was going to require more practice and perseverance.

John Hall Say had an unusual sports car. It was a Sebring Sprite, made by Austin Healey. Built on a conventional frog eyed sprite chassis. It featured a front end with a conventional headlight array instead of the usual frogeye type. The bonnet was actually the whole front end of the car. Cast in fiberglass, which would hinge forward to display an impressive Racing Cam fitted twin carb B.M.C power plant. In it's closed position; the bonnet was held in place by a leather strap.

The rest of the bodywork was beaten out in Aluminium and it had a framed convertible soft top. Finished off in a beautiful metallic blue paintwork and wire spoke racing wheels.

It was a magnificent specimen. We were told it had competed in the Sebring races with Graham Hill behind the wheel.

My Dad loved this car. It was for sale. My Dad would have to have this car!

It was decided that Ali would maybe like to come and stay with us over the Christmas holidays. I liked the sound of that. So the plan was, start of Christmas holidays, Dad would take the train to Exeter where John would collect him and bring him back to Launceston.

He would do the deal, and the next day, He and Ali would travel back up to Four Oaks in the Sebring Sprite.

It was going to be a long wait through the autumn until Dad could take delivery of his dream car.

And I could take delivery of my dream girl.

16 ADOLESCENT FANTASIES

When we got back from Cornwall, I couldn't wait to go up to Darnel Hurst Road and tell John Chawner about my Cornish Holiday and brief encounter with a girl.

We rode our bikes down Worcester lane and down to the woods. As we sat in the bracken flicking small pebbles at an old gatepost, I told John about Ali. I might, I confess, have included in the story a little bit more from my fantasy than the actual reality.

John too, had a story to tell me. From the upstairs box room in their house, John and Steve had established an observatory with a telescope. The heavenly body of interest was not however sky bound. It was that of a family's teenage daughter across the road. One of them would go into the living room and announce discreetly to the other who was watching Dad's Army on TV "She's there again" They would make their excuses to their parents and go up to their observation post.

There she was, posing topless in front of her mirror in the bedroom. The two boys would take turn to marvel at this vision of teenage beauty.

They were both convinced that she was putting on this show of naughtiness for them. Well aware of the adolescent admiration that was coming from across the road.

Any way John and I spent the afternoon riding our bikes and exaggerating our stories of exploring our new interest. The; fairer sex.

The other topic on our minds was we were soon to become Third Years at Riland Bedford.

Once more it was term time. We took the number 2 Midland Red School bus into School from Mere Green.

We all gathered in the hall for assembly, Now that we were third years, we entered by the rear doors and lined up in front of the Fourth, Fifth years and seniors, waiting for the new little First and Second years to file in through the front door, in front of us.

Where were they? There was no sign of them!

Then the strangest thing happened. The front doors swung open, and a girl dressed in Riland Bedford High School for Girls uniform walked in. When she turned and saw all us lads at the back of the hall gorping at her, mouths open in total disbelief, she turned and looked back at whence she came. She beckoned to someone out of sight, and when that created no response, she rapidly walked back out of the door.

Well we lads all looked at each other in amazement. The whole school remained stupefied and glued to the spot. What was going on? We had never seen a GIRL in Riland Bedford School for Boys before. Yes we had seen them on the games field, because the two schools shared a common games field. We knew they ate in the same canteen, but at different times. The canteen was located between the two schools and had a Boys Entrance and a girl's. But never, ever, up until this moment. The twain would meet. And where were our first and second years?

Before we gathered our composure and voices the answers arrived. This time the same girl entered the room, smiling a little more confidently now for the rest of the entire Girls sixth form followed her. After that, the fifth year fourth and third year girls filed into the assembly hall.

The girls were giggly and talking to one another. Perplexed as us. With the change, in circumstance. This broke the ice and "What the Fuck?" was being exclaimed in every corner of the ranks of boys.

Headmaster, Mr Freeman at the Lectern, called the room to order. Behind him, onstage were some of the familiar faces of teachers, interspersed with some less familiar faces.

Following the demise during the summer break, of the Headmistress of Riland Bedford School for Girls. Sutton Coldfield has made a decision, to bring this school in line with the other comprehensive schools of the Borough. Riland Bedford High School is now Co-ed! First and second year classes to begin with will be run from what was formally the Girls school side of the building. With some third years.

Blue and Green Houses will have their form rooms on the Boys Side. Red and Yellow, on the former girls side.

From now on, houses will be named Riland, Bedford, Beauchamp and Beaumont.

What a lot to take in!

So once again we found ourselves sat in class with girls. We had not shared a class with girls since the Junior School three years back. To begin with, the boys sat together, mainly occupying the back rows of the form room. The girls sat together in the front rows.

We hadn't really paid much attention to the girls at Junior School. At break time they would play girl games involving skipping ropes and soppy rhymes. "I like Coffee I like Tea, I like Katy in with me!" Then Katy would jump over the rope along with the first girl. Why oh why would us boys be remotely interested in soppy girls?

But now the third year, these girls were beginning to catch our eye. They were beginning to develop womanly charms of varying degrees.

We would sit at the back of class sniggering about how when we last saw her, she had nothing at all. "Look at the tits on her now!" Our voyage of discovery on the charms and attractions of the following sex had begun.

One new lad in our class was Paul Buckmaster. His family had moved to town from Nottingham during the summer holidays. I got to know Paul quite early on when I discovered that he lived in a flat over the off licence across the road from Holly Lodge.

Pauls father was a graphic artist and Paul was showing signs of following in his footsteps. Paul was an authority on girls apparently, and he gained popularity amongst us boys by bringing his fathers Playboy magazines to school.

Very soon the D.C. Comic collections were to make room for Penthouse and Playboy Magazines hidden beneath our beds. Our hero's were no longer Superman or Batman, Now, we preferred Miss July or Miss August our playmate for the month.

Paul called on me one day at home and said. "Come with me I want to show you something." He led me down Lichfield Road towards Four Oaks station. On the junction to Walsall Road opposite the station was a gateway. Paul opened the gate and led me into large unkempt garden.

The grass was growing uncontrollably over waist high in some areas, and the hedges were desperately in need of a trim.

As we walked up the path, a large old house came into view. It would have been a beautiful home in it's day. Large bay windows, going up, three floors. Now sadly, abandoned and derelict.

We walked through the front doorway. The door was unhinged and lying in a heap of dust and rubble, redundant on the floor.

A huge hallway with a large staircase; leading to a landing. The remains of a stained glass window reflected coloured shadows on the patchy walls. Many of the stairs were now missing.

How sad to see a building in this condition. No doubt, once a family home. How many family occasions had been hosted in this hallway? Who was to know?

How many blushing brides had descended this staircase? No doubt a proud father below once looked up, felt a tear on his cheek and a lump in his throat. On sight of the vision, which was the daughter he was about to give away "My Darling, you look more beautiful on this day, than ever!" He reaches out to take her hand, kiss her gently on the cheek and lower the veil over her face. Escorting through the front door, to the waiting limousine.

Who was to know? This old house was keeping its secrets.

"Come up here" Paul beckoned. "I want to show you my secret hideout." Paul sprinted up the staircase to the landing, which was no mean feat, seeing as many of the stairs had pieces of wood missing. Plainly this was not the first time Paul had climbed these stairs. By following in his footsteps, I too managed to reach the landing. From there, we climbed one of the next set of stairs to the first floor landing.

Here were a selection of bedrooms and bathrooms in various states of decay. One had to watch ones steps because many floorboards were missing, and many of those that remained seemed to be infested with woodworm. Step on a floorboard with the tell tale minute holes in it. And it would instantly turn to dust. We climbed another staircase and were presented by a bay window frame set into the sloping ceiling. "Follow me it's all right, I've done this loads of times" Paul said. With that, he stepped out of the glassless window and I could hear him scaling the roof.

I gingerly followed and saw there was quite a large ledge that appeared to be solid. I easily followed Paul up the tiles. I'd climbed the rocks at Watermouth Caves. This felt no different. By one of the huge chimneystacks, there was an area where the tiles were completely missing. Paul lowered him self through the hole and was now standing in the loft on the edge of what must have been the water tank. By the side of the water tank was a loft hatch into a room below. This was Paul's secret hideaway. The door to the room; was barricaded up by a large workbench. Our secret method of entry was the only access to this room.

It appeared this was where Paul kept his illicit collection of Playboy magazines, which his father believed had long since been thrown out.

We would study these pictures and talk about what sex must be like. Paul said he'd done it with a girl in Nottingham and he would give me a blow-by-blow account of the details.

I told him I had a Cornish girlfriend who would be coming to see me at Christmas. "Have you gone all the way yet?" Paul asked. "Na not yet" I had to admit. "We just held hands on the beach kissed and smoked." Well he was probably relating his fantasy of a girl in Nottingham, so figured I could relate mine.

"Have you got any fags on you now?" Paul then asked. "I bloody well left mine at home." Obviously I hadn't. "Tell you what, I'll show you another place I go tonight." He offered. "It's nearer home. We can smoke there."

Well it was about time I started smoking. I didn't want to be embarrassed again next time I saw my Ali.

We left our hideout the same way we came in. "I have a code name for this house." Paul announced. "I call it E short for E Type Jag!" Well I have got no idea what the logic of that label was. In years to follow, there would be a lot of occasions when I would question Paul Buckmaster's logic. Plainly our journeys were heading for different ultimate destinations. But for now they were converging.

17 BAD INFLUENCES

"Come round to my place at seven and I'll get us some fags. " Paul said as we got back to Holly Lodge.

Seven O Clock came and I climbed the concrete steps at the back of the off licence and knocked on the door. Paul opened the door on a small flat. We went through to the living room. A scruffy man was sat in an old armchair. His hair was thin but long, nearly shoulder length. This was unusual for Four Oaks. I think Grandy would probably have described him as a beatnik type. On the table was a large bottle of beer. "There are some bottles for you to take back to the off licence Pablo (Paul), you got to earn your pocket money somehow!" Paul's dad said. "Ok Dad I will get them now.

I followed Paul into a small kitchen by the entrance. There was a large bag containing four or five large beer bottles. He grabbed it by its handles and proceeded out the door and down the concrete steps.

"Hang on a minute." Paul said as I was almost out from the back of the shops and on the pavement. "Just hang on to these for a moment" He handed me the bag of bottles, then turned and disappeared into the darkness behind the shop.

I heard a clinking sound and when Paul emerged back from the dimly lit shop rear, he was carrying another armful of bottles. "We will take these in as well, then we will have enough money for a two packets of fags.

We walked into the Off Licence. "Hi Pablo." George behind the counter greeted. "Returning more bottles from your dad are you?" "Yeah that's right George and he says can he have two packets of Ten Number Six with the money. One for him and one for me mum."

We left the Off Licence with a packet of number six each. And crossed Clarence Road. Opposite the shops was a driveway and a wooden garage that looked like it had seen better days. Paul opened one of the double doors ajar so we could gain entrance. Inside was an old car a workbench with a large metal vice fitted. On the shelves were various pots of paint and an old orange box filled with an assortment of hammers, spanners and paintbrushes. It was some kind of classic car reminiscent of the type driven by gangsters at the Saturday morning pictures. It had a running board and huge front wings with oversized headlights. The front door was hinged from behind so it hung on the same pillar as the backdoor. I opened the front passenger door and climbed in. Paul climbed in the back like he was Al Capone.

Apparently this was Pauls Dads car. And the idea was that he rented this garage across the road so that he could spend his spare time renovating it. Some of the bodywork had evidence of filler and red undercoat but not much more had been done to the car.

That may have had more to do with the Off Licence having a closer proximity to Pauls Dads Armchair than this garage all the way across the road.

The interior of the car smelt of leather upholstery and like our other den "E" It stirred a question of nostalgia. I wondered what this cars story had been. I wondered if it ever would have a future, or like "E", it was to end its days hosting two young teenagers illicit smoking and sex conferences.

"So where did you find those extra beer bottles?" I asked Paul, "In a crate at the back of the Off Licence." He replied. "I think old George drinks most of his stock himself. Those bottles were the ones I returned last night. Silly old sod, always so pissed, pays me for them and puts them in a crate out back for deliverymen. I just collect them from there when I need fags go round the shop and get the money back on them again!"

Oh my God. Had I unknowingly been an accomplice to a crime. I had never ever stolen in my life?

Actually, I lie. I did take a Milky Way from the Newsagents counter on the corner of Jordon Road. I heard kids at school say they do it all the time. I thought I'd totally got away with it. Well, I hadn't at all.

I don't know whether it was a result of my early Catholic upbringing and fear of being sent to hell but that chocolaty feast had been marred with a very guilty flavour. It was not enjoyed in the slightest. I kept the empty wrapper in my coat pocket for a long time as a reminder of my terrible sin.

In the end I had to resolve my wrongdoing. When the newsagents were closed. They would hang newspapers on racks outside the door. People would help themselves to a newspaper and post the money through the letterbox. This made me feel even worst about my crime. These people were trusting, and I took advantage of them when their back was turned.

In the end I took the Milky Way wrapper out of my pocket. Turned it inside out and wrote SORRY on the inside. I put two thru penny bit coins inside it. A milky Way was only 3 pence I figured God would surely forgive me, if I penalized myself in some way. Shop closed, I went down and posted the wrapper bearing my anonymous apology payment and self imposed interest through the letterbox. "Oye you little shit!" The man from nowhere wacked me across the head with his rolled up newspaper "What do you think this is a bloody litterbin? Fuck off before I box your bloody ears!"

Fuck off I did, and quickly without looking back. Plainly God wanted to make a point. And he did. Other people might get away with stuff. Me? Forget it!

So here we were in Pauls dads car. And I was about to have my first cigarette. I was not unfamiliar with second hand cigarette smoke. All the adults I knew smoked. My father was a most enthusiastic smoker. Cigarettes the occasional cigar but his favourite was pipe smoking. He had a rack of pipes that he would select from. Stoke them up with Old Holburn light with a Swan Vestor Match and puff away. Many of his suits became ruined; by ash burns from his pipe.

So now I was about to embrace another aspect of my journey into adult hood.

Paul lit his cigarette first and inhaled deeply like a pro. Then exhaled and the inside of the car filled with smoke. I lit mine, holding my fag between my index and middle finger like my mum did. I took a puff and lightly inhaled. It was not so bad if you took it a little at a time. I felt the smoke invade the back of my throat and my lungs. Then exhaled this time without coughing a fit.

I came to the conclusion, that in illicit smoking mode, it was wise for one to hold the cigarette between thumb and for finger, cupping it from view with your hands. This was Paul's favoured technique.

It turned out that what Paul and I were doing was being repeated all over Four Oaks by third years. The next time I rode down Worcester Lane on my bike with John Chawner, I discovered that he too was smoking, along with most of the kids of Darnel Hurst Road. John was going through some family turmoil. His father Roy had been taken ill. A stroke left him unable to work and affected his short-term memory. This had been a terrible strain on Hazel. Johns mother. John was weeping, saying he didn't know what he was going to do if anything happened to his Dad. We shared our cigarettes and I tried my best to console him.

Oh! How we were all growing up so fast!

Christmas was coming, and Ali would be coming to stay. Dad had just left for Four Oaks Station to get the train to Birmingham, and from there to Exeter.

Tony Hofton came by. He, Julie, Mark, Nicky and Andrew Hofton were now living in South Wales. I was very upset at the news that they were to move away from Wilde Green. Tony worked in the Steel industry and his work moved him down to the valleys.

Tony was in the area and he thought he would call in on Dad. Shame he was going to miss him. Mum invited him to stay with us rather than go to the Royal Hotel. Only polite I thought. I'm sure home cooking among friends was preferable to a night with strangers in a Bed and breakfast.

We had visited the Hofton's in Wales. They lived on a newly built housing estate. Mark and I had enjoyed adventures around the building of the estate. With the bonus of a river running along side the project. Took me back to those earlier days of Crockford drive.

Mark played the recorder in junior school. That had now progressed to Clarinet. That was cool too. Acker Bilk's career was non too shabby after all.

The day before Dad got back with the car he'd been dreaming of for some months, and the girl that I'd been dreaming of. Mum and us kids paid a visit to Gangan at Chadsway.

Every body was chatting in the kitchen. Aunty Christine was there. Sally was playing with cousin Tamzin, Adam was amusing himself with some toy cars making engine noises with his mouth. He almost got that familiar sound of the Morris Minor off to a tee!

Gangan Christine and Mum where doing the usual thing in the kitchen, smoking cigarettes and chatting. "Where is his lordship today" Christine enquired of my father's whereabouts. "Cornwall, picking up his Sports Car" Mum replied with a slight stammer.

Mum was inflicted with a stammer for most of her life. It was something that we became used to, so we kids hardly noticed it. It did cause her some concern and she had tried several means to rid herself of it. To no avail.

Where did I belong in this scenario? Too old now to play buses on the stairs, theatres or department store lifts with the sliding curtains of the patio doors.

It seemed like as good a time to make my transition from childhood in the living room with the kids, to declare my grown-up-ness in the kitchen with the adults.

I took the packet of ten number six out of my jeans pocket, removed a cigarette, picked up Gangan's ornate lighter off the mantle piece and lit up.

I then strolled out of the living room and into the smoke filled kitchen, cigarette in hand.

"Oh look! Simon's smoking!" Was the exclamation.

The way I remember it in my head. It was a moment of celebration.

I had become a grown up!

How strange! As I think back about that now as I write these pages.

18 PLAYING GOOSEBERRY

Dads Sebring Sprite. Me at the wheel, whilst Adam looks on.

Although the ladies of the family welcomed me into adult hood, and their smoking circle, my father did not share their enthusiasm.

I now appreciate, he was quite right to be unimpressed, but at the time the feeling was. "Why do you have to dampen everything down and suck all the fun out of growing up?" I say feeling because I didn't argue. I just knew it was something best not to share with him. Not to worry. For I had an ally in Ali!

It was nice to see Ali again. I took her to St John Ambulance and she got to meet all the boys. We arranged to take the bus to Walsall Baths with a gang of us and we all went swimming. Having an older good-looking girl in our midst seemed to bring out the show off in all the boys. Naturally John Chawner was showing off his gymnastic prowess, summersaulting off the diving boards and emerging in front a Ali after an under water swim worthy of Flipper! Ali was great fun with the gang. They all thought I was cool to bring this exotic creature from Cornwall into their lives.

The boys would be taking rise out of Ali's Cornish drawl. Out of Cornwall it sounded a lot more alien to us than back in Crackington Haven. Ali gave as much back chiding their Brummy Accents.

She was quite taken back by some of the population in Walsall. Apparently you don't get black people in Launceston!

We shared cigarettes on the top deck of the bus back to Four Oaks.

Dad seemed to accept the fact that Ali smoked. They had shared a journey together up the A38 in the Sprite. "Does your Mother know you smoke Ali?" He enquired "Yes but she doesn't approve. She'd rather I didn't." She replied taking two cigarettes from Dad's package, putting both in her mouth and lighting them together. She handed one to my dad at the wheel. "Well we better make this our little secret." They conspired.

I think he quite liked having a charming companion for his journey, and he enjoyed having a smoking partner at home.

Ali slept on the bottom bunk in my room at Holly Lodge. I wondered how this was supposed to play out. I so wanted my first kiss from Ali. I think she might have sensed my interest, because she seemed to make a point of mentioning her seventeen-year-old boy friend back home.

Well the bubble, which was my dreams for so many months, was burst there and then. She was fifteen and going out with someone four years older than me. Plainly I had no chance. Ali and me were well and truly confined to the friend zone.

All was not lost though. As far as friends go, Ali was cool and definitely the most pretty I had. If I was going to be able to be my new adult self with her, I needed to get from my fathers watchful eye. Where could we go?

The solution soon came by with a knock on the door. Paul Buckmaster came round. "Hello Paul. Simon and Ali are playing records up in his room go on up." I heard Mum say.

Paul made his entrance. He was wearing a leather jacket that was maybe two sizes too big, his black hair long like a Beatles style and his usual self assured gait. "Hi, I'm Paul, but my friends call me Pablo" Paul introduced himself to Ali.

We sat playing some records for a while then Paul suggested we went over to his father's garage. We could all have a fag in his car.

Sounds like a plan. We entered the garage, and there was the car. I opened the front passenger door and slipped over the bench seat to the driver's side so Ali could sit next to me.

Paul opened the back door and said "Come on Ali, why not get into the back with me."

Bollocks!

She obediently climbed into the back with Paul and we all started chatting and smoking. "Do you mind if I put my arm around you like that." Paul asked as he engulfed Ali in the sleeve of his leather jacket. She didn't seem too bothered. "Good luck with that mate!" I thought waiting for the "I've got a seventeen year old boyfriend!" rebuttal that Ali delivered to me. "Do you mind if I kiss you?" Paul asked. Making sure that their cigarettes were firmly extinguished.

The next thing, I found myself sitting in the front of this car whilst a snogging session ensued on the back seat.

When it became obvious that this was not going to end any time soon, and for the first time in my life I learnt what it was like to be a gooseberry. I did the only thing I could do. I went home to bed, rather confused about women. Not for the last time!

When I woke in the morning. Ali was in the bunk below me. "Morning my lover!" was my Cornish greeting.

I had to ask, "Ali you told me you had a seventeen year old boyfriend?" "I know!" She giggled. "You wont say anything. Will you?"

Ali left after Christmas leaving me with feelings of total confusion over my first unrequited experience with the fairer sex. And leaving Pablo with a canvas of circumstance which he could embellish with fantasy.

With this he would irritate me forever. Last time I would ever introduce him to any of my girlfriends. I decided

19 FIRST LOVE

My total no clues how to deal with this topic of great interest continued. Girls, Women were, and if I am to be totally honest continue to be a total mystery to me.

The appeal; of English Football. Soccer. To my American readers. Remains a similar mystery to me. How can so many men follow a sport such as this with a passion unprecedented when in truth. We are just not very good at it!

Every now and then I get caught up in the frenzy, which surrounds Soccer. When it is world cup, you cannot help it, it invades every medium. So then in a spirit of patriotism one finds oneself taking an interest in England. In 1966, they actually won it. For the next five decades they have built up our hopes, and dashed them away on a regular basis.

I find I am the same with women. And yet it doesn't stop us allowing it to consume our lives.

I figured that the best way forward for me, was indeed to become a pop star. Women will just fall at my feet then. Won't they?

David Hamber; My Pop Star cousin. Told me a story of Mick Jagger, a naked woman and a Mars Bar. It sounded a lot more interesting than my experience with a woman and a Mars Bar walking back from the beach at Crackington Haven.

So I would take my guitar into the School Hall during Music lessons. I would attempt to woo the girls with my compositions. "Between you and me you just can't beat her.. This girl I know called Anita." was one such desperate attempt. But sadly, to no avail.

Mr John our music teacher announced that the school was to put on another production by Gilbert and Sullivan. This year it was to be the Gondoliers. Auditions were to be held in the school hall.

Every body in the choir was keen to audition. We had a lot of girls in our choir too so this could be interesting. We were all sat on the stage, and one by one we were called upon to sing a verse of "All things Bright and

Beautiful" I would have been happier with "Till there was you" or some other track off a Beatles album, but no. Everybody knew "All things bright and beautiful." So "All things bright and beautiful." It was going to be.

My voice was in that transitional stage of breaking between Alto and Tenor. I could sing still in a reasonably stable alto tone. So my audition was although reasonable, not memorable.

When John Chawner followed me and began to sing with a never before heard from him sensational Tenor tone. The audition had found their lead role.

John was cast as Marco. I was cast in the chorus but named Antonio for I was to have a solo.

The Girl to play the romantic role opposite John was Virginia Bumpstead. Virginia was a petite blond with an amazing soprano voice.

My chorus partner, was Virginia's friend Julie. Julie was a brunette with the most beautiful eyes I had ever seen. When she smiled, you were awarded with a vision of beauty and pure friendliness. I was my usual shy self, but somehow it didn't seem to matter with Julie. She seemed to draw me out of myself. Were we having some kind of connection?

Rehearsals started in earnest for this production. Those of us who failed to land parts on stage, were called upon to assist with scenery, costumes, lighting. The whole school had a hand in this production. I have to say it was perhaps my happiest time at Riland Bedford.

One day I was taking the regular bus home from Sutton Parade. Who should I see at the bus stop but Julie. Once again she greeted me with her disarming smile. And it seemed quite the natural thing to do to talk to her. I hadn't seen her at Mere Green bus stop. I didn't know she lived on the same route as me. Her home it appeared was an apartment in a large house on Lichfield Road a stop before Four Oaks station. She lived with her parents and older brother. Her older sister and husband also had an apartment in the same house.

She told me she was having a party on Saturday night and asked me if I would like to come. Our conversion was cut short by our arrival at her bus stop. "This is me. Bye for now." Julie bayed me farewell.

The bus had stopped in front of a large house in its own garden. There was a driveway that had a drive through entrance. Either side of the main house were more modern looking two story wings with entrance via a rear access. In front of the driveway the well manicured lawn framed and a large oak tree. The lawn ran all the way level to the top of a three-foot high wall. On the pavement in front of the wall was a wrought iron bench in line with the bus stop sign.

I watched Julie through the grubby Midland Red window as she jumped off the bus, walked directly across the pavement put one foot on the seat of the bench, step up onto the wall and walk confidently across the grass towards the main front door of the house. As she did so she stopped and in a half turn, looked back at me, gave me one more delicious smile and a wave, before pulling a key out of her pocket, and opening the big front door.

I didn't recognise any one at Julie's party. And as Julie was mingling with her guests, my shyness left me wondering, what on earth was I doing here. I was comfortable with Julie but as she appeared to be otherwise occupied, in the end I went over to her and made my excuses to leave.

She turned her attention to me. Once again, her beautiful smiling eyes sealed that connection which made me feel there was no one else in the room. She walked me to the door. It seemed like the most natural thing for me to do was to kiss her. Should I? God I am turning out to be so bad at this! "Simon" She said, as if sensing my awkwardness " I hope you don't mind. But I have just got over a break up, and I am not ready to get into anything else at the moment."

"Oh well here we bloody go again!" My thirteen years old life experience silently moaned inside me. Off I went home. Still no wiser, in the ways of women. Or soccer.

My father had taken up Golf. His interest in More Hall Golf and Country Club started as a means to build up his client list. Manulife World map Calendars were gracing some of the best homes and offices in the borough. But a bi product of this enterprise was he had become quite an enthusiastic golfer.

To improve his swing, he had some plastic practice balls. He would set up a tee on the back lawn and chip balls at the back of the house. Every now and then a ball would bounce off the morning room window, which used to get the attention of us in side the house. This was all well and good until he inadvertently had a regular golf ball amongst the pile of practice balls. Had the regular ball struck the brick work of the back of the house, it may have bounced straight back at him, and depending where it made contact with him, given him a start and put him right in the wisdom of his ways. But no. When it came the time for the regular ball to be teed up it was one of the shots making for the window. Instead of bouncing of the window, the ball made a 2 inch bullet hole in the glass, showering the breakfast table with tiny fragments of glass. The ball ricocheted off the mantel piece over the Arga, shot up to the ceiling and landed in our terrapin tank. Terrapins Fred and Freda, named after Grandy and his new love interest wondered what this new addition to their world was.

Dad would load his clubs into the passenger seat of the Sebring Sprite and be out for the day on a Sunday. Playing Golf in the morning and arranging appointments at the 19hole as the clubhouse was known, in the afternoon.

This would turn into a goodtime for me to lord it in the living room. Maybe have the odd crafty cigarette. I was sat in there that afternoon when the most unexpected thing happened. I noticed a figure pass by our bay window walking up the drive towards our front door. Hair blowing back in the breeze, a rather uncertain demeanour but with those eyes, there was no mistaking who it was. It was Julie. Why was she here? What did she want?

Puzzled. I opened the door. Julie stood there head down pensively biting her bottom lip her big eyes looking upwards at me. She seemed more than a little concerned about something. "I am so sorry about last night." She said. "I wouldn't blame you if you never wanted to speak to me again."

She came in and explained that she felt awful after I left. She'd invited me to this party and I didn't know any of the people. Then what she said to me on the doorstep.

I had believed that I was just going through yet another rejection. One, which I found difficulty understanding. Because for the first time ever, I had felt I was experiencing a real connection. Yet now, here she was!

She was telling me that she found our address in the Four Oaks Telephone directory. There were only two Edgington's in the listing, and only one on Lichfield Road. I knew who the other one was. It was an out of date entry. Frederick Thomas Edgington. Grandy.

I was so immersed in the beauty in her eyes; I wasn't really paying much attention to what was being said. I just felt I had to make her feel better so once again I would be rewarded by being the recipient of that wonderful smile.

"Julie it's all OK. I'm sorry if I seemed strange too." I said and then the words just spilled from me somehow skilfully evading the filter, which is my shyness "I just need you to know. I like you."

Julie smiled that smile that made my heart dance, her beautiful eyes began to show relief.

"I know, and I think you wanted to kiss me last night?" she suggested.
"Yes." I answered feeling a blush rising from within.

"Do you still want to kiss me now?"

I leant towards her and our lips met. It was a warm minty feeling. Her lips tasted of toothpaste and girl. This was the nicest feeling ever. Our lips parted and I realised my eyes were closed. I opened them and saw those beautiful brown eyes smiling back at me. I brushed my hand on her cheek and Julie shyly looked down. I felt her soft hair and caught the smell of shampoo. I kissed the top of her head and she looked up, again her beautiful eyes smiling at me, and we kissed again.

Si John's got a girlfriend !!!!!!!!!!

Julie

20 BIRDS AND BEES. A ROYAL PERFORMANCE. A SAD HOME COMING

Julie and I became a team. John Chawner and Virginia were getting on well too. In fact it was becoming quite noticeable how the boys at the back of the class, girls at the front arrangement was beginning to alter as some boys and girls hooked up with one another. Some of these relationships where transitory, others stuck.

It was becoming very apparent to me that some boys in class were experiencing a totally different reality to others. Some lads were definitely enjoying the attention of a lot of girls, and like a kid in a sweet shop, they were intent on sampling as many of these treats on offer as possible.

I was not one of them. That was for sure, which made me persevere with the relationship I had. Doing that. I discovered something more valuable than playing the field. I was building a real loving relationship with Julie.

My family adored her and welcomed her as one of us. Finally in my family unit I had someone I connected with my own age. We kissed and held hands and explored together the wonder that was intimacy. We were sure that we were in love and would be together forever.

We went to visit John Chawner and his family in Darnel Hurst Road. By now Roy John's Dad was back home from hospital. He sat in his chair in the living room and kept a notebook on the arm of the chair. He would record everything that happened "Simon Edgington came round today and introduced his friend Julie to us. What a lovely Girl she is. Beautiful big brown eyes and a bright smile." We sneaked a peak at the entry he just made when he went to the bathroom. Hazel, John's Mother couldn't resist relating the story to Julie of how I went to PE in the infants school in my Knickers. Thanks Hazel.

One day I was in the Morning room having a late night Horlicks before bed and Mum came in and said. "Darling would you mind taking your drink into the living room? Your father would like a word with you."

I took my hot drink into the living room. Dad was sat in his armchair by the fire scraping the ash out of one of his pipes. "Ah Si John, sit down I need to have a little chat with you."

I sat on the sofa next to him and placed my drink on the coffee table a little concerned about what was on his mind. Had he found my stash of cigarettes?

"Your mother wants me to have a word with you about something." He said to me awkwardly. Somehow without looking at me in the eye. "You have been spending a lot of time with your friend Julie, and we think it is time for you to know certain things about Boys and Girls or," and he paused looking for the dialog that he had already pondered and rehearsed in his mind. "Birds and Bees." Plainly he was embarrassed and not looking my way for that reason.

I looked over towards the rubber plant between the fireplace and the television set. Oh my God! My gaze wondered from the plant to the Axminster carpet in front of the fireplace. How ironic I thought. Of all the very places. My father was about to give me the talk. You know, the one when he has to explain about being careful in a relationship with girls. The sex talk. I turned my gaze back to the rubber plant.

"Monstera Deliciosa. " Julie had said to me, the other evening, after we came up for some air after some kissing and exploratory adolescent fondling. We had been lying together on that very spot on the green Axminster by the rubber plant.

We were Baby Sitting for Adam and Sally. "What did you call me?" I said to her stealing another kiss. Her big eyes closed slightly and she grinned. "Not you silly. This plant. Monstera Deliciosa.. Look at the label tied to it. That's what it's called!"

"The thing is Si John," Dad continued stirring me from my reminiscing and back into the present. I looked at the green leaves of the Monstera Deliciosa. Was it actually looking back at me, reassuring me that our secret was safe? I absent minded-ly pondered, "The thing is this." Poor Dad I could see his anguish. This was not something that he was well equipped for.

Time to take control. "It's OK Dad. We have covered all this stuff at school and again at St John Ambulance Brigade. You don't have to worry about this." I let him off. I picked up my Horlicks and said goodnight. As I left the room, I looked back. Dad had picked up his pipe again; I think we both needed a smoke. He still wasn't able to make any direct eye contact with me, but I remember the smile on his face. Was it a smile of relief that that little episode had gone better than imagined, and was now behind him? He had another ten years before he may be called upon to deliver that talk again. With brother Adam.

The Gondoliers production came and went. I don't think John and Virginia's romance was to last long beyond that, in fact not long after John started seeing Jackie Hickmot, Daughter of the "Singing Policeman" Sergeant Ron Hickmot. He had gained fame in some A.T.V. television show at their Birmingham studios. He was very impressed with Johns roll in the Gondoliers. He offered to hook John up with his music contacts. I was incredulous at John when he said he turned down the offer. John was heavily into Gymnastics. Perhaps; I should have dated Jackie, I teased Julie!

One day at St John Ambulance John Titmus told me that his cousin, who had played in the group that night in the St John hut, had quit the band and was selling his amplifiers. John agreed to take me to his place in Castle Bromwich. We took the bus to Wilde Green and another down Chester Road and arrived at his cousins house. John's cousin Ian showed me a collection of amplifiers he had in his room. He had a PA set up comprising two pillar speakers and a mixer amp. He wanted five pounds for that. He had a smaller amp that he said would be great for guitar for two pounds. Brilliant I thought I'll have that one.

Dad had been back to the music shop on Small Brook ring way and bought me a pick up for my acoustic guitar. It just mounted at the foot of the neck. I was dying to go electric!

So I was very excited when we got this amplifier back home. We set it up in the morning room, plugged in connected the guitar and …….. Nothing.

I looked around the back of the amplifier and as with the Gangan's old TV set, I could see the valves emitting a red glow. So it was on.

I had told Ian that I wanted to save up and buy the PA he had for sale, and I was interested in an electric guitar there too. He had given me his phone number. So I called him and explained that we had it all plugged in but, not a sound! "What kind of speaker have you plugged into it?" Ian asked. "Speaker? I thought it had it's own speaker!" I looked once more into the back of the amp. No Speaker. In fact as it was an Amp top. No room for a speaker!

We found an extension speaker in the house that was used for our radio and rigged it up to that. Electric at last!

Dad had a change of car about this time. As much as he loved his Sebring Sprite, and I loved the times that he would roar to a halt outside the school gates turning my school chums heads in envy, on the odd occasion I talked him into giving me a lift. It had to go. It was not very well insulated, leaked in the Midlands drizzle and it had no creature comforts like heaters. So one day he came home in a sparkling red M.G. Midget.

Very similar to the Sprite but a more civilised car. The soft top worked better too as it was folded very easily into its frame when down. The Sebring, although it had an optional hard top had plastic side windows that were very draughty in Birmingham weather. Julie and I posed for photos in Dads new car. I imagined us taking to the road together. Wow! One day maybe.

Summer Holidays again.

1967. Before the family holiday, St John Ambulance Brigade were to have a camping week in Swansea. A coach was laid on and we travelled down with all the divisions from our Sutton Coldfield Duke Street headquarters.

There was a lot of excitement because our president was to visit the Jamboree on the final day. Non other, than Her Royal Highness Princess Margaret.

Amongst my luggage I had my guitar and I wondered whether I would get to perform in front of the Princess. There was talk of all the cadets being presented to her in a walk by as we "Sing Songed" around the campfire.

We arrived at the venue Singleton Park Gower, where a sea of Army tents had been erected. There was a large marquee which was our mess tent which had benches and tables laid out. In the corner there was a large stage with Drums and Guitars set up. This immediately caught my eye.

There was a mail order catalogue in the sixties published by a company called Bells Music. My copy had pages that were thumbed through and the content coveted possibly as much as, if not more than, the Playboy Magazines acquired illicitly from Paul Buckmaster's collection.

The Bells catalogue contains pictures of Hofner Guitars, amplifiers, accessories. Every need of the budding pop star was within the pages of this publication.

Well the stage in this marquee, was a pretty good representation of a page from Bells Catalogue. There was a Paul McCartney Hofner Violin Bass. A Ludwig Drum Kit, and the very guitar; that had caught my eye from the Bells catalogue. Signal red with an array of rocker switches on the top, to switch in any combination of the four pickups set beneath the strings. Also; a rather impressive, tremolo arm. I loved the look of that guitar. Seeing that guitar in the flesh so to speak was like meeting my pin up. I couldn't have been more thrilled if Playmate of the month of June 1968 had appeared on this stage.

We settled into our dormitory tents. George Blackburn was our supervisor. We liked George, he was Superintendent of the Erdington Division who also shared the coach down with us. Our tent was kitted out with camp beds. We had bought our own sleeping bags, it was a very similar situation to the St John cottage in Mid Wales. I of course was very excited to find out more about what the musical instruments where all about.

So that evening, after tucking into a feast of sausage, beans and mash, some Salvation Army guys entered the Marquee. It turned out they were the band. I felt a little apprehensive when I saw the uniforms. What the hell kind of music where we going to get from them? I needn't have worried. They were really good and as in any teenage dance we did exactly what all teenagers do. All the girls sat shyly on one side of the room, and all the boys sat on the other.

I didn't really want to get involved with any other girls. I had Julie, but Diane was there from the Sutton Girls division, I remembered our silent bowling date. I went over and asked her if she would like to dance.

She turned to her friends and giggled slightly as if seeking approval, they must have secretly granted it because she jumped up from the bench and started to move to the music. We slowly drifted away from the girls corner towards the no mans land which was the dance floor in front of the band. That was the catalyst that was needed to get the other boys to wonder across the floor and join in with the rest of the girls.

Had I not already known Dianne, there is no way I would have had the nerve to do what I did. I guess the dance would have continued with the band playing to an empty floor until someone else made that first move. It was so unlike me to be the one. But I was excited by the live music and after all Diane and I were bowling partners! So my shyness somehow turned a blind eye.

The band was playing all the hits from the time. Knock Three times. House of the Rising Sun. Beatles hits. I loved listening to live music.

When the band took a break. Girls and Boys returned to their benches and the dance floor emptied. I went and spoke to the guy who owned the Hofner Guitar that I so coveted. Sure enough, it had been ordered from the Bells catalogue, along with all the musical equipment on stage. What was interesting was it was all purchased; by the Salvation Army. God moves in mysterious ways. I remember thinking.

I told him I played guitar and had mine with me. "Do you want to play a song with us?" The guy asked. In a strong, South Wales accent. Did I? "I would LOVE to." I replied enthusiastically. "I'll just go get my guitar." "No need." My new best friend said. "You can use this one if you want." Did I? !

So I got to play my first ever electric guitar performance in Singleton Park Gower Swansea in a marquee. With a Salvation Army rock band. We did "I saw her standing there" by the Beatles.

My vocals were amazing because the microphones went through another bit of kit available through the Bells Catalogue. The "Watkins Electrical Music" or "WEM Copycat". This was essentially a tape machine that used a loop of recording tape. The tape would pass an eraser head, which would wipe all signals off it. Then the microphone signal would be recorded on to the loop of tape on the second head and then pass three play back heads.

This ingenious contraption created echo. that could be controlled by selecting the number of play back heads and the speed of the tape loop.

Singing and playing guitar with this great band from the Salvation Army on this fabulous state of the art music equipment was a huge thrill. My dance partner Diane was basking in the reflected glory on the dance floor with her friends from the girls corner. I'd fantasised about how good it would feel to perform in front of a band on stage.

It was better than I imagined. My usual shyness totally evaporates on stage. I felt here. Right here. This is where I belong!

That was nearly the most memorable moment of the camping holiday with Saint John Ambulance.

I was expecting the most memorable moment to be when I got to play the guitar and sing around the camp fire to Her Royal Highness Princess Margaret.

But that very nearly didn't get to happen. The most memorable moment of that camping Holiday was when disaster struck. It involved a Swansea Girl and my Guitar.

The Salvation Army Band was only booked to appear in this Marquee for the first night of the camp. But later in the week, there was to be another event held in a nearby hall for us. They invited me to bring my guitar and perform with them.

It was another dance and once again I got to play with the band. By now I was becoming quite the music celebrity within the camp. It was definitely on that we would be singing around the campfire when Princess Margaret was to do her walk about. As we left the dance, I heard a girls voice saying "Hey I play guitar, can I have a strum on yours?"

I turned, and there was a bunch of girls that I had noticed in the dance. They weren't from the camp. They were locals from Gower. Well I thought it would be a bit unfriendly to refuse. After all, it had meant so much to me when my friend from the Salvation Army band had allowed me to play his guitar.

I took the strap from around my shoulder and handed the guitar to the Girl from Gower placing the strap around her. She started to strum and look at her left hand on the fret board. Plainly she was no guitarist. "Oh I thought I could do it but I can't. It's a bit more difficult than I thought Innit!" The Girl from Gower sang out in her Welsh accent. With this she let go of the guitar and lifted the strap from her shoulder. The strap came away at the neck end of the guitar and I watched my pride and joy. My Prized possession, fall to the ground neck first.

It was like slow motion. The girl somehow managed to keep hold of the body of my guitar but as the machine head hit the gravel driveway a large painful and final twang of strings erupted as the neck broke away from the body.

"It wasn't my fault" The Girl from Gower pronounced. "The strap came off innit!"

I was stunned. All I can recall was feeling the worst thing possible had just happened. My music was the core of my world, and my guitar had just been killed in what took a Nano second. This was a disaster. I couldn't look at the Girl from Gower. I was in a haze. I was angry, I was heartbroken, I was totally and utterly distraught. John Titmus helped me pick up the remains of my guitar and carried it back to our tent. By now I was shaking uncontrollably with rage. That stupid girl from Gower could have had no idea what she had just done to me!

When we got back to the tent George Blackburn could plainly see the state I was in. Tears were rolling down my cheeks and I was still shaking with anger. I tried to put the remains of my guitar back in its zip case, somehow in the hope that in the morning tonight's events would have just been some kind of horrific dream. I would awake and all would be well with the world again.

I did eventually get to sleep. For a brief moment on awaking in the morning to the bugle playing, all was well with the world. But all to quickly the events of the previous evening invaded my well being and filled me once again with disbelief of this disaster.

George Blackburn came to my rescue. He had been up and out first thing in the morning and bought a pot of Evo Stick Impact Glue. "Lets have a look at this guitar of yours and see if we can stick it back together." We removed the strings and examined the fracture in the wood to the neck. The fret board was undamaged, the break had occurred where the neck attaches to the body of the guitar. I looked on as my wooden companion lay broken and silent on the bench. George put his handy man skills to work and managed to glue the two broken pieces neatly back together. "I suggest you leave it to set for a day before you put the strings back on it!" George advised. A Day? Tomorrow is the last day of camp and I'm supposed to be playing to Princess Margaret.

I wondered what that Girl from Gower was doing right now. I now wanted to kill her for the stress I was now under! She no doubt has got on with her life, oblivious to the turmoil she caused me.

The longest day so far of my life went by at snail pace. I kept examining my guitar, which now smelt of Evo Stick hoping the repair would stand the tension of the strings.

JOHN AMBULANCE BRIGADE, PRIORY FOR WALES, GOLDEN JUBILEE, CADET CAMP 1963

The Royal Command Performance That nearly couldn't happen. I'm on guitar to the right.

Next mornings Bugle revile was surplus to requirements. I was awake. After a hastily downed bacon and eggs, I returned to my bunk and gingerly set about stringing my guitar. I had found a music shop in Swansea and bought some new strings. Nylon. I figured that the tension would be less than steel strings. Thankfully George Blackburn's repair was going to hold good for the duration of my Royal Command Performance.

Princess Margaret arrived in a motorcade of black limousines. Dressed in her Saint John Ambulance Brigade Uniform she was very petite amongst even us cadets. She inspected the ranks then as arranged all the cadets congregated around the camp fire around me and we sung camp fire songs like "She'll be coming round the mountain when she comes. " "When the saints go marching in." and "I saw her standing there." For good measure!

Family holiday this year we were going to pitch the tent at Harlyn Bay near Padstow in Cornwall. Ali's Mother Diane and John Hall Say were now married and they operated a caravan rental business at Crackington Haven and Harlyn Bay.

Mum drove the Zodiac and camping trailer to Harlyn, Dad set up convoy in the MG. We arrived at Harlyn and set up camp. The camp was in a field on a cliff top with tents and touring caravans scattered about. There was a rank of larger static Caravans. These were Diana and Johns rentals. Every Saturday was change over day, as the outgoing guests left, each caravan had to be serviced and bed linens exchanged for the incoming guests later that day. There always seemed to be maintenance issues too. There was no electricity on site. Caravans ran on calor gas, including the lights which had gas mantles that all had to be checked and replaced if necessary. Gas bottles would need replacing when empty too. As on the camp site in Devon. I enjoyed helping Diane and John with these chores, and I got paid a little pocket money.

In fact for most of that vacation, I stayed at the Hall-Says in Launceston. I would travel to Harlyn with Diane and her dogs. She had a Basset, A Dachshund and a Great Dane which was an insane combination. The dachshund was the boss and seemed to enjoy doing things it knew the Great Dane couldn't possibly copy. Like running under tables. This would not prevent the Great Dane from trying, resulting in chaos. The Basset just seemed content to fill the atmosphere with fart gas.

Me Sunbathing whilst Diane's Dachshund steels my towel

My guitar repair tuned out to be temporary. The Evo Stick remedy got me through my Royal Variety Performance in Swansea but it was not holding strong enough to remain in tune. Fortunately there was a music shop in Launceston owned by a luther who repairs violins. I took my guitar in and he said Evo Stick was not the correct adhesive for a long lasting repair. He held on to my guitar for a couple of weeks. When I got it back, he had done as good a job with dedicated wood glue as possible.

I had my guitar back. I no longer had murderous intentions towards the Girl from Gower.

I loved Harlyn. A path led down through a field to the cliff top, then you could negotiate a gentle slope down on to a beautiful beach. Sheltered by the cliffs, this was a truly heavenly spot to sun bathe, play ball on the sand, surf and explore the rock pools for sea life.

Dad returned home after a week at Harlyn. We remained until the end of August. There was no shortage of help when it came to de camping and loading up the trailer. It had been a nice vacation in Cornwall. I saw a little of Ali and her sister Sue. Ali asked after Paul Buckmaster. I told her that she had given him something to talk about. "I don't know why?" she said. "We only had a snog and a few fags." So much for Paul and his story telling. Becoming more outrageous at every rendition. I was looking forward to getting home and seeing Julie again. We had exchanged postcards. She had been to Benidorm with her family. I'd never been to Spain. We both told each other how much we missed each other, wish you were here, love you. At last we could be together again and share our stories.

It was a long journey home. The A38 was clogged with traffic but there was a bit of motorway now running from Bristol to Birmingham. The M5. Eventually this would go deep into Devon all the way to Plymouth.

So back to Holly Lodge. Time soon, for another autumn term in school. Was looking forward to seeing Dad again too.

We got home late and went to bed. The next morning I got up. Did my usual bathroom routine, taking my toothbrush out of our travel bag. Having got dressed, I went down to the morning room.

I sensed an atmosphere in the room immediately. Dad and Mum had their backs to each other. Unable, seemingly to make eye contact.

I was used to them arguing and having tiffs about this and that. But this was different. Normally their altercations would end in my dad tutting in resignation and retiring to the comfort of the living room and his trusty pipe. This time he appeared to be standing his ground.

Mum and Dad had plainly been deep in conversation.

Mum was crying.

21 THE MAN OF THE HOUSE

I don't think I had ever experienced my mother crying before.

What has happened now? Everything was going so well. I was looking forward to seeing Julie. I was looking forward to getting back to my mates at Saint John Ambulance and believe it or not, I was quite looking forward to getting back to School. This time, as a fourth year.

Part of me cursed my father for putting a dampener on what was seemingly so perfect.

Dad turned to me. Mum still had her face to the Aga. Her one hand on the rail in front, the other hand clutching a Kleenex tissue she was using to wipe her weeping eyes.

I could see that Dad too had a tear in his eye. They were red and puffy, through either lack of sleep or upset. He spoke to me with a voice tempered with emotion, as if he was holding back a bout of uncontrollable sobbing himself. "Si John. Your mother and I have not being getting along too well lately."

"Tell me about it!" I thought to myself. I felt that my father had been a bad mood running through the family dynamic for quite some time. I remembered my big gesture before Christmas. My big moment when everyone said "Oh look. Simon is Smoking!" but was my father impressed? Not one bit!

"So we have been talking." He continued "And we have decided that it would be better for me to move out for a while."

My first thought was. "Well if you are going to be a misery, making us all unhappy. Maybe it would be for the best."

My father shook a little and bit his bottom lip. "Si John. I need you to do me a favour. Because while I am away. You are going to be the man of the house. I need you to promise me that you will help your Mother to take care of your little brother and sister. She is going to need you to be there for her. Is that okay?"

I felt the sadness in the room. Mum and Dad had not been happy for a long time. I think I was always aware of that. I had always blamed my dad, but I never questioned his honour. Here was a man who had tried for his family. He provided us with a good standard of living. But sadly the dynamics between him and my mother were flavoured with conflict.

Something had to give. He was forcing a change for everyone. From the perspective of the scene in the Morning Room at Holy Lodge that day, it was impossible to see this as a change for better or worse. Time alone would decide that one for everybody.

Dad gathered a suitcase of clothes, his golf clubs and his banjo in its case and loaded his M.G. He reversed down the driveway, and with a roar of exhaust. He was gone.

22 DON'T TAKE SIDES

I don't know where Dad went on that day, but news of his movements came to light. He had been in contact a lot with Gangan at Chadsway. They always had a good relationship. She would have him over for dinner with her neighbours and I think she kept him reassured that we were doing ok. Occasionally he would call briefly and pick up extra belongings.

He would collect Adam for an afternoon and take him to Wyndley lake in Sutton park to feed the ducks. On his return one day he promised Sally and I could go stay with him one weekend.

Julie was a great support during this time. She liked my dad and was sad that he had left. Julie would always help around her house in the kitchen for her mother and father. She enjoyed then coming to Holly Lodge and helping my Mum in our house.

First night back at Saint John Ambulance and Frank Titmus asked me for a private word. " Have you got anything you want to talk to me about. Simon?" He asked. "MMM? I don't think so." I replied. "Is everything alright at home?" He probed further. " Well my father has left for a while. He and my Mum have not been getting on for some time." "Ok Simon." Frank went on. " You know if anything is troubling you. You can always talk to me, but if I may, I want to give you a piece of good practical advice. I know sometimes it is easier to blame one or the other for this situation. But you must not take sides. It is no one in particulars fault. Your parents are two different people. The one thing that they both have in common is that they both love you. They both want what they consider to be best for you. I will say it again. Don't take sides!"

I later asked John Titmus "Did you tell your dad that my mum and dad are taking a break from each other?" "No I didn't." He replied. "He received a letter from your dad. Thanking him for all the help that he was able to give you with St John. And saying how proud he had become of your achievements."

Why had my father never indicated that to me?

It began to become apparent that the temporary break from each other that my father had announced on that day, was not quite as advertised on its packaging. It was of a more permanent nature.

Again I arrived for breakfast to find Mum weeping. This time over a letter opened on the kitchen table. It was a petition for divorce.

I needed some more information about what was going on. Julie and I walked up to Chadsway to visit Gangan.

"The trouble with Warwick." Gangan announced. "Is that he is a very nice man, but he always hangs his fiddle in the doorway." "What?" I exclaimed. What on earth is she talking about?

She explained that he is very very nice to every one else, but when he gets home, he just goes into a shell. It breaks me and your mothers heart to see him playing with anybody else's kids, but his own.

I was growing up by this time. I was beginning to experience a similar feeling. Kids in our house were mollycoddled. Treated like we were fragile. It did nothing to prepare us for the real world. I was being toughened up by entities outside of the family influence and I found it hard to relate to my fragile siblings. Dad wanted us kids to toughen up. Mum wanted us to remain her babies.

One day we all went swimming at Bracebridge Lake after school. At one point somebody exclaimed, "There's a baby in the water!" "ADAM ! " my mother yelled hysterically and in an instant somebody had pulled my brother from the lake and he immediately started coughing and spluttering. My memory of this event was Adam was paddling, Adam fell on his face, Adam was pulled out of the water. I don't know whether Adams memories of this episode are borne from the actual experience, or the hysteria that was to follow. My mother was inconsolably sobbing, holding her baby to her bosom. The memory she and Adam carried away from this traumatised them both.

My father was allowed no say in the bringing up of his kids. He was relentlessly overruled. Should my mother really have been pleased when 13 year old Simon revealed that he was a smoker? Was my Dad right to disapprove of this?

Frank Titmus's mantra "Don't take sides" was serving me well. I was beginning to see that as kids we had been taking the easy course always. Mum was the enabler. Dad was often the one in touch with reality.

23 THE DAY DREAMING FENCE

I found myself wondering about the garden at Holly Lodge. I walked across the lawn to the silver birch tree half way up the garden. It had a branch sticking out within arms reach, making it easily climbable. I remembered the day I sprinted up there to escape my first girlfriend Julia Sims. She decided it was time for our first kiss and I was having none of it. We were 9 or 10 and now I was fourteen. It seemed like a lifetime ago.

I walked through the neglected vegetable patch. When Grandy came to stay all those years before, he planted some seeds. I don't think they were ever dug up, but somewhere beneath the weeds, some potatoes were surely lurking. When I got to the old shed at the very back of the garden, I took a peak inside. It seemed very small now. In the past it had been a den where John Chawner and me would hang out. I remember him demonstrating his moves to Diana Ross's and the Supremes "Baby Love".

I walked to the other end of the path at the back of our garden, where there was a wooden fence over looking the railway embankment. I climbed up and sat on the fence. Idly gazing down the embankment at the railway tracks below in the cutting. I grabbed a piece of long grass growing out the hedge and stretched it between both thumb and fore fingers and blew on its reed so that it made that squeaky sound. I was deep in thought.

"Si John you are now the man of the house." Well I wanted to be grown up. Not sure whether I was quite ready for this. I lit a number six, and as I inhaled that first drag, I began to reflect on my life as it now had become. I had a lot going on. I had a lovely girlfriend. I couldn't begin to imagine what life would be like without Julie. She illuminated my whole existence. She encouraged my music, we would sing together.

I had managed to sell an old Hornby OO train set that I had acquired from Gangan's neighbour, years ago. I had put my paper mache skills into practice and built a hill with a tunnel for the train to pass through. I felt this enhanced the value of the layout, which was mounted on a piece of hardboard. I got my five pounds for it and managed to buy the PA speakers and electric guitar from Ian, John Titmus's cousin.

There were several boys at school who would be interested in forming a band. That was about to happen.

We were becoming unstoppable with the Saint John Ambulance Brigade First Aid Competitions. Perhaps beginning to get a bit cocky because no doubt the quality of training and discipline instilled in us by Frank Titmus was way beyond any of that of our competitors.

School. Was bearable now, because Julie was there. Not many of the other lessons engaged me. It was just a chore to be there. John Chawner had got a weekend job at More Hall Golf Club. Working with the pro in his shop. We managed to get special dispensation to go there during games period at school. The idea was that we would be going to play golf.

Well we did for a while. But mostly we sat in the back of the pro shop smoking number six's and helping our selves to Mars Bars. I felt quite at home in Mac's Pro Shop at More hall golf club. Possibly because on the wall there was the familiar Manulife World map Calendar presented by non other. Warwick G. Edgington Life underwriter.

The sound of a Diesel train slowly picking up speed as it pulled out of Four Oaks Station bought my thoughts back to the fence I was perched on at the top of my garden. I flicked the remains of my number six into the wet grass at the top of the embankment and watched it fizzle out.

The last time I had sat on this fence was just after we moved to Holly Lodge. Timmy had gone missing. Timmy was our ginger cat that we acquired whilst we were living in Crockford Drive. It was a kitten and had come from a farm. It was totally wild and Dad had bought it home and left it in an open cardboard box in the garage. I had been off school at the time with Chicken Pox. I think Bonnie Trig had got it first. So immediately all the kids in Crockford Drive were invited round to play with her, so that we too could catch it and get it over with!

I had spent a week sitting on the couch in our darkened living room, itching, covered in calamine lotion and feeling generally fed up, so Timmy was introduced to cheer me up. When I was finally allowed to go into the garage to try and tame him. I walked up to the cardboard box to say hello. He wasn't there. I sat on the floor wondering where he might be. "Puss

Puss Puss." I called out and I heard a sound coming from beneath an old chest of drawers Dad used as his workbench. I could see a pair of round eyes shining, and slowly, very slowly Timmy came up to me. I stroked his cheek as he rubbed his whiskers against me and started to purr. We were friends!

Now at Holly lodge. I would climb the fence at the back of our garden and call him. After a while I would hear a meow and a rustling through the long grass of the embankment, and he would jump up onto the fence beside me. One day, he just didn't come home. For days I would go to the fence after school and call to him. It was my first big loss, and I was heartbroken.

We had a dog at Holly Lodge too. Pepper. I loved him very much. He came camping with us. On getting back from School one day, mum was waiting for me with a cup of tea. "Sit down Simon, I have something to tell you. Pepper got run over." He used to follow next doors whippet everywhere to our annoyance. It was always left to its own devises. It crossed the Lichfield Road unscathed. Pepper was not so lucky. Sally and I were so devastated that Mum and Dad suggested the next day we should go to Saturday morning Matinee to take our minds of it. It didn't ! I think we both decided to come home early from the matinee. Heartbroken. Not even the anticipation of the adventures of Batman could console us.

Now we have another Cat. A beautiful female tort shell which we called Tammy because we got her from Tamworth.

Next the train from Lichfield stirred me from my thoughts whilst sitting on my daydream fence. This time the train's breaks were squeaking as it slowed down on the approach to Four Oaks Station.

I guess that now Dad is not coming back to live with us. Things are going to change quite drastically.

24 LET'S GET A BAND TOGETHER

The most noticeable change was The Ford Zodiac went, followed by the camping equipment and trailer.

We helped Mum set the tent up in the garden for the last time. We enjoyed a mini weekend camping out. John Chawner came for a sleep over. Julie stayed for part of the evening. We tried to spook her with the ghost stories that we had entertained ourselves with before, but she had one or two up her sleeve as well.

On the Sunday, the advertisement in the Sutton Coldfield News resulted in a successful sale. We said a reluctant goodbye to our camping holidays.

For the first time ever. We were aware that money was short. The simple truth is running two homes was more costly than one. Dad was struggling. Gangan helped but Holly Lodge was a big house to upkeep.

I liked my Dads office downstairs. The large room; with the desk. A wide corridor, Leading to a door to the back garden. This was to become my retreat. There was room in the corridor for a single bed. I curtained this off from the rest of the room which was beginning to look quite studio like.

I started to look through the drawers of my fathers now abandoned desk. First I found a collection of his old pipes. Sundry pipe husbandry tools, pen knives and un finished pouches of tobacco. The whole drawer had that smell of tobacco about it.

The larger drawer to the desk contained a batch of rolled up Manulife World Map Calendars. I took one out and spread it out on the desk. Presented by Warwick G Edgington. Life Underwriter.

I looked at the world. How small the British Isle looked. I studied Europe. France, Spain, Germany, Italy. North America, South America, Australia, Africa, The Middle East, India and the Far East China.

I remembered the Pathe News Clips we watched in the News Cinema and Saturday Morning matinees. Would I ever get to see all these places? How could that happen? I'd been as far as Cornwall and Wales, which is more of

135

Great Britain than many of my school friends had seen. Julie had been to Benidorm. Said it was fantastic and hot. Which by the amazing suntan she had, I had no difficulty believing. I had never even been on an aeroplane.

My initial incentive to be a pop star was a contradiction in many ways. I was shy, yet for some reason quite relaxed about the idea of appearing on stage. Being a performer would combat my shyness. It would validate me socially. I first saw that as a way to be popular with girls. I met a girl. Julie. I had no further desire to attract more Girls. Star sign Cancer. They say the homemaker! But I wanted the other opportunities of being good at music. I wanted to perform in front of audiences. I wanted to travel.

I gazed at this map and pinpointed the places in my mind I would like to visit. New York, Sydney, Hollywood, Hawaii, Italy, Spain, Germany, Paris and many more exotic locations around the Manulife world map. It seemed such a far fetched fantasy for a young man sitting in a room in the heart of the Midlands.

Now I had my amplifiers and electric guitar, I arranged them on the floor of Dads office in the same way I had seen The Embers Equipment piled into the back of their Commer Van that day in the driveway to Chadsway.

I must get my band on the road!

One of my musician classmates John Cannan was a keen Monkeys fan. He had learnt the Last train To Clarksville and a number of other songs from his Best of The monkeys songbook that he had bought from the music section of Frosts the Chemist in Sutton High Street.

He introduced me to a friend of his called Fred. Fred was to be our drummer. Because he had drums! He lived in a very posh part of Four Oaks in a huge house. His father was a scrap metal dealer and drove a Rolls Royce. At the back of their double garage was a games room. With a magnificent red Ludwig drum Kit. The problem was that although Fred owned a drum Kit. He didn't want to be a drummer. He wanted to play guitar. So now Daddy had bought him a brand new Fender Stratocaster. So we had a drum kit at our disposal, as long as we allowed Fred to be in the band on guitar, but no drummer. John told me about a lad in his class who played drums, his brother played drums, and his father played drums. Mark

Stanway. So I got to meet Mark when John Cannan bought him round to my house.

Mum knew the Stanway family. John Stanway, Marks father was a school friend of Dads. A well-known bandleader. In his youth.

So we had the first rehearsal at Freds. John Cannan. Mark Stanway Myself and Fred. It soon became apparent that Fred's best asset was the rehearsal room at his dad's place and nothing else. I remember very little about the actual musical content of our rehearsal, in fact the only lasting memory I have of my visit to that huge house was peering into the living room where Fred's father was watching football on a colour television. That was the first colour television I had ever seen!

I don't remember how Mark convinced Fred of this but somehow; he talked him into lending him his drum set so that we could practice at my place. The next thing was Dad's office had a Ludwig Drum Set Up in it with all the amplification for a rock band.

There was another boy at Riland Bedford who was a guitar genius. John Minchel. He could play all the Shadows songs perfectly. John was quite tall, and wore glasses so he even had a bit of the Hank Marvin look about him. I got friendly with John Minchel we used to play Shadows hits in the schoolyard. He would play Lead and I would accompany on Rhythm. He came up to my place one day and Mark joined us on drums. For the first time, we actually made some thing approaching music together.

We decided that as a trio, we had what it took. John Cannan was really not a fit. He was a strikingly good-looking boy. My Mother always remarked on how charming he was. He was a bit of a fantasist, and his stories were beginning to get so tiresome, that when he appeared to loose interest in the idea of being in a band, he found no objection from the rest of us.

In the 1980s The name John Cannan was to find notorious fame as the A30 Murderer! He was jailed for life for the Murder of Estate agent Suzie Lamplou. Could that have been the same guy that charmed my mother and played shit guitar?

Eventually Fred's drum kit had to be returned to Rosemary Hill Road mansion. The Rolls Royce drew up outside Holly Lodge and we helped the chauffer load the cases into the boot and back seat. I was quite disappointed, how nice it would have been to arrive at our first gig in a Roller!

Marks dad allowed him to use his kit. The big band bass drum was something like a 26 inch diameter, and we emblazoned the front skin with the name of our band. The Syndicate!

John Minchel needed an amplifier. One day we all piled into his dads car and we drove to Aston where there were a number of second hand shops in the High Street. These shops were like an Aladdin's cave of musical goodies. This is where Birmingham's disgruntled wannabe pop stars would off load their guitars and amplifiers for cash for the next venture.

Johns father forked out 18 pounds for what looked like a brand new Selmer 30 watt Guitar amp. We all looked on in envy. When we got back to the Minchel's home in Upper Holland Road, we took this prized possession into the huge cellar under the house. The house was at the top of a driveway. To reach the front door, you had to climb a flight of steps. To the side of the steps was a basement door which gave access to a huge cellar. John's parents were obviously party people, because they had made their own little nightclub. It looked like we had found our new rehearsal rooms.

I had learnt a lot of songs from the Beatles Complete Song Book that I had as a present one Christmas. John was especially good at all things Shadows. We also threw in an instrumental version of Paint it Black by the Rolling Stones. I got to play lead on that one.

The Minchel's were a great family and encouraged us kids with our music. We held parties in their cellar and Julie would come with some of her girlfriends so a great time would be had by all at these do's.

It was about this time that I discovered another genre of musical entertainment. John Chawner had been going to Streetly Youth Club on a Saturday night and asked me if I wanted to go some time. I said I wasn't sure it was my thing. I knew that John was getting medals and really doing well with his gymnastics, so I assumed youth club, sweaty gym smell of plimsolls etc. "Oh no!" John exclaimed. "Its nothing like that. On a Saturday night, Streetly Youth Club becomes a Discotheque! " "What the hell is a Discotheque?" I enquired dumbly. In 1967 I had never heard of such a thing. "Well it's a dance, they have coloured lights and somebody plays records. You should come, and bring Julie."

Well I mentioned it to Julie and she said if it was a dance, it would make a nice change for me not to be playing so we could actually have a dance together. That Saturday we caught the bus that was laid on for Streetly youth club. We got off and the outside of this modern looking building was teeming with teenagers. Eventually the doors opened and everyone had to file past two enormous doormen dressed in tuxedos. Pay your sixpence entrance and in you go.

Well I remembered what had been told me about somebody playing records. This was no Bush portable gramophone like I was expecting. There was a booth at the far end of a sunken dance floor with some guy swaying to the music and holding a telephone receiver to his ear. The sounds of Motown were blasting through enormous speakers on each corner of the dance floor. "You're more than a number in my little red book....... You're more than a one night stand......" The bass was felt in your stomach rather than heard and the coloured lights? I was imagining something similar to a Christmas tree. No! The whole room; lit up by a sea of flashing light boxes. The dance floor quickly filled with a sea of gyrating young bodies. John would be doing his Diana Ross moves. "OOOOOOOhhhhhhooo Baby love, My Baby love ...."

"You know what?" I thought. "This could quite possibly catch on!"

We loved Streetly Youth Club. At the end of the night. 9pm! The music would slow, and couples would begin to slow dance and snog, to hits like "Only You" from the Platters. Then it was all back to the bus stop back to Four Oaks.

One day The Syndicate managed to get a gig at St James Village Hall, next to St James Church in Mere Green Road. John Stanway Marks Dad came to pick us up from Holly Lodge. We climbed into the back of his Ford Executive. "Bloody Hell!" He exclaimed. "What do you two smell of? It's like a bloody tarts boudoir in the back of this car." Well as we were doing our first public gig, Mark and I had doused ourselves in a bottle of Brut aftershave, that we found in the drawer of my dads desk. "If Henry Cooper says Splash it all over. That is good enough for us!" We protested to Marks Dad, who obviously was enjoying taking the rise out of us adolescents.

The Syndicate was on with another band. The guitarist was a familiar face. It was Fred. The main difference between our two bands was, they had that gleaming new red Ludwig drum kit whilst we had John Stanway's 26 inch base drum. Fred was actually getting a lot better on guitar than we remembered him, but our John was the master. We had to play instrumental because our microphone had broken, so our set that night consisted of mainly Shadows music. The other band was able to feature a very bad vocal effort. I think both bands considered that they were the best that night.

I didn't care. I was in my element. Playing live music on a stage. I loved it. Julie was dancing with some of her friends and she constantly looked up and gave me her beautiful approving smile. Life was good.

25 LEARNING TO FLY

Dad came to pick Sally and me up for a weekend at his new home. He had been staying at Grandy's in Little Stretton, and sometimes at his sister Pam's.

I had been wondering about how Sally and I were both going to fit into the MG Midget. When he arrived, he had again changed his car. This time he was in a White Volkswagen Beetle.

The journey up the A5 left us wondering where Dad was taking us for the weekend. Could it be to his Sister Pam's at Dorrington Grove or was it to stay with Grandy at the Ancient House in Little Stretton. We took a turn off the A5 heading towards Wolverhampton, we approached a village called Cobern and pulled into a quaint residential mobile home site. It was very nice. All the homes had white picket fences. We pulled up in front of one such home. "Here we are, Home Sweet Home!" Dad announced. We spent a weekend together in this park. It very quickly became apparent that this was largely a retirement community. Dad had become known as the young man with a banjo amongst his neighbours. He made an attempt at cooking a chicken in the small oven. When it was served up, it was undercooked. Plainly Dad would normally eat out. This was his first attempt at a Sunday Roast. Instead we drove the beetle out and sought after the local fish and chip shop. Judging by the Manulife World Map Calendar on their wall, this was not Dad's first visit to this establishment.

After some tasty fish and chips we took a drive and happened across RAF COSSFORD camp where there was some gliding activity. We went and watched the gliders for a while, and in his way Dad struck up a conversation with one of the pilots. Next thing, he comes up to me. "Come on Si John. I've got us a ride in a Glider!"

We walked on to the grass airstrip to where the two gliders sat on the ground. One of the huge wings resting on the ground and the other pointing skywards. The glider fuselage was very low on the ground. A single wheel hung below and central. This it was explained is retractable in flight.

The Perspex dome of the first glider cockpit was open revealing tandem seating. I was told to climb into the front. The front? Apparently the main pilot sits behind. Between my legs was a joy stick and there were a pair of rudder pedals beneath my feet.

The pilot climbed in behind me then the Perspex dome was closed shut. I glanced around. I could see a lot of legs surrounding us outside. In the cockpit on the ground, we were so low it felt like we were actually sitting on the ground. I glanced across to see Dad climbing into the cockpit of his glider. It looked slightly older than mine. There was no Perspex canopy and the seating configuration was side by side.

A land rover approached us towing a wire. It had driven to the winch at the end of the airfield to retrieve the tow cable after the previous take off. The cable was detached from the Land Rover and connected to the front of our fuselage.

"Simon, can you see that lever in front of you?" the pilot asked. I nodded. "When I give you the word. I want you to pull it and it will release the cable."

Wow I had a job to do.

Once the cable was secured, two people gathered on either wing. One guy reached up to the wing pointing skyward and pulled it down. The cockpit was now level and suspended on its one wheel beneath the cockpit and a skid on the tail.

"Right now we have to perform our pre flight check Simon." The pilot said to me. "First I want you to take the stick and move it backwards and forward. While you are doing that look in the mirror to check that the elevator flaps on the tail wings are moving up and down." I grasped the stick and did as I was told. Sure enough I could see the flaps moving on the tail wing. "Elevators Check?" "Elevators Check." "Now move the stick from side to side and check the control flaps are moving. "Check?" "Check." Rudder pedals followed, cable release lock in place, Harnesses, Altimeter Zeroed, Air brake retracted. These were spoiler fins on the main wing that would be deployed on landing. Once all pre flight checks were complete, thumbs up all round were confirmed.

Someone spoke to the winch man via radio and first the cable went tort. This immediately made the cockpit reverberate like a tin can to the vibration of the winch motor at the other end of the airfield. Rather like the children's tin can and string telephones we used to play with as kids.

The glider began to slowly move forward on its wheel. The men gathered pace on either wing. Soon they were running along side us, and very quickly, the wing became supported by the air flowing across it.

The vibration increased and we appeared to be moving very fast on this tiny wheel so close to the ground. Then the ground began to disappear beneath us and all I could see in front of me was the clouds that were previously above me. We were in a steep climb and the noise and vibration coming from the cable was deafening. I wasn't sure I cared for this noise at all.

The altimeter was climbing from 0 feet rapidly to 750 ft. and the pilot gave me the order. "OK Simon Pull the cable NOW!" He shouted above the din. I grabbed the cable release and tugged it. The result. Instant silence.

Our glider levelled out and all you could hear was the sound of the wind moving across the wings. The view was sensational. I could see for miles and miles. I looked down at the airfield. The land rover, merely a dot by now, had retrieved the cable and was delivering it to the next flight. Dad's glider. We appeared to be gaining height from thermals and we exploited them by riding them in circles. We watched dad's glider take off. It looked quite scary to see the glider climb like a kite. Is that what we too must have looked like?

This was the best ride ever. My first ever flight since my imaginary one on my swing in Crockford drive. Was the view I was looking at now similar to the one from the Sutton Coldfield TV mast? Truly, amazing. I loved flying.

Eventually Dads glider came into formation with us. Despite the Perspex canopy that enclosed me, I could hear my father talking to his pilot. Knowing him he was probably asking him whether he had any life insurance. I was allowed to take the stick and execute a few turns. That was it I was hooked on flying. I definitely wanted to spend more weekends with Dad.

We made our approach to land. We flew along the airstrip for some time at about 12 feet off the ground allowing our speed to drain before setting the plane down on its wheel. When it came to rest. The one wing settled into the grass.

Climbing out of the cockpit and once more putting my feet on solid ground, I was filled with euphoria. I glanced up at the sky and saw Dads glider preparing for its final approach. Had I really just been all the way up there myself? It really was one of the best feelings ever.

Then it was time to go to the clubhouse. Dad got into conversation with the pilot; I could see that he had been just as taken by this sport as I had. It was the most amazing experience after all. It emerged that the gliding club was for RAF personnel. They did however have a quota for non-military personnel who could be proposed to the membership on the merit of what they could bring to the club in the way of skills or human resources.

Dad did suggest Life Insurance might be handy. That caused amusement among the room full of RAF pilots. "A life insurance policy might make a good read, when your wing falls off at 5000 feet. I think we will stick with the parachutes that we are sitting on." Well by the end of our visit the clubhouse did have one more trophy to hang on its wall. The Warwick G. Edgington Manulife World map Calendar. But I don't think it was quite enough to get that much sort after membership.

26 FERAL WOMEN

Life at Holly Lodge did start to change. It started to become quite full of Mum's new friends. Adam had just started school at the Coppice Infants School. The Coppice was a small wood, that we all used to ride our bikes in. It was a great place full of trees and pathways where John Chawner, Robert Brown and myself would race around in earlier days.

Then all of a sudden it became fenced off, and the next thing we discovered was it was to be the site of a new infant and primary school serving the surrounding estate of houses.

It opened up a social life for Mum. She would take Adam to school, and she soon discovered that there were quite a few single or recently divorced Mum's gathering at the School gate.

Two of them actually lived in flats in a house just two doors away from Holly Lodge. So it became the routine that coffee mornings, Tupperware Parties and other social gatherings were the order of the day.

Sharon one of the ladies had a husband in prison. Despite it being a petit crime, It awarded him 18 months in an open prison, she was quick to point out. She drove a Ford Popular that had seen better days. She had a boy.

Margaret was another one of the Mums. She was a brassy blond with two daughters Sindy and Jackie. I got on quite well with Margaret. Julie and I would babysit for her and Sharon whenever either of them had a date. Which seemed quite often.

So the atmosphere at Holly Lodge was becoming quite female. I would spend a lot of my time at John Minchel's. Rehearsing the Syndicate. We were very excited because Frank Titmus had agreed to give us a gig at the St John Ambulance hut in Duke Street.

This meant a lot to me. I had seen that as a way point in my musical journey. To return to the venue where I first enjoyed a band playing. And now I was about to provide the band for my friends at Saint John Ambulance. Everything was organised and then disaster struck.

Mark Stanway, our drummer was grounded. He had been cheeky to his mother Pam and she told him that was that. I pleaded with her to let him just come to our gig but she was adamant. She was having none of it. "I've had to put up with this nonsense all my bloody life." She protested angrily down the telephone. "Bloody drummers in this house! It was bad enough when it was just my husband, now I have got two more of them. Running me ragged they are!"

I spoke to John Mark's Father. He was very scared of his wife when she was angry. He felt my pain but said there was nothing he could do. Just then I had a thought. What had Marks Mother said? Three drummers in that house? I needed a drummer. If it couldn't be Mark, maybe Mark's dad would play. "Would you be able to play for us?" I asked John. "Ha ha. I was more of a Buddy Rich than a Ringo Starr." John explained. "But I tell you what. I will give you Mark's brother Paul's phone number." Sorted.

Paul was happy to play for us. What a great drummer he was. A lot more mature in his playing than Mark at the time, and it made our night at the St John Ambulance hut. Paul was very impressed with us and said that he knew of a gig we would be good for in Henley in Arden. Wow we thought we are going for the big time. Actually going to get paid!

That promise of better days and better gigs was the first time that I was to discover how fickle the music business could be. After weeks of telling people we were bound for better things, and being excited about actually getting paid work. It became apparent that with all best intentions in the world. Paul's recommendation amounted to nothing for us. That's show business, folks!

Now the Zodiac had gone, Dad arranged for a smaller car for Mum. We had an old MG Magnet. This was great it had leather seats and was quite comfortable. Our friends the Hall-Says at Harlyn told Mum about a caravan she could have for her half of the money she got from selling the camping equipment. So we were on for a holiday in Harlyn. This time Julie came too. We had a lovely time together in Harlyn basically doing all the things together that I had fantasised would happen with my first crush, Ali. We would walk along the beach hand in hand. Sing together and enjoy the magnificent night sky. For some reason Cornish skies is a beauty to behold. So much more spectacular, than in the Midlands, where the night sky is polluted by the glare of street lamps of Birmingham. We would walk down the lane to the next village, and look up at the stars. We were fifteen years old, totally in love with each other.

Julie told me that she would not be staying on at school for the fifth year. Her sister Pam had got her a job as a trainee secretary at an Estate Agent in Boldmere. I was sorry that Julie was not going to be at school anymore. I was going to miss her.

When we got back from our short break in Harlyn the Mg magnet had to go in for its MOT. It was immediately scrapped. The petrol tank had a huge leak in it and it was a dangerous fire risk. Christ! We thought. On the journey there and back three of us had been smoking in that car. We had noticed a slight petrol smell. Needless to say Dad didn't earn any brownie points for fixing us up with what could have been a time bomb. I felt sorry for him. It was a kind gesture for him to provide us with a car. Shame his thoughtfulness backfired on him.

Another thing Dad managed to organise for me was a summer job. Now that we were back from Harlyn, I had a month of summer holidays to earn some pocket money. Also this could be a Saturday Job too. It was at factory in Mere Green Road, which made kitchen utensils.

I had to be in work for 8am and I was working a swing press, which would shape components for tin openers. It was totally monotonous work. You would find yourself drifting into a repetitive trance. Hour after hour. The same thing!

I was beginning to find out more and more about women. Julie and I were enjoying a physical relationship. Mums friends were kind of fun to have around, they were perhaps only ten to fifteen years older than me. They had all had their experiences and heartaches over men and didn't seem to mind sharing them, even when I was in the room. But working in that factory was going to give me an insight into just how feral a bunch of factory women can become.

By the time the factory women came in to work at Nine I had been working for an hour. It was 1968 and BBC Radio One was soon to celebrate its first Birthday.

One minute the factory was awash with the industrial sounds of the presses.

Clunking, Guard cages rattling, the burr sound that the toolmakers lathes made, the stinging sound of the angle grinder as it shot sparks into the air. The next minute it was Nine O Clock. BBC radio one would spring to life with Blue mink and "Good Morning World it's a brand new day!" and you would hear the time clock ringing away as the women arrived. "Good Morning Darling." "Hello Gorgeous." "Did you miss me sweetie?" The relative silence of factory noise was shattered from this moment on. Constant women talking, laughing, the crudest of jokes and sexual innuendo became the sound track for the next seven hours.

Sometimes it was our job to take away the bins of completed work and feed the ladies with a supply of blank components. "Hello darling have you come to fill my hopper?" "Tell you what, he can fill my hopper anytime." "Oh Gladys, if your old man could hear you now!" "Him? That silly sod wouldn't know what the fuck I'm talking about!" "Woo Pardon her French, Simon. Gladys watch what you say in front of the kids." "In front of the Kids? I bet he's done it just as much as the rest of us. Haven't you love?"

Quite a contrast to my Gangan! Occasionally after working there, I would go to Chadsway for tea. One day I arrived from work. Gangan was on the phone to someone and I heard her say. "Oh I have to go now, I have been expecting Simon for tea and he has just arrived from the office!" The office? I was dressed in scruffy denims and smelt of sweat and machine oil. She was sometimes a delicious snob. Keeping up appearances. Why did she need to let on that I worked in an office? Was manual labour just too common to apprehend for her?

And so it went on every day. How do people work all their lives in such places?

One thing that experience did for me, was convince me that factory life was not for me. It gave me incentive to achieve my dreams, if this would be the alternative.

27 VESPA'S

David Hamber left the music business about this time. He and his Brothers Howard and William and some mates formed a building business, specialising in fitting strong rooms in banks.

Once again I was sat in the front room of Holly Lodge, and a familiar face walked up the path in front of the bay window. It was the Hamber's and their mates.

They were in Mere Green for a few days putting a new vault in Barclays Bank.

Mum was pleased to see them and immediately rallied all her girl friends. It was party time. First thing they wanted to do was go down the pub.

"Simon are you coming down the pub?" David asked. "I'm going to buy you a pint." I had never been in a pub and I had never drunk beer. I had had some Bulmers Woodpecker Cider before from the off licence across the road.

So I walked into the pub accompanied by this gang of Essex lads. We were like the Ansells Bitter Men, which was an ad campaign on TV at the time. I say we. I mean they were. I was fifteen and small but no questions were asked about my age. David bought me a pint of Double Diamond. We sat at a table drinking and smoking. David started telling me stories of his tours of Hamburg with the Beatles.

The Hamber's came to visit several times, and each time it was great party. Visits to the pub, Party packs back to the house. And all Mums friends seemed to enjoy themselves too.

Roy Hammond was the first of us to reach the grand old age of sixteen. The next goal of the teenager in the midlands was to get his wheels. Roy told me that he had bought a Vespa scooter and on his sixteenth birthday he would come round to Holly Lodge on it.

We couldn't wait to get our wheels. That would spell out our independence and mean most of all. No more Midland Red Buses for us!

John Chawner had got an old Lamberetta Scooter that he was lovingly resurrecting. I was on the look out for a Scooter. Mum didn't want me to have a motorbike. She thought a scooter was safer. Not entirely sure I agree. I would have liked a B.S.A. Bampton Motorcycle but at least she was willing to consider a scooter.

Roy Hammond didn't exactly do anything to promote my cause, because as he proudly turned into the drive of Holly Lodge on his sixteenth birthday, he lost control crashed it into a wall and ended up in a heap on the floor. His cheeks flushed as red as his helmet. Fortunately we were able to scoop him up off the floor, his pride hurt more than anything else. Before Mum was any the wiser over what just happened.

We were very envious of Roy. Who went on to pass his motorcycle test quite quickly, which meant he could take us on the back. It was quite a scary experience. So now we were eagerly counting the days to our sixteenth birthday when we could take to the road.

One of the boys at school had a Vespa 125 for sale. He wanted 20 pounds. I had managed to sell some surplus amplification, and had some money saved from my factory job. I could just about manage to buy it.

It was about a mile from my place. John Chawner and I went and looked at this scooter. It was Blue and I fell in love with it. We were scared to ride it, so we pushed it back to Holly Lodge. When we got to the foot of the drive, we kick started it and practiced our clutch control on the driveway. Didn't want a repeat of Roy Hammonds Experience.

Fifth Year at school. Exams. It really wasn't the same there now that Julie wasn't there. She was doing well in her job and I was eager to leave school. I really had this feeling that there was nothing more they were going to do for me. I wanted to get on with the rest of my life.

What was I going to do for a job. The pop star ambition seemed to have dwindled. If David Hamber was finding that scene difficult, what hope had I? Grandy's question "What are you going to do for a living" was now becoming my question. What about the jewellery trade? A career at Samuel

Hopes. I went and spoke to Gangan. She spoke to Leonard Cooney who told her that the people they employ go to the Birmingham School of Jewellery and Silversmithing. I decided to look into this.

I spoke to the careers adviser at school. Most of the people in my class would be sent to work in a Birmingham wholesaler. It wasn't really a serious career direction. But it was basically the extent of this Career adviser's imagination. If you were like me, and really felt that school had nothing more to offer you, sending you off to Wilkinson Riddel and Larkin wholesalers was their way of passing you onto to become somebody else's problem.

After a bit of a chat, I persuaded him that a course in Trade Jewellery would be of benefit to me. An interview was arranged for me to go and speak to the Principle.

I travelled into Birmingham to the Jewellery Quarter. The School of Jewellery was very close to Samuel Hope's in Vittoria Street opposite the bullion dealers Johnson Mathey. An old three story Victorian Building, I grasped the brass handrail as I climbed the stone steps to the large front door. Once inside there was a large reception hall with young people dressed in very Arty wear! Grandy's adjective Beatnik Type came to mind, but they did not look at all out of place. It was clearly a look to go for I decided. If I immediately warmed to the informality of dress here, in contrast to the School Uniform of Riland Bedford, I was really taken aback by the School Principle.

A small man in his sixties, in equally worn out attire was Reginald Baxindale The Principle of The Birmingham School of Jewellery and Silversmithing. He opened the door to his office, and I got up from the chair where I had been waiting. I expected to be ushered into his office. No, Reg was checking the time on his watch.

"Simon?" He said "They must be open about now, come on follow me." Reg walked out of the front door and straight across the road to the Albion Arms Pub.

Reg Baxindale was obviously a well known regular in the Albion. He sat in his regular seat in the bay window of this old pub and a barmaid placed a large scotch in front of him. "What can I get you Simon. Have a pint of M and B Bitter." He said putting a cigarette in his mouth and offering me one. I'm going to look forward to coming here after the summer. I thought to myself.

28 SIMON. THIS IS MY FRIEND JIM

My sixteenth birthday was looming. I was eagerly counting the days when I could at last take my scooter out on the road. Holly Lodge had a long driveway and if you opened the garage doors front and back, I could lengthen my practice run.

Mum and her friends had started attending The Solo Club, which met at the same hall where St John Cadets helped with the handicap club. The coffee mornings after would be when the ladies would debrief each other on the encounters good, bad and the darn right ugly. It caused a lot of laughter and some cringing, but I was happy to see Mum enjoying a social life.

One morning, I came down to breakfast expecting to see the ladies engaged in their weekly post mortem of their previous nights Solo Club adventures. They weren't there. Sat at the Breakfast table next to Mum was a young man tucking into some egg on toast. They both looked towards me awkwardly. The man had a kind face but he was plainly nervous about the situation. "Simon." Mum said. "This is my friend Jim."

Jim was thirty-two years old. Ten years younger than Mum! Recently divorced, he has two children. His son David lives with him, and idolises him. Jim is a lorry driver working for Unigate Dairies near Birmingham and is currently staying with his Mum and Dad in Erdington.

Mums sister Christine enjoyed taking the rise out of Mum's new romance. "I bet he goes back to his parents home in Erdington and says." She says in the mock Hope Edgington Brummy. "Muuum Oi met a rail loi---day!" (Translation:- "Mother, I have met a real lady!")

Poor Jim did have to run that gauntlet for a while. But I liked him instantly. He won me over, when he took me out to find a tail light unit for my Vespa which I needed for its MOT test.

Jim would talk to me. He was very open about the relationship he was stepping into. He also enjoyed a pint so we became drinking buddies, even though I was still too young to be drinking in pubs. He was only sixteen years older than me, and life was delivering him some surprises right now that he was struggling with. I enjoyed being in the loop that was to change our family dynamic forever. I was very happy when Mum asked me what I thought of Jim and his son David moving in with us. They would eventually marry.

It was so good to see Mum happy. I think she was happier at this time, than I could have ever remembered her.

My sixteenth birthday arrived. 23rd June 1969. Roy Hammond came by to be my wingman on my first solo flight out of the driveway of Holly Lodge. Impressively, he managed to turn into the drive this time without falling off! Compared to the roads of today. In spite of the A38 Lichfield being a busy main road. Traffic was scarce that day. I donned my helmet and my warm corduroy jacket. Pointed my Vespa towards the road, and like a bird taking its first flight from its nest, I was away. The sense of Freedom that I was feeling was boundless. I could go anywhere. And I did!

Roy followed me to John Chawner's. We proudly pulled up outside his driveway. He was arm deep in oily rags from putting a new spark plug in his Lamberetta. We felt his frustration. John still had three weeks to go before his sixteenth. His scooter was still grounded. But Roy was now a fully qualified bike rider, which meant John could try out his new helmet and ride pillion with him. So the three of us joy rode the streets of Four Oaks and celebrated our liberation to the roads.

I went for a long drive on my own. I wanted to go visit Dad at his caravan park and surprise him I rode the thirty miles or so and arrived at the park, but alas no one was home. So I rode on to Dorrington Grove to my father's sister Pam's house. I had travelled some fifty miles in all to get there. It was nice to see them all, but no. Dad. Sadly, he was not there that day. I adored my newfound freedom.

The last month of school I rode my Vespa in and parked it at the back near the gym where the teachers parked their cars. I could sit in class and look out of the window lovingly at my Vespa. Similarly to how I did with my Dawes Dapper bicycle in the cycle shed of Ley Hill Junior School.

I didn't get involved in the Mods and Rockers thing at all in the sixties. This was a time when Scooter Gangs and Motorcycle gangs would clash. The news would report how these gangs would converge on places like Brighton on a bank holiday and there would be violent eruptions between the two gangs.

The nearest I ever got to that was when I was leaving the school gates and this Chopper Motorbike with huge "Ape Hanger" handle bars appeared from nowhere off the street. The helmeted goggled rider with a Hells Angel leather jacket wouldn't let me through the gate much to the amusement of onlookers. I would push my scooter back and try and get by him, but he was quicker than me every time. Twisting his throttle, blasting exhaust noises across the pavement. "You Fucking Mods are pussies." He chanted. "I'm not a Mod. I would have preferred a motorbike myself. But my Mum wouldn't let me have one." Was not going to be an appropriate answer. I knew that. I started to wonder what I was going to do. Just then the Hells Angel lifted his goggles from his eyes and removed his helmet. It was my old mate Pablo. Paul Buckmaster. "Ha ha ! got you going there didn't I."

Last day of school arrived. I had no regrets. No looking back. I was looking forward to going to Jewellery College after the summer. But first my scooter and me had some summer holidays to enjoy.

My plan was once again a working holiday with Diane and John Hall Say in Cornwall. It was quite a long way to travel on a Vespa. I was unable to use the M5 motorway because I was still on Learner Plates. So I boarded a train to Exeter from Birmingham Snow Hill.

I'd remembered Snow Hill station in Birmingham from the times I would go Train Spotting with Steven Suttle as a kid. It was a magnificent Victorian Structure and it would bustle with activity. To this day, I marvel at the transport hubs of communication. Everybody congregating at this one location, for this brief moment in time before going their separate ways to the further corners of the world. Snow Hill Station was my first such hub. The furthest corners of its world were within the British Isle, but I still romanticised about the huge Steam Locomotives that in just a few hours will have delivered their passengers and freight to far off places such as Edinburgh, Newcastle, London or now in my case. Exeter.

Now Snow Hill was looking tired, soon to be disused demolished and to become a car park. How sad.

My train to Exeter had some lovely Pullman carriages. British Rail posters; In every compartment. Depicting the romance of taking the train. Sadly no longer drawn by steam locomotive. We had entered the age of the Diesel Electric Locomotive.

My Vespa travelled in the guards van, and we were finally reunited at Exeter. It was quite the adventure travelling from Exeter to Launceston. When I think about the trust that I put in that old Vespa, which I paid just twenty pounds for, it makes me shudder. But my trusty steed served me well. During my Cornish vacation, I even managed to get across to Pontins in Paignton for a rendezvous with Julie.

Virginia Bumstead, Julies best friend from school had gone on to become quite a success with her singing. We were all very proud that one of our circle had hit the big time. She had become a Pontins Blue Coat. Julie had fixed to go there on holiday.

I rode my Vespa to Paington and Julie managed to smuggle me into the park. I was able to see Virginia do her show. She was now working under the name Gina Marsh. Well I have to be honest, I had wondered about whether I was the only person questioning what the hell Mr and Mrs Bumpstead were thinking when they decided to call their daughter Virginia!

Gina sang beautifully to the piano bass and drums, but then it appeared she had other Blue Coat duties to perform like calling Bingo. The three of us sat down together and got chatting. Gina asked me if I could think about writing a song for her. She had a record producer interested in her musical talent. They were looking for the next hit song to follow in the footsteps of Frank Sinatra's My Way. I told her I would see what I could come up with. Quite flattered that she should turn to me for such a project.

I couldn't stay with Julie that night. She shared a bedroom with another girl that was a disappointment. I had been rather hoping we could catch up with a bit of canoodling. So we had to make do with a few private moments before I had to sneak off and kip in some guys car.

I had a blanket and a pillow and I was curled up in the back seat of a Ford Anglia in the Pontins car park. At one point I heard the security moving around. I just got under the blanket and played dead. They shone a torch through the window and from beneath the blanket I could see my crash helmet caught in its beam. I held my breath and stayed perfectly still. Then they were gone. First light I made my exit and way back to Launceston.

I didn't have my guitar with me, but Ian Diane's son had a guitar I could use. I wrote the song for Gina Marsh which was going to overshadow old Frank Sinatra's signature tune.

Times.

Times of Happiness Times of Tears

Times of loneliness, Times of Fears

Times when I didn't know, which way to turn

Times when I found out, I have a lot to learn.

Thoughts of foolishness, Memories of grief

Times with loved ones, that were too brief

Although some times I've been sad, I have to say

It's those times good and bad, that have made me a man today.

Look out Frank. Some young blood is coming up behind you.

Back in Sutton Coldfield, I recorded Times on to a cassette tape for Julie to give to Gina. I think Gina liked my song but Julie told me her friend had suffered a bit of a setback. She seemed a bit upset.

I was to discover that there had been a bit of consoling going on between best friends. Gina had learnt a lesson in Show Business. Not all people are who they say they are. Not all record producers are what they say they are. And it is not necessarily a girl's musical talent that they are interested in exploiting!

29 JEWELLERY COLLEGE

Term time. I rode my Vespa to Birmingham to the Birmingham School of Jewellery and Silversmithing in the Jewellery quarter.

College was so much different than school. Smoking was allowed. No uniforms. The whole college thing just seemed so much more comfortable. The tutors treated us like adults, many of them not that much older than us students.

We were given a list of tools that we would need to do our course. There was a shop in Warstone Lane, which was like an Aladdin's cave when it came to tools. Delicate pairs of pliers minute saws and tiny files.

Dad came and met me in the first week and took me out to lunch. It was so nice to have some one on one time together. He asked me about Mum, and how was I getting along with Jim. How were Sally and Adam? He wistfully recounted how he was so very much in love when he first met Mum. Then he said it got to the point where he was feeling like a stranger in his own house. I felt so sorry. Had we done that to him?

He was a kind man. He took the list of tools I needed and we went to the shop in Warstone lane and handed it to the man behind the counter. I came out of that shop with a tin box full of all the tools I was going to need for my course.

We would study tool making, engraving, enamelling, silver work, soldering, mounting, gemmology and watchmaking. Most of the time we would be working with copper, but it became apparent that silver was a much better metal to work with. Gold was a rare treat being so expensive.

If we came across any surplus silver items, we could melt it down, draw it through a hole to create wire for making rings or melt it into ingots that could be pressed into sheets. The trouble with that is some family air looms turn out to be not what you are told. If they are hallmarked silver no problem. A lot of silver was not assayed in the School of Jewellery. It would be scrapped and reused. So we would take items over to Johnson Mathey the bullion dealers for testing. They would put some chemical onto the object. In one case it was a silver fruit bowl Gangan gave me that she could spare. With the silver in this, I would never have to work in copper again. I could exchange it for ring wire and some sheet silver. It was heavy maybe I could even compliment my paltry maintenance grant of thirty pounds a term. Thirty pounds a term! Most of the other students were away from home. They had grants of thirty pounds a month. A pound a day! They were living like kings!

I was snapped out of my daydream of well being, when the lady behind the counter looked at me sadly and said. "Sorry luv. I'm afraid its E.P.N.S." Fuck! Gangan's generous contribution to my student fund is an Electro Plated Nickel Silver Fruit Bowl. Not enough scrap value to even buy some fruit!

Driving the Vespa back to Sutton one day I was just going down an underpass at Perry Bar when crunch, followed by a deathly grinding of gearbox parts and my rear wheel locking. I managed to come to a halt but my Vespa had chosen that time to die on me.

I was lucky. I wasn't going too fast. What if I had been overtaking a truck, which I often did. I could accelerate to the top speed of 65MPH and the whole handlebars would vibrate with protest. If it had happened at such a time, God knows what trouble I would have been in. What if it had happened on the Bodmin moor I had driven many times between Launceston and Harlyn Bay? I think my trusty stead had chosen a good time for both of us to Part Company.

Jim came to my rescue. I managed to heave my Vesper into the back of his Anglia estate. When we got it back to Holly Lodge it was dead on arrival. For now it was going to be Four Oaks Station for the train to Birmingham. At least I had a student's rail card, so it was free. But I was mourning the loss of my Vespa, and the freedom that it represented which I was going to miss.

Another change was about to occur. Mum and Dad's divorce was now absolute and now that Jim and David had joined the family, it was time for a move. Holly Lodge was sold and Mum and Jim had pooled their resources to buy a house between them. Jim was in favour of living near his parents in Erdington and they found a three-bedroom semi detached house in Court Lane Erdington that fitted their budget comfortably. Number 177, next to the park.

They married at Birmingham registry office

It meant that I was sharing a bedroom with Adam and David. Sally had the other room. I was not over the moon about loosing my space in Holly Lodge and I was not pleased about being so far away from Julie. Although where she worked in Boldmere was within comfortable walking distance. I was still able to take the train or bus into college.

Mum got an opportunity to go to work. She started working as a taxi driver for a private Hire Company. She enjoyed driving, she was a very good driver and she became a favourite amongst the clients, driving this huge old Rover. Her favourite Taxi driving story of that time was about when she pulled into the drive of Highcroft Mental Hospital and announced to the doorman that she was a taxi. We all laughed and speculated that he was about to gently let her in to the grounds and give her a nice canvass jacket with straps to wear!

It was my turn now to start feeling like a stranger in my own home. I missed not being able to see Julie. I was finding the lack of personal space in Court Lane, having to share a bedroom with a six year old and a seven year old challenging.

I asked Julie if she knew of any rental properties my college mates and me could share. They were already in digs, but they were willing to consider looking at other options. I was very keen to have a place where Julie and I could be together. One day I met her and she was allowed to show me around a small house between Boldmere and Perry Bar. My thirty pounds a term was not going stretch that far.

Dad meeting me for lunch became a weekly ritual. It was nice to see him. Sometimes I would walk across town to Norfolk House and we would eat on his side of town. I told him that I was getting fed up of living with two kids in my bedroom. Mum and Jim were making a nice world for each other, but I wasn't sure where I fitted.

I thought of the fun that we had when we went and stayed with him. The gliding. He comes into Birmingham for work. We could ride in together. "How about if I was to come and live with you?" I suggested. Dad was quite surprised. "You would really like to come and live with me?" I thought it would be great. I said "Maybe I could get a motorbike so I have some transport." Dad said to my surprise. "Well to be honest, I breathed a sigh of relief when that scooter of yours finally packed up. I don't know what your mother was thinking not letting you have a motorbike. Scooters are so much more dangerous with those small wheels and no power to get out of trouble. But you are nearly seventeen soon. Why don't we wait and see if we can get you a small car? Bob Miller would soon get you through your driving test"

Well that sounded like a perfect solution to me. Dad and I would be living together like two mates in his mobile home in Codsel. It's a bit far from Julie but I would be getting a car so I would have my independence. Fantastic.

At first Mum was quite upset when I told her I wanted to go live with Dad. "I have been so immersed in my own happiness with Jim, that I didn't even realise that you were unhappy with me." She wept. "Now I feel like I have let you down. You know I wouldn't do that for the world." I did know that, and in fairness to Jim, with some help from him, we managed to help her see that it was nothing more than me wanting to try and fit in somewhere as an adult. It was decided and it was made abundantly clear that she loved me would miss me and anytime I wanted to come back, I was welcome. "I love you Mum."

Well the day came for Dad to pick me up from Court Lane. I packed a bag, and my guitar. I had my Ex RAF trench coat which all us student types were wearing. Very warm for those long walks from New street Station to the Jewellery Quarter. Probably do not need to worry about that now I thought. Will be riding in by car.

I was waiting for Dad's white Beetle to show up at Court Lane. When he eventually arrived he was in an old Green Cortina Mk1. My new car? I wondered. I put my suitcase in the boot, shook Jim by the hand and kissed Mum farewell. "Love you Darling." Mum said "Love you too." I got into the Cortina and prepared to enter the next episode of my life's journey.

30 MOVING HOUSE

We took the road up towards Sutton, Strange route to Codsall Wolverhampton I thought. I expected us to go via Birmingham. Perhaps we are going to go via the A5. Seems like the wrong direction to me. We entered Sutton Park by the Boldmere Gate.

"This is working out quite well." Dad said. "We should get back just in time for tea." My God I hope he hasn't left a chicken to cook in that bloody oven. He will burn the mobile home down. We drove out of Sutton Park Town entrance past number 77 to the roundabout.

"Do you remember when we were riding our bikes towards this roundabout?" I asked Dad. "Yeah, you frightened the crap out of me. I told you to follow me." Dad said. "Well when I saw you with your right hand indicating going round to the right." I justified my 4 year old actions. "I thought I would just cut across in front of the Island and get in front of you!" " I was wondering how I was going to explain to your mother how I got you run over." Well he hadn't told me you were supposed to go round the roundabout.

We took that exact same turning. "Here we are." We pulled up outside a house.

What? I was confused. I got my case out of the boot and walked up to the front door. The door opened and a lady was stood at the door.

"Hello Simon." Gangan's former next door neighbour greeted me. "Welcome to your new home."

What the fuck had just happened?

I thought that I was going to live the high life with Dad. We were going to buddy up. Maybe go gliding again, and have some fun.

The Ford Cortina was Kate's car. Dad picked me up in that because his Beetle was probably full of fucking Manulife calendars. Kate had something else too. Two young children. Angela and Christopher and they seemed to constantly squabble.

It turned out that during one of recently divorced Dad's many visits to Gangan he had met recently divorced Kate a teacher. Kate moved to this rental house following the sale of 407 Lichfield Road next to Chadsway. Now Dad and Kate were waiting on completion of the sale of their new home in Boswell Road Sutton. We were to move in at the weekend.

This was a lot for me to take in. Dad was plainly well into the honeymoon period of this relationship. Wooing Kate with flowers and compliments. She would find this a little over the top. "Oh for goodness sake Warwick." She would say "Wind it in! You only needed to buy me a bloody packet of Rothmans, and I would have been happy."

I wasn't getting the attention I expected. But I was beginning to realise. It may not matter. Boswell Road was very close to Julie. This could turn out OK.

This was not what I had signed up for at all, but I decided to try and keep a positive attitude. The move to Boswell Road was uneventful. But once installed in the new house, it became all hands on deck to the task of decorating the new home.

I turned out to be a disaster at every task given to me. This didn't help the family dynamic I was supposed to now fit into one little bit. The house had a third floor with a single attic bedroom. That was to be my room. I was pleased about that. A room of my own!

The first task I was set to was to dig the front garden. The soil was rock hard and eventually after much effort, the garden fork I was issued with let out a sudden crack as the wooden handle spectacularly broke in two. Apparently this garden fork had been in Kate's family for generations and Warwick's bloody son had managed to break it in seconds.

Dad was plainly trying to align himself to this new relationship, and I was obviously not helping. I don't think it was my fault the handle on the garden fork broke. I considered it more my misfortune that I happened to be using it, when it finally decided to protest at the lifetime of neglect it had received and die. When the same thing happened to Kate's garden rake, it was decided that I should come indoors and help with the painting. Big mistake!

At last Dad and I were to have some Father Son bonding time together. No one else was talking to us. We set about painting the banister railings on the staircase. I would be sat on the stairs painting the stair side of the railings, whilst Dad perched on some stepladders painting the other side of the railings. Each of us had our own pot of paint. I was very careful not to drip paint on the newly laid Axminster stair carpet. I used newspaper to protect that. That should get me back into favour I thought.

We were making good progress. When we both got about two thirds of the way up the staircase, Kate came to inspect our workmanship. "That is looking so much brighter" She commented. "Oh I am so glad you approve Darling." Dad sucked up to her. "Me and Si John have got the hang of this painting lark." "It's interesting how the light plays tricks on the colour white." I added. "What do you mean?" Dad asked. "Well when you stand in the hallway the railings look brilliant white." I noticed. "But from the stair side the colour looks kind of creamy." Kate came round to the stairs to see what I was talking about. "Oh my God!" she exclaimed. "I leave you two to do one simple task and you can't even do that!" What was the matter I didn't know what we had done wrong. "It's not a trick of the light. Warwick you have been painting your side white. And he's using magnolia!" Dad looked at my paint pot and exclaimed. "Oh fucking hell Simon! What the hell possessed you to use magnolia?" I had no idea what magnolia was. I saw a pot of paint that looked white to me and just started using it. Clearly my presence was not helping the crucial honeymoon period of this new relationship Dad had with Kate. It was not helping the simultaneous crucial honeymoon period between my dad and me either.

I liked Kate. But she was a very different creature to my mother. She was a schoolteacher in a private girls school. The fact that both my father and Kate worked made the family dynamic very different to my mother's home. We would all eat in the kitchen breakfast room. All my life, I was used to doing nothing to help. A plate of food would appear in front of me. I would eat it and I would ask "Please may I leave the table?" I would go and do my thing. I seem to remember Dad would pretty much do the same.

The difference at Kate's table, was when Dad finished his plate, he would get up, take it to the sink, rinse it, dry it with a tea towel and put it away in it's cupboard. Like wise Angela and Christopher would do the same, putting the cutlery away in it's own drawer. Was I supposed to do this too? I awkwardly followed suit, by now Kate was smoking a cigarette and Dad then declared that it was tonight his turn to wash the pots and pans, tomorrow it would be mine!

I commented on this to Julie, I was feeling quite incredulous. "What do you mean?" Julie asked. "I do that all the time, in fact my mother has commented in the past. Why doesn't Simon ever help out in the kitchen when he comes to eat here?" I thought about it then. Was my living with Mum so different to the rest of the world? Mum would do everything for us. She allowed us to treat her like a servant it would seem!

I discovered that to get to college, I could wait at the top of Boswell road, and John Stanway who was a director at G.K.N. would be giving Mark a lift into his work at Buck and Hickman in Birmingham. I too could get a ride in with him. I envied Mark his relationship with his dad. They got on well together. One-day Mark was drumming on the dash board to some song on the radio. "Don't do that Mark, it's annoying." His dad said. That made Mark do it all the more. "Mark I'm warning you." This made him act up even more. I could feel myself retreating into the leather upholstered back seat of the Ford Executive, What is Mark doing, surely he is going to come to grief. Then his dad just burst out laughing. They were good mates. I was a mate with Jim. Why couldn't I be a mate with my Dad?

Dad's home life was all about Kate. When he left my mother, I remember he exclaimed that he felt like an intruder in his own home. Now I was the one who felt like an intruder.

Julie and I would go out with Mum and Jim a lot. Now seventeen I was having weekly driving lessons with Bob Miller. I was doing a Saturday job at the Kitchen Utensil factory to get the money to pay for them. Jim would allow me to drive their car a Hillman Husky. I never ever got to drive Dad's car. Thanks to the practice I got in the Hillman Husky after six driving lessons, Bob Miller decided I was ready for my test.

On the day of my test I had a lesson in Bob's Mini. He took me around the test route in Boldmere showing me the pitfalls and told me if I perform like that on my actual test, I'll have nothing to worry about.

The actual test was very similar to the previous run in my lesson. At the end of it the instructor commented that, it had become a bit misty in the drizzle towards the end of the run. I should have put on my sidelights. Oh no! I must have blown it. "Ok Mr Edgington, you have passed. Now go out there and learn to drive!" I was stunned. I climbed out of the Mini. Bob Miller was waiting for me. My legs were shaking; I could hardly get the words out in reply to his question. "Are you all right? How did you do?" "I passed." I blurted out.

When I got home to Boswell Road, I thought to myself, surely Dad will let me drive his car now. I told Kate and we celebrated with a cigarette. Shortly after Dad arrived home. "How about this?" Kate announced. "Simon has just passed his driving test." "Well Bob Miller is a very good driving instructor." Was Dad's reply without even acknowledging I was in the room. Why was he being so mean to me?

31 GOING TO WORK

Money was getting tight. It was becoming increasingly difficult to make ends meet at college. Dad's attitude had become very negative towards my college education and was strongly suggesting that I should go and get a job.

I wanted money. I wanted to be able to afford to go out with Julie. Jim would allow me to use the Hillman Husky but I was dreaming of having a car of my own.

In the end I left the Birmingham School of Jewellery after one and a half years. I went to the Birmingham wholesalers Whittington Riddell and Larkin and after an interview with the director of personnel, I secured a job in the Ladies Underwear department for seven pounds a week.

John Chawner had started work at Sainsbury's in Erdington and started dating one of the cashiers called Valerie. He was on Eight Pounds a week.

This was about the time that British Currency was becoming decimalised. Over the previous twelve months, there existed a kind of conversion process where both currencies were acceptable, and gradually old penny coins and halfpenny coins were being faded out. As students of the Jewellery college many of us made bracelets by soldering jump rings onto old coins, liking them together, then taking them to an old queen who ran a electro plating workshop. We would never go alone, always three or four of us at a time. His office had pictures of young boys naked around a swimming pool, on a mantle piece.

The two-shilling coin became the new Ten Pence. Which meant that the old Sixpence coin was only worth two and a half new pence. One Shilling coins became five new pence.

First of all the Old penny, Half Penny Thupence and Six pence coins where withdrawn. And smaller copper; Half New Pence, New Pence coins were introduced. It didn't take many years for the Half New Penny to be withdrawn, because there was no longer any thing you could buy with it. If there was no accurate conversion of a price from Old Money to new, then the price was inevitably adjusted upward.

A very subtle inflation started to occur. At that time my most common purchase was a Mars Bar. Mars Bars had been seven pence for as long as I could remember. It wasn't too long before they were re-priced to five new pence. That was a Shilling! What a rip off. What a time to join the employment game!

One day when I was walking into town, I saw a familiar face standing out side the Royal Hotel smoking a cigarette. Dressed in waiter uniform. It was Pablo. Paul Buckmaster himself. I hadn't seen him since we moved from Holly Lodge. He was working at the Royal and living in a house across the road from the turning to Boswell road. He invited me to go round that night.

I left the Boswell road and called round at the house Paul told me he was in. He greeted me and we went upstairs into a common room where there was a load of other people. Paul was always the artful dodger type. We had spent time together, shared beer, cigarettes and talked about girls. At this place the new thing was smoking pot. I was absolutely amazed at this and knowing what I knew about my inability to get away with anything I wanted no part of it.

I have never in my life felt the need to take drugs. The house was next door to Sutton Coldfield police station for Christ's sake and on the other side of it was the Catholic Church where Mum and Dad had got married, across the road was Bishop Vesey Grammar School which my Dad had attended and the entrance to Boswell Road where we now lived. My relationship with my Dad was becoming strained. I was sad that things were not better between us. I felt that the negative attitude I was experiencing from him was undeserved, but there was no way I was going to risk further disapproval by getting involved in drugs.

I made my excuses and left. That was the last time I saw Paul Buckmaster.

Things finally came to a head with life in Boswell Road, when after a night out with Julie, Mum and Jim I got back to Boswell Road to find the house all locked up. I rang the doorbell, but there was no response.

I walked up to the telephone box and rang court lane. Mum drove the

Husky in her dressing gown to come and rescue me. The next day Jim and I drove to Boswell Road to collect my things. After a doorstep altercation with Dad I left Boswell Road.

I was sorry that my time with Dad had not worked out for us. I had tried, but even when I was there, Julie and I spent time at Mum and Jim's in Court Lane, it seemed a place where we were treated like adults and not like one of the kids.

32 FORD ANGLIA

Working at a wholesaler in the centre of Birmingham was a means to an end. The money was horrible. Every morning, I would walk up to the junction of Chester Road and Boldmere Road, and wait for Mark Stanway and his Dad to pick me up in his Ford Executive. It could be quite bleak at that time of day, and by the time headlights of this big car loomed into sight through the early morning mist, I was glad to climb into the warm back seat of a now heated up vehicle.

Entrance via the employee gate, past the security guard and clock in. "Ding" we would walk through the loading bay past a small fleet of Ford Cortina's. These were the Reps cars. Oh how much more glamorous their lives must be compared to mine A life on the road with a company car. I was quite envious of them in their smart suits and briefcases tucked under their arms.

I would ride the elevator to the Ladies Underwear department. There were a number of items that I bought for Julie, using my staff discount. But to be honest, most of it was more designed for comfort than style.

On the top floor there was a white goods department, with washing machines and televisions. I did feel that that department might be more to my taste.

Shortly after joining, there was a meeting, where it was announced that the company would be moving out of its City Centre Premises to the suburbs, and we were all asked if we would like to be considered to carry on working at the new location. I believe it was Stourbridge, which would have been difficult for me. The writing was on the wall that I should perhaps start looking for alternative employment.

Jim worked at Unigate and he told me that the kids working in the Bottling plant were earning much more money than me. It was on a kind of rota that meant you had to work some weekends, but every now and then it would give you a long weekend off.

He set me up with an interview, and I travelled into work with him one morning.

The first thing that you notice when you walk into a bottling plant is the sound of bottles noisily colliding with each other, every step of their journey through the plant.

I was familiar with Jim's lorry. He often parked it outside the house when he sneaked home for an illicit tea break between deliveries. The lorry would pull to a halt with the tell tale sound of air brakes and the sound of milk bottles dancing in their plastic crates.

That sound is multiplied times over in the confined activity of a bottling plant. Jim and his lorry driving companions would stop their lorry full of empties at one end of the plant. Fork lift trucks would lift a palette sized block of crates from the truck bed, and load them onto a machine that would place the 6 high stacks of cases in line amidst a torrent of hisses and clunks from the hydraulic machinery. Like this they would enter the plant on a conveyer belt. The next machine in line would de stack the cases for the de casing machine that would lift the bottles on to a separate belt that would carry them to the huge bottle washer.

At the other end of the bottle washer, clean bottles would emerge and join a single file line waiting to be filled with fresh milk. Once filled a capper machine would attach the aluminium bottle tops. The full bottles would be reunited with their now hosed down cases which once again would be stacked ready for loading back onto empty lorries at the exit end of the plant.

I followed Jim into the locker room, where "Ding" he took out his time card and clocked in. The room was full of lockers and guys changing from street clothes to the white over trousers and tunics, emblazoned with the Unigate Dairies Logo. Jim put on his familiar blue overalls and beckoned me to follow him.

At the rear of the bottle washer and above the Milk Filling machines, there was a huge balcony holding stainless steel tanks. A flight of metal stairs leads up to the balcony and a suite of offices with large windows overlooking the plant floor. I followed Jim up the stairs, and we walked into the office. "Hi, this is Simon who I was telling you about. He is looking for a job." A small man, dressed in white overalls came forward and shook me by the hand. "How old are you son?" He enquired. "Umm seventeen sir." Was my reply. Well there really wasn't much more to the interview than that. "Ok I'll start you off on the bottle washer, and we will see how we get on. One thing though. You have to be prepared to work some weekends. If you don't turn up for work on a Sunday, because you got drunk on a Saturday night, there will be trouble. There are a million unemployed in this country right now, so if you don't want to make it a million and one, make sure you are here when we expect you. The way the rota works, every now and then you get a long weekend off so it is not so bad. I will start you on eighteen pounds a week. "

Eighteen pounds a week! Wow I'm in the money. Just to put this in perspective. As an H.G.V. Class one lorry driver in 1970, Jim was taking home thirty pounds a week. At my last job, I was earning seven pounds a week; John Chawner was earning eight pounds fifty as a trainee manager at Sainsbury's. For a seventeen year old, I had odd hours, but I was earning more than twice as much as my mates.

It was about this time, that Julie had a party again. I met her friends Annette and Dave. They lived together in a flat near Four Oaks. Dave had just landed a job as a TV repair engineer, and his new job provided him with a Morris Minor van. This meant that his Ford Anglia was no longer needed and he put it up for sale. Now living in Erdington, I needed my own car. Jim would allow me to use the Hillman, but it was very thirsty.

I quickly managed to save up the money to buy my very first car. I couldn't believe my luck, Dave only wanted twenty five pounds for this car. Only a few quid more than the scooter I bought last year. Insurance cost me eight pounds third party fire and theft.

I climbed into my new blue Ford Anglia. Held the wheel proudly for the first time and jiggled my gear stick. My car! I drove it up to John Chawner's to proudly show it off to him and his family. Hazel said "It is very nice." I was beaming with pride.

By now John too had acquired some wheels. A Ford Cortina Mk 1. We would spend hours tinkering with our new passport to adulthood. I spent five pounds on a set of cross ply tyres. My car was looking good.

We would drive our cars, with our girlfriends up to Bar Beacon. A favourite spot for courting couples. There was a hot dog van up there where you could take an interlude from making out on the back seat with a cup of tea or a sausage roll.

Every now and then, some guy would get out of his car and walk forward to the trees to take a pee. If he was unlucky and spotted by some one in a car not otherwise engaged in back seat carnal pursuits, he would find himself bathed in a headlight beam. One toot of the horn, and every car would light up its beams amid laughter and horn tooting. One unfortunate caught up in this ritual one night was John Chawner. I confess I might have been the initiator on that occasion. John just turned to the spotlights, and with his cheeky grin, bowed to his audience.

Having a car was brilliant, and it was instrumental in re kindling my musical interests. There was a country pub in Little Hay, a small village that hosted Traditional Jazz. One evening Annette Dave Julie and myself, stumbled across this pub. As we walked through the car park, we could hear this wonderful music coming from within. On opening the door, the energy and atmosphere was just staggering. Every body was tapping their feet to the double bass. The trombone was sensational, clarinet blowing counter melodies, a trumpet lead, fabulous jazz guitar and drums. My memory of this band was just musical excellence. From that moment, I was hooked on the entity that was live Trad Jazz. Didn't really care to listen to recordings. For me it was all about being present when these musical events actually took place. The band were having fun, taking the rise out of one another, and the atmosphere spread out to the whole room. At the end of the night, we discovered that the band would be appearing at the Dog Inn Sutton Coldfield on Fridays. We were definitely going to be there.

We turned up on the Friday night at the Dog Inn. This pub was next door to the famous Empress Cinema, where as kids we used to enjoy Saturday Morning Matinees. Where I made my first career choice years ago. That of becoming a super hero! Now the venue next door was to rekindle the flame that was my love of music and entertainment.

The same faces were lined up in the front line of the band. Tony Robinson on Trumpet. Pete Wiseman, Clarinet. John Kearnon, Trombone, Tony Caldicot on drums, and a character on piano, Ron, who also sung some great blues numbers.

What was also interesting on jazz night was the crowd. They would loyally come and support the band every week. There would be a lot of people turning up with cases of different shapes and sizes. These were other musicians, and throughout the night they would be invited to take their instruments out and sit in with the band. I got to know a lot of these other musicians, some of whom also had bands, so in time we were travelling all around the area following the local jazz scene.

Mum and Jim soon came to enjoy the jazz scene too. They became regulars with Julie and myself. We would get there early to secure our favourite front table. We would invite friends to come and join us, and on many occasions we had a large gathering.

At the end of the night often the finale was not really a Trad Jazz number, but Water Melon Man. Everybody in the room who had bought an instrument would share the stage and take a solo. Then the encore would be When The Saints Go Marching In. Again; with a line of trumpets blowing solos and taking applause.

Oh how I wanted to be in that line. I daydreamed.

33 TRUMPETS

That summer, Julie and I booked a holiday together. We were seventeen, I had my car and we saved up twenty pounds each for a week in Pontin's Holiday Camp, Osmington Bay, Weymouth. After that we arranged to drive down to Harlyn Bay, for a further week in Diane Hall-Says caravan.

It was very exciting going away together. We booked in as a Mr and Mrs. It was back in the day of Carry On films and strict land ladies after all! Pontin's was a bit forgetful, apart from the entertainment, which we loved. I remember Julie telling me that when she stayed at Pontin's before, she won the talent competition. I remembered that holiday more from the fact that I ended up sleeping alone in someone's Ford Anglia. Not this time. My Ford Anglia was in the car park this time, and you know what? I decided we would enter the talent contest. I borrowed a guitar off one of the Blue Coats. We walked onto the stage and the compare asked us our names. Julie got to the mike first "Um Julie Dan' … no sorry I mean Simon and Julie Edgington. Whoops ! we are on our honeymoon" I liked the sound of that. We sung "All you have to do is dream" and won first prize!

This was followed by a week in Harlyn of walking hand in hand along the beach and enjoying the romance of the Cornish star lit skies at night.

I was once again feeling the pull of my musical genes. When we got home, I took a journey to Aston. I wanted to check out the second hand shops to see if I could buy a trumpet. I had dreamed of standing in that line of musicians at the Dog Inn and joining in the chorus of When the Saints Go Marching in, and maybe even taking a solo.

I parked the car and walked into the second hand shop just by the entrance to Aston Station. There among the various cast offs, was a Boosey and Hawkes Regent Trumpet. Going for eighteen pounds. It came in a case with an assortment of Mutes, Cleaners and a mouthpiece. I bought it!

Now it was time to learn my new musical Instrument. I managed to get the Trumpet Players equivalent of Burt Wheedons "Play in a Day" This gave me note positions and fingering for scales. I had spoken to a number of musicians at the jazz club, and they told me that scales were all important.

So I set to practicing my scales. It was hard at first to get a decent sound out the trumpet. But with practice and perseverance, that musician's mantra that my father had written in the dedication in Burt Weedon's book, I eventually started to make headway.

Yes. Scales are important. But so is having fun with music. I have always been able to pick a simple tune on any instrument I picked up. So naturally, I wanted to have a go at "When the Saints" After a few blundering attempts, in time. Maybe a lot more time to the poor long suffering members of my family who had to endure these lengthy practice session, I managed to blow out a respectable melody line.

My lengthy practice sessions did have a time limit. This was caused by what trumpeters call the Embrasure. Blowing a trumpet requires good muscle control of the lips. Like any other muscle this has to be developed. I would find that I could only blow scales for so long before the chops went. Then the wind that you exhale would leak all around the mouthpiece in the form of a comical raspberry sound.

I found out that our Double Bass player Sleepy Reed. A charming black man who could have stepped off the plane from Bourbon Street New Orleans, had he not actually come from Aston, like my trumpet, had a brother. Eddie Reed was a trumpet player, and he could give me some lessons.

I met Eddie in a pub in Aston. The land lord, a big homely Irish man with ginger hair and an unshaven beard, said it was alright for us to use the back room for lessons, any day except for a "Torsday" (Translation Thursday) because "Torsday" was darts and dominoes night. Well these lessons don't seem to have much of a lasting memory with me. It turned out that Eddie was pretty much self-taught, but he did show me a few useful licks, which would help me put together a solo.

Jim was starting to get caught up in the jazz scene too. He was keen that I bought a second hand trumpet and he decided to go one better. He must have spent a small fortune. He went out and bought himself a brand new Yamaha Trombone. It became his pride and joy.

This actually turned out to be quite good for me. I would play the melody to "When the saints," and Jim would give me a trombone bass line. We were having fun.

So after much practice and perseverance, I finally got the melody to Hello Dolly, An English Country Garden, and When The Saints Go Marching In. In addition to that I had worked out what I considered to be an amazing solo. This I was going to amaze my band buddies with. By now I had been practicing for hours, days, weeks or even perhaps months!

The Pub in Little Hay had stopped it's Sunday Night Jazz Club. The Dog Inn, mindful of the great Friday crowd attracted by the Jazz was quick to snap up the Sunday night too.

The Friday night of my trumpet player debut arrived. I took my seat proudly holding my trumpet case like all the other visiting stars. All night long I had that butterfly feeling in my stomach. My solo was good; it would surely blow them away. "What are you going to play with us?" Tony Robinson, my trumpet hero enquired. I announced that I would just sit in at the end this first time. A great night was enjoyed. That evening Mike Bernie was sat in on Tenor Sax. He was a pro who worked in the orchestra of the new Cunard Flag ship QE2. It was always a treat when he was in town between contracts.

Finally the moment arrived. Tony announced. "Time for our finale on this Friday night. But first; a public service announcement. Sunday nights at Little Hay has been cancelled!" A groan of disappointment ensued from the crowd. " Apparently the pub think we take up too much space, and they want to pack the crowds in!" Clever jibe I thought! " So the new home for our Sunday Jazz will be right here at the Dog Inn!" Cheers erupted and Tony counted in the band for the final song and a number of musicians joined the band from the floor. Including me with my Boosey and Hawkes Regent.

34 STAGE FRIGHT AND BUM NOTES

I stood on the front line of the jazz band amongst my hero's. How long had I been coming to this jazz night? How many different venues had Julie and I explored? Enjoying the sounds of Traditional Jazz being performed by fellow enthusiasts from all walks of life. Tony Robinson Trumpet was the managing Director of a flooring company. Pete Wiseman Clarinet was a TV engineer. John Kearnan Trombone, a travelling salesman. Mike Bernie Saxophone actually made his living as a professional musician. Little Si John Trumpet, a bottle washer for Unigate Dairies!

I looked out at the sea of faces in the room that would normally be the audience that I was a part of. This time I had crossed over to the band. Julie was sat with Mum and Jim. They were all smoking cigarettes, as was most of the crowd, creating this hazy cloud over the room, which leant a sleazy atmosphere to the Jazz club. We all started in unison, When the saints.......

With me there were several trumpets. Tony and one other guy from the crowd on a silver cornet then myself. We seemed to manage the first chorus pretty well. I had played this many times in the front room of Court Lane and all horns were pretty much in unison. Tony took a magnificent solo, followed by John on trombone. My turn would be coming soon. I could feel a cold sweat welling up around my collar, and a dryness forming around my lips. Oh no. What if I made a mistake? When you make a mistake during practice. You stop and start again. This band was chugging along like an unstoppable freight train. I had this solo worked out parrot fashion. I was quite pleased with it. I had fantasised many times about this very moment that was now looming up on me...... Fast. Silver Cornet took a solo. This made me feel a bit more heartened. I think my solo was stronger, and then Pete on Clarinet I was next. An uncontrollable shaking seemed to run through my whole body, the butterflies in my stomach now seemed to be fluttering about in a mad frenzy, my lip forehead and my neck were awash with that cold sweat now and my lips were now so dry that they were sticking to the tops of my teeth. I bought the trumpet up to begin my solo. What was supposed to be a sharp Bda da da da da da da da daaaaa da turned into a horrible selection of squeaks and embrasure farts. It was all going horribly wrong. The crowd politely clapped at the end of the chorus, but with notably less enthusiasm than the other solos. I think the fact that I got any applause at all was due to the fact that one of their own, was having a go! The song progressed back into the final chorus where everyone once more played in unison. I somehow managed to regain some composure for this. Hiding amongst the other horns was a lot less daunting than having the proverbial spot light on you during a solo. There was not actually a spot light at all in the Dog Inn. More a selection of wall mounted lights with the occasional bulb actually working, illuminating the red flock pub wallpaper that seemed to be the choice of most breweries.

We shared the ovation at the end of the last song. Tony politely congratulated me on my effort. I was despondent. I knew I could do better. I returned to the sanctuary of my Girlfriend and Family sat in our front row table.

Mum always the one to encourage and blindly compliment gave me a "Well done Darling, I was so proud of you up there!" It felt undeserved and didn't help. I looked at Jim. He had heard me rehearsing, he knew I could do better; He felt my pain, because he too was looking forward to the time that he could sit in on trombone. I was feeling dejected. I had visions of adoring crowds complimenting me on my efforts. Not tonight. Maybe not ever!

The next day was a working Saturday.

35 STANDING OVATION FOR THE BOTTLE WASHER

I lay awake in bed, reliving the horrors of my awful solo. Where I seek jubilation, I found humiliation. Why? Why was this so important to me?

The next day, Jim and I car shared to the Unigate Dairy. We drove in silence, only the sound of Radio One; blaring in the background. Some chirpy prat of a DJ, most likely Tony Blackburn was giving his best effort to stir the nation into another Saturday. For Jim and me it was another day at work.

We arrived at the usual scenario that was Unigate Dairies. I clocked in and went to my locker. My fellow workmates were drifting in and getting prepared for the beginning of the day. What a mixture of sorts we had here. There were older guys who had worked here their entire life. Different ethnic origins. A lot of Pakistani guys, from their strong Brummie accents, obviously second generation. Probably never even left the Midlands in their entire lives.

One particular guy struck my attention. He would arrive to work dressed as a City Gent. Grey striped trousers, a dark jacket, a bowler hat, umbrella and a copy of the financial times tucked under his arm. He would remove his attire and dress in the overalls we were all issued with by Unigate until the end of the day, when once again he would redress in his business attire to catch the bus home again. We would all quietly speculate on what that was all about? We were convinced that his wife must have thought that he must be Mr Unigate himself. That was until one day I had the occasion to give him a lift home. Home was a very modest two up two down terrace house, and his wife clearly was under no illusions over what he did for a living. She was extremely pleasant and down to earth, and more than a little tongue in cheek over the way her husband liked to present himself towards his neighbours!

I found myself among the clanking sound of milk bottles. A truly overwhelming sound as the conveyor belt delivered them to the wider loading bed of the bottle washer. My job was to examine the sea of empty milk bottles and spot any rejects. These would be either bottles that were damaged, containing objects like "Notes to the Milkman" from housewives, which would be more like "No Milk Today" or "One extra pint please" Than the Carry on Movie version which might say "Please Knock……. Husband away!"

Some bottles were so incredibly filthy; that there was no way the bottle washer could cope with them. How some people lived their lives! Fancy leaving out a milk bottle without even rinsing it out! Others that we had to reject were what we referred to as Foreigners. These were bottles that belonged to other Dairies. After some time one would develop an eye for these bottles that required rejection. In fact during my first weeks at Unigate, I would see a sea of bottles every time I closed my eyes. I would lay in bed and have difficulty falling asleep. I would have the vision of hundreds of Unigate Dairies moving in front of me with the occasional foreign "Northern Dairies" stowaway attempting to sneak past me.

At Nine O Clock in the morning, our three man team would start to relieve one another for a twenty minute breakfast break. If we timed the break just right, this would be the time that the Channel Island milk was being filled into the bottles. There was nothing quite as nice, as a freshly bottled pint of milk with your breakfast, and the red-topped channel island bottles were truly to be sort after. Simply delicious!

I would take my bottle upstairs to the canteen and sometimes have beans and egg on toast, or more often than not, simply a Kit Kat washed down by the best tasting milk in the world. I would gaze out of the window at all the cars dawdling nose to tail into the city. For someone chained to a bottle washing machine for eight hours a day, I fancied that the lives of any one of those frustrated drivers was more interesting than mine.

This was the thing about menial work. The rewards were there. I was making good money. But all the joy in my world most definitely came from elsewhere. I had my girlfriend, Julie who I loved with all my heart, and the jazz club was the current conduit that served my passion for Music and Performance. What was the sound track of my life. Was it the onslaught of dancing milk bottles colliding with one another? No it wasn't. Because when one is engaged in a mind numbingly repetitive activity, one takes ones mind to a better place. The din of Unigate Dairy may bombard my ears, but what I am listening to in my mind is the jazz club and the sounds of

"Woodchoppers Ball" by Woody Herman. "St Lewis Blues", "Tiger Rag", "Hello Dolly", "Satin Doll", and many other favourites. All these years later; as I write this, it was these songs that were the sound track of my life back then.

And that is why my poor trumpet solo was so important to me. This Dairy work wasn't me. It was when I was in the company of all these wonderfully talented musicians, playing and sharing their fabulous music that I really and truly felt alive. I didn't really see how it was ever going to be possible for me. But there existed an almost silent whisper within the centre of my very core as a human being telling me that this was to be my chosen path. A whisper that for a few more years yet to come was being easily drowned out by other entities.

However. In spite of my set back, I wasn't put off. Saturday went by as a day of mourning towards my abysmal performance. Sunday was another day at the dairy and Sunday night was jazz club once more. We arrived at the Dog in and took up our favourite table at the front. It was politely acknowledged that despite my setback the previous Friday, I was still carrying my trumpet case. I had two long shifts at Unigate to contemplate my disaster. I had played it over in my mind, and strangely the nerves that I had previously experienced on Friday were thankfully absent. I spoke to a few members of the audience. Many were quite encouraging but I couldn't help sensing a bit of doubt from the band as to whether it would be wise to encourage me to come and share the stage with them.

It was a very normal night, listening to the band and enjoying the atmosphere, and at the end of the night, for the final number Tony Robinson stepped to one side politely, but I sensed with a little reluctance, to allow me to sit in on "When The Saints Go Marching In" The song began. I decided that I was going to relax and soak in the moment. Tapping my feet as good as the rest of them and blowing out the melody with equal commitment.

When the time came for my solo, everything fell exactly into place, just as it had all those may times I had rehearsed it in my living room. The truth is that I had known that solo for months. But the truth to the Sutton Coldfield Jazz All Stars at The Dog Inn was this guy came and played on Friday and totally sucked, then two days later he ripped the room apart with this amazing flawless solo.

There was no polite handclap after this solo. There was a total ovation from the room. The whole room stood up to the sound of applause and whoops and hollers' the guys in the front line of the band were patting me on the back and shaking my hand. I was soaking in the adoration and getting intoxicated by the high that was a real adrenalin rush.

When the song ended, the applause exploded one more time. I was beaming with pride. Julie cast me one of her enchanting smiles from the table where she sat with Mum and Jim, I knew exactly how we would be celebrating my triumph later on that night.

Life was good. I was a very happy Bottle Washer from Unigate.

36 PLAYING THE FIELD

I was becoming more and more dissatisfied with my job at Unigate. I felt I didn't belong there. One young guy, who joined about the same time as me could see nothing in his life beyond this place. I couldn't help feeling that there must be more to life than this for me.

I had pretty much decided that my pop star ambitions were being unrequited right now, but I couldn't help feeling that the time was coming for me to think about a change in employment. The working hours were beginning to have an effect on my social life too.

Julie was starting to get itchy feet. She was working with her sister at an Estate Agents and she had caught the eye of a number of visitors to the office.

I think sister had advised her that she was too young to be settled down with one guy, and why shouldn't she play the field. I think Julie was becoming curious about the interest that she was receiving from elsewhere. And eventually one evening, we had the talk.

"Simon." She started "We have been together a long time. Neither of us have ever really experienced anybody else. Have you ever thought about us allowing each other to play the field a bit?"

This came to me as a crushing blow! I had never contemplated a life without Julie. You occasionally come across couples that say they were high school sweethearts. To me that was Julie and me. For the first time I am being made aware that this is not necessarily the same agenda that was shared by Julie.

I was incredulous. We had discussed our future together, fantasised about what we would be calling our kids. In the space of this conversation, all of our dreams together were falling apart. I was devastated. I had never contemplated being with any one but Julie. I told her how heartbroken I was feeling by all this.

"Simon. I love you, and I know that you cannot see it now, but in years to come you will realise that this is for the best for both of us. We are still so very young, and we need to allow each other the freedom to explore what is out there."

As a seventeen going on eighteen year old, I could not see it then. I felt betrayed by the love of my life. I was devastated. I just wanted my Jules back.

All these years later, as you quite rightly pointed out, I realise of course you were right. Julie. But, from my seventeen, going on eighteen-year-old perspective then. No.

Working at Unigate was now becoming unbearable. I was unhappy. I would gaze out at the cars travelling to Birmingham centre in the early morning rush hour from the canteen. Loosing Julie created a huge void in my life. I wanted her back. I held a huge resentment towards all the unenjoyably aspects of my life. I never enjoyed working at Unigate but it was tolerable along side the aspects of my life that I did enjoy.

"There are plenty more fish in the sea!" was a phrase that good intentioned friends and family would tell me, affording me little or no comfort at all. I was and I remain to this day someone who is a lot more comfortable with people with whom I have a history, than striking up new relationships. It is this aspect of me that would serve to have me persevere with situations, long after the sensible money cuts its losses and go elsewhere! But that is another chapter or four!!!

My Eighteenth Birthday arrived, and I was called up to the office. "Well laddie, now that you are Eighteen, I have to pay you a mans wage. So now more than ever I expect to see man's work from you!" and then he went on with the same tirade that I heard when he first hired me. "Don't forget, there are a million unemployed in this country. So if you don't want it to become a million and one ....!"

So now I was earning 25 pounds a week as a bottle washer. Good money, but I needed a change. And I didn't mean a change of girlfriend. After a few more weeks, I decided that I wanted to leave Unigate. Jim was a bit disappointed, especially since I still lived at home, and I hadn't got another job to go to.

Shortly after my eighteenth birthday, I drove out of the gates of Unigate Dairy for the last time.

37 SITUATIONS VACANT

So now I was unemployed. Jim said I should go and sign on at the labour exchange in Erdington. I drove down there in my Ford Anglia. There was a queue around the block of some of the roughest looking individuals I had ever seen. I didn't want to join the queue, Hell; I didn't want to risk parking my car around there.

I drove to WH Smiths and picked up a Birmingham Evening Mail and a Sutton Coldfield News newspaper. Let's see what there is in the classified vacancies column.

I had quite a bit of time on my hands. I wanted to hang out with John Chawner, but he was working at Sainsbury's in Erdington. He was now steadily dating one of the cashiers there. Val. Julie and I had been out with them on a foursome several times. Val was very unusually quiet, but for good reason, he was quite besotted by her.

I took a drive up to Chadsway to visit Gangan. She was quite surprised to see that I was alone, as Julie and I had been seemingly inseparable. After the "Plenty more fish in the sea" Speech yet again that seemed to be what everybody was conspiring to tell me I left and drove home.

I sat in the dining room at Court Lane, away from the maddening crowd watching the TV in the living room, and started to examine the situations vacant columns, of the Birmingham mail and the Sutton Coldfield News.

"Trainee Metallurgist Required" McKechnie Metals. Aldridge. Qualifications Physics Maths Equivalent O levels. I phoned the number and a very nice lady told me I had an appointment for the following Monday. Well I guess at the very least, I was about to discover what a Metallurgist was. I always enjoyed physics, in school, and I had some experience with metal casting in the Birmingham School of jewellery might be interesting.

I also saw another advertisement that caught my eye. Eames the Jewellers on Sutton Coldfield Parade were advertising for a Trainee Retail Manager. Well I figured that would be a good situation for me too. So I telephoned Eames. I spoke to the manager Bill Thomas. A very strong South Wales accent emerged down the phone. "Awe very good innit. We 'ave 'ead office 'ere for stock take and audit till Wednesday next week, and Thursday is early closing 'innit. Tell you what boyo, come and 'ave a chat with me Friday morning next week." Well it looked like I had two possibilities for employment. Both completely different career paths. For an Eighteen year old, it appeared I was approaching a very interesting fork in the road. "Which way was destiny going to take me?" I daydreamed.

In spite of our apparent different directions, Julie and I still enjoyed the Jazz club together. I told her about my upcoming week of interviews. She was quite excited for me. We had a nice weekend together and I wondered about whether we were going to be back to normal again soon. I hoped so. A new job and normality with the girl I love. Exciting!

Monday morning arrived, and I put on my smart suit. Foster Brothers. I hadn't dressed smart since the days of Wilkinson Riddell and Larkin and their ladies underwear department. No need for a suit at Unigate Dairies. I drove my Ford Anglia to Aldridge and McKechnie Metals. I arrived at an industrial estate at a large entrance gateway. A lot of noise emerged from a large factory sized building with funnels emitting smoke and steam. In an annex to this building there was a Reception doorway. I guess that's where I go.

A nice young girl on reception received me. Things were looking good, I wondered if she was going out with anyone. She smiled sweetly and beckoned me to follow her up a staircase to a suite of offices. I took to the stairs appreciating the pencil skirt at eye level in front of me covering a pleasantly undulating bottom as she climbed and nylon covered legs down to high-heeled sandals. "Tights or stockings with suspenders?" I speculated quietly in my mind. Maybe if I get to work here, these "Other People" that I am supposed to be dating might be plentiful!

I was shown into the office and met the personnel officer. He told me that the position would involve some night study. At the end of which; I would be a qualified Metallurgist. I had to ask. "What exactly is a Metallurgist?" The factory was a Brass Casting works. Rods of brass would be either rolled into shapes or molten brass poured into moulds. The metallurgist's function was to be responsible for the chemical consistence of the metals poured or rolled. This involved a little chemistry, a bit of physics and a lot of maths. Well I loved Physics at school. I managed to scrape an equivalent of a maths O level. I was asked how I would feel about taking A level Maths if I was offered the position. Maths was always a challenge, but I thought to myself, if it is applied to a profession, perhaps at last I get to see the point of it. I replied enthusiastically that I was very interested in the position.

Then they took me to the factory where I was able to view the actual process of rolling metals and brass casting. I had rolled silver wire and drawn it through progressively smaller die holes to arrive at a smaller gauge wire. But this process was on a much larger industrial scale. The metals had to be annealed after every process in order to prevent it becoming brittle. This involved heating the newly worked metal to red hot, much like a blacksmith would. My experience at college of this made me know that once annealed the metal became less fatigued or brittle and more malleable for the next process.

Brass findings for Yale locks were manufactured here, along with many parts of electric light bulbs. I was quite excited at the prospect of working with metal once again. The personnel manager introduced me as Mr Edgington to members of the floor team. "One of the candidates we are talking to about the Trainee Metallurgist Position" I think this was the first times I was referred to as Mr Edgington. Felt much like my father. I wondered if that receptionist with the pencil skirt and pretty bottom would be my secretary. Mmmm !

Interview over, I was told that they had a number of other candidates to meet, but they would be in touch in the next couple of days, with a decision.

One down, one to go, I speculated on the way home. A couple of days? Well if I don't hear from them by Wednesday, there is always Eames the jewellers.

I stayed close to the phone Tuesday afternoon. I had gone and met Julie in the morning at her office to tell her about my interview. When I got home, Mum greeted me with the news that the phone had not rung all morning, apart from a wrong number. By the end of the day no news. The same on Wednesday. As the day came to a close, my day dreams of becoming a

Metallurgist, which my family had explained to me, would be some kind of scientist was fading. Thursday. I no longer wanted to allow myself that fantasy, as it appeared that my future was more likely to be determined by my interview the following day at Eames the Jewellers. Or not! What if I failed to be offered either Job. Had I made a huge mistake abandoning those nice large pay packets at Unigate Dairies.

38 START ON MONDAY

Friday came, and once again it was time to put on my smart suit and point my Ford Anglia towards Sutton Coldfield Parade, and Eames the Jewellers.

I parked in the Dog Inn car park and crossed the road to the parade. Walking past the bus stop that I used to wait at so often to get my ride to Holly Lodge. I walked up to number 80 The Parade. RH Eames Ltd, retail jewellers, straightened my tie and opened the door to the chime of a jingling brass bell attached to its frame.

RH Eames was a small shop. Two glass counters with shelves behind displaying various clocks and Capo De Monte Porcelain figures. Below the counters were more display cases showing various lines in watches and gold and silver chains and pendants. In the corner was a large safe and a doorway leading to a back room.

A rather attractive young girl popped her head through the doorway, in response to the chiming doorbell. Obviously in the process of enjoying a morning coffee, she stood and came out the greet me. A Danish Pastry in her hand. "Hello, how can I help you today?" She greeted me with a smile. "I've come for an interview with Mr Thomas." I replied. With that the voice I had heard on the telephone bellowed out Welshly from the doorway. "Well don't just stand there, Susan, tell 'im to come in 'ere for a coffee a pastry and a chat!"

Susan beckoned me to follow her behind the counter and through the doorway in to a very pokey back room with a desk and a jewellers workbench a lot of shelves with boxes a back window looking out onto the Parade car park and a door way leading to a W.C.

There was barely room for us all to sit. Bill Thomas was a Welshman from South Wales and he occupied the chair at the desk, which he lazily sprawled out on with his feet on the desk whilst he nursed a cup of coffee in his hands.

"Susan make Simon a coffee, and then maybe you could go do the banking whilst us blokes 'ave a chat." Mr Thomas said casually. Susan stood up, and

I noticed that her mini skirt revealed perhaps the most beautiful pair of long legs I had ever seen.

I was sorry she was going, but I think both Bill Thomas and myself enjoyed watching her leave!

Bill Thomas was a very easy-going sort of guy even though I noticed that he liked to be addressed as Mr Thomas by his staff. I told him what I had been doing and my experience at the Birmingham School of Jewellery. It became clear that I would have no difficulty with minor Jewellery repairs and adjustments; all the familiar Jewellers tools were to be found. I thought this could be nice. When he came to ask me what kind of money would I expect, I told him I was on 20 pounds a week at my last job. "Well you wont be getting that much 'ere boyo! Why that's nearly as much as they pay me, and I'm the bloody manager!"

He told me "The job pays 10 pounds a week rising to 11.50 after the first year if you make it." For that we have Thursday and Saturday early closing. Sundays off. Of course.

I liked the idea of seeing more of Susan's lovely legs, and the job did appeal to me. I was told it would involve driving to the jewellery quarter to collect repairs occasionally; I really liked the idea of having the opportunity to drive around, and not be confined to the shop. I accepted the Job. Start on Monday!

As I walked towards the door, it opened once more to the jingle of the bell. Susan and her delicious legs had returned. "See you on Monday." I greeted her as we passed in the doorway.

I called in at Julie's office in Boldmere and gave her the news that I had landed a job at Eames. She was pleased for me. I asked her if she was coming to the Jazz night. She looked at me painfully and said that she had a date. I knew that I shouldn't have been surprised, after all we had had the talk, but it appeared that reality was now beginning to set in.

"He picked me up on Wednesday in his E Type Jag. He is really nice. Oh and he owns a Karate club so you better not try and fight him" She joked. Well my stomach churned at the prospect that my Jules was actually seeing someone else. He had met her when he came into the estate agents to find a house to rent for one of his Japanese Karate Instructors.

Well I bluffed trying my best to muster up as much bravado as I could. "There is a really nice girl working in the Jewellers so I expect I will be asking her out soon!"

Teatime came at Court Lane. Mum and Jim were going to be coming with me to the Jazz and we would celebrate my bittersweet day. Bitter because I couldn't get the churning in my stomach to stop because of Julie. Sweet because I was about to become a retail jeweller!

As we were tucking into our tea, the phone rang. I answered it, hoping it was Julie wanting to put things right. "Hello Mr Edgington. Its McKechnie Metals of Aldridge here. I am sorry that we have taken so long to get back to you, but I am phoning to tell you that we are very pleased to be able to offer you the position of Trainee Metallurgist, would you be able to start Monday?"

39 LIFE'S FORK IN THE ROAD

Those moments in life's journey when, you have to make a decision, to go one way. Or another, way. One way may be the decision to continue on ones current path because it is the least challenging but the most comfortable. As I look back on my journey reader, with the benefit of hindsight. I recognise that I have been guilty of that at times. I have continued to wear long redundant relationships like a comfortable threadbare cardigan, because it is safe. But I have come to learn that often one is closing oneself off from brighter more fulfilling opportunities.

The trauma of embarking on a new direction in life whether it be relationship or career requires a leap of faith. It is surprising how many people are not prepared to ever consider making that leap and settle for the mundane in everything they do.

Occasionally our journey presents us with a change in direction that doesn't require a blind leap of faith so much. It just seems like the right thing to do. When that happens, some say it is destiny. It certainly feels like it sometimes. I had already accepted the job in the jewellers unaware that I was still a viable candidate for the other job. Destiny made that choice for me!

But destiny has not spared me over time the desire to ponder about what would have been, had I taken the other fork in the road.

If only I could have been as wise then over affairs of the heart.

Our paths converged for a while, and then started to part. Instead of celebrating the joy that our journey bought us whilst we travelled together and looking

forward to what destiny now presented to me, I was looking back desperately clinging to what I thought was safe, what I was used to.

We all mature at different rates. For a long time Julie and I were on the same path. I think in this respect, she was growing up faster than me. Her destiny was presenting her with people interested in her, and at that age that was a healthy thing. Although 18 year old Si John did not agree! He wanted his Jules no matter what.

Monday morning. Time to take that fork in the road that was Trainee Salesman at RH Eames The Jewellers, Sutton Coldfield. As my Ford Anglia carried me towards my new adventure, I pondered about the decision that destiny seemed to thrust upon me. "Oh thank you for phoning me." I had said to the caller on Friday evening. "Unfortunately, when I didn't hear back from you as expected on Wednesday. I accepted another offer of employment with Eames the Jewellers." The lady was very friendly. "Oh I am sorry to hear that, we had a lot of applicants to work through which took time. But in the end we all said we would have loved for you to come and work with us. Anyway Simon, may I wish you all the best in your new job." "That was nice, wasn't it Jim?" Mum said, when I told her of the conversation.

I parked in the Dog car park.

As I approached the pedestrian crossing;

outside Woolworths. I looked across the road at the perfectly formed mini skirted pair of legs waiting out side RH Eames The Jewellers. Sue caught my eye and politely smiled as I approached her. "We are a bit early, he's not here yet." She commented "Oh." I replied shyly. "Oh" ? "Oh" ? Really Simon? I thought. Is that the best you can do? I thought Sue was exceptionally attractive, which left me feeling quite intimidated. My shyness tumbled over me like an overpowering breaking wave that dumbfounded me and consumed me with panic. I couldn't find anything to say, but my panic was relieved by the sound of keys jangling behind me as Mr Thomas approached to open up.

The door opened to the chime of the brass bell and a second beeping noise, which was the Burglar Alarm. Mr Thomas attended to that by inserting another key in a box by the door and turning it anticlockwise.

He then walked to the large safe and proceeded to unlock it. Sue followed him in and I followed her admiring the poetry in motion.

Coats off and the first order of the day was to remove the trays of rings from the safe and place the valuables in the window display. Nothing of major value was left in the window. Every morning, the window was redressed with ring trays, to allow courting couples to gaze wishfully at our wares. Every evening before closing, these are returned to the safe.

Eames the Jewellers also carried the dealership for Omega, Tissot, Rotary, Bulova, Ingasol and Rolex Watches. No Timex for our clients. I was soon to discover that many of the well to do residents of Sutton Coldfield, who's biggest problem in life was "What on earth am I going to do with all this money I've got?" Shop here. Some quite fanatically had to have the latest trinket as they strive towards one up man ship with their fellow man. Or woman.

Sue showed me how to dress the window and the glass display cabinets with the content of the safe. Every article had a small price label attached by a thread. The label had to be displayed so that the price was visible through the window. On the other side of the label, was a stock number and a code which if you knew the key word would reveal the cost price of the item. (I have long since forgotten what the Key Word was.) But a similar practice was adopted in the Ladies Underwear department at Wilkinson Riddell and Larkin.

Bill Thomas seemed to be in the habit of going out a lot, leaving Sue and I to mind the shop together. "So Simon. Have you got a girlfriend?" She asked. "Wow! That is normally a question that I have no difficulty answering. But now I really don't know!" I answered. Probably shouldn't have bent her ear with the Julie story, but we had a lot of time in the shop together to kill between customers, and I had to overcome my shyness around her. She sniggered when I asked about her and Men. "No one in particular. Normally after a couple of dates and I have told them, No funny business, they move on." She lent over the glass counter hand on chin and pondered. "I have got one that wants me to go on a trip to Miami with him. Quite fancy that idea."

Wow I thought. This girl is way out of my league. Miami. All I was hoping to do with her was go to the Dog Inn and listen to some jazz. And that is only across the road!

Bill Thomas came back in. "Simon I need you to go into Birmingham to pick up a repair for a client. Take my car, it's the Triumph Spitfire in the car park." Seriously ???

He gave me the address, told me to take a pound out of the till for petrol and handed me the keys. "Don't hurt it mind you. Or there will be trouble!"

I had sat in Dads Sprite and his M.G. Midget, but I had never actually driven a sports car before. I eagerly looked around the Dog Inn car park for the Spitfire. There it was. It looked brand new with a black soft top and wire wheels. I might have to take a detour down Court Lane to show Mum.

I sat in the drivers seat, figured out how to adjust the seat, Bill Thomas was taller than me. Hell every body was taller than me. I really should have not spent my school lunch money on cigarettes. But school dinners were disgusting! I placed the key in the ignition and started her up. A crispy exhaust sound emerged from somewhere behind me, as I blipped the throttle. This job had some real good points.

I took the car through Boldmere. As I passed by the Unigate dairy where I had worked I glanced at the first floor canteen window. I was pleased that I took that leap of faith. Now instead of being there looking enviously at the passing motorists. I was a passing motorist, and I was right, this life definitely was already becoming more interesting.

40 SIMON THE JEWELLER

I was enjoying work at Eames the Jewellers. Once I got all romantic notions out of my head regarding the beautifully legged Sue, my shyness faded around her and we became friends.

Bill Thomas would invite clients into the back room for a coffee and a chat. He would be telling them of his hopes to acquire a shop of his own in South Wales, when he and his fiancé finally marry. She didn't really care for the Midlands.

I had my own work station at the Jewellers bench. I could perform minor adjustments to watches, replace watch straps repair necklaces and keep the stock clean and shiny. We had a watch repair box and a jewellery repair box. A watch maker would collect these repairs and deliver the finished ones which would be placed in the box awaiting collection. Similarly, a jeweller would collect any rings or other items that needed repair or resizing. Occasionally if there was an urgency, I would drive the Spitfire to deliver and collect jobs.

Some customers were really nice. Some were downright nightmares. One lady came in and protested "My watch has stopped, yet again!" "Oh no, I don't believe it!" I empathised "What do you mean you don't believe it young man?" She retorted incredulously. "Are you calling me a bloody liar?"

Mr Thomas stepped into my rescue with his Welsh Charm that he could switch on in an instant, and switch off even faster.

I began to think some of these rich bored hags would start their day with the question. "Now who shall I go and take out my anger on today. I know, there's a new guy working at RH EAMES the Jewellers. I'll go and make his life a misery. He is supposed to be polite to me.

We sold Omega watches. My father had bought a stainless steel Omega here long before I came here to work. It was his pride and joy. Omega designed the Chronographs used for the Moon landing. That model was a very popular line with up and comers in the business world.

Bill Thomas had a Bulova Accutron Watch. This was a new design and his had a Perspex case so that he could show clients the inner workings. It wasn't a classic clock work movement. It was a tuning fork mechanism. This would vibrate at a constant rate creating a much greater rate of timekeeping accuracy. If you put the watch to your ear, you were not presented with Tick Tock Tick Tock. It was a barely audible very high pitched tone.

This was pre quartz that proved to be even more accurate. There was a very good reason why the tuning fork movement didn't stay in the market for long. And the quartz movement was to eventually become the standard. Here is the story.

One of the clients who used to visit Mr Thomas for coffee and conversation, had a significant celebration coming up. He was a fanatic about accuracy of watches. This new technology promised accuracy in seconds per month. He decided to treat himself to a new top of the range Tissot gold watch with a tuning fork movement. Once the watch arrived at the shop, I had to take it to an engraver to have the 18 carat back engraved with his personal message. He was like a child at Christmas eagerly calling back time and time again to see if it was ready for collection yet.

Finally he took delivery of his pride and joy. It cost a fortune. He wrapped the golden bracelet around his wrist and checked its face for the time. He held it up to his ear and "Yes ! I can just about hear the high pitched tone!" He exclaimed. He was so thrilled. Grinning like a Cheshire cat, as he left the shop.

The very next day, he was back looking very despondent. "I am afraid I wont be able to have this watch, with the Tuning Fork movement in it. You will have to change it for a regular one." "Why on earth not?" Bill Thomas enquired. "My bloody dog won't come anywhere near me!"

One morning, after a week or so at Eames the jewellers I was walking from the Dog Inn car park. As I approached Woolworths I noticed Sue waiting outside the shop waiting for a once again tardy Mr Thomas. I was just about to give her a wave when a figure came out of the shadows of Woolworths.

It was Julie.

41 THE RECONCILIATION

Like that occasion that seemed a lifetime away on the doorstep of Holly Lodge, Julie was just there quite unexpectedly. Similarly, she held the same expression. Head bowed her big brown eyes looking up at me, and quite noticeably puffy. "I had to come and see you." She murmured in a small voice. Her bottom lip was quivering, I noticed her normally beautiful smiling eyes had been crying as she reached for my hands. "I have been so stupid and I have been missing you so much. Have you missed me?" What a question. She was my world. I was struggling to be without her. My Eighteen year old logic totally failing to see the sense in either of us looking for someone else when we already had each other. "Of course I missed you. You know how much I love you Jules!" A small smile came to her lips and a tear fell down her red cheek with the early morning chill. It disappeared into the scarf she wore around her shoulders. She had travelled to work with her Mum who works the sweetie counter in Woolworths so she could see me. Now she needed to get the bus to Boldmere. She was going to be late for her work. "Will you come and see me tonight?" She asked. Still looking apprehensive and fearful that the answer might be no. Maybe it should have been, but eighteen year old Simon could only think to himself. "I need to wipe the sadness off that beautiful face, I want to hold you in my arms and be rewarded by that wonderful smile again!" "Of course I'll see you later Jules." "Will you kiss me?" She asked. I removed my hands from hers and rested my right hand on her cold cheek. I could feel the wet of her tears with the back of my hand on her scarf. I put my left hand about her waist and she came closer so our bodies met and we could share each others warmth. I kissed her caringly quickly, and then again longer and more passionately, totally oblivious that by now we had wondered towards the pedestrian crossing and she was leaning against the black and white striped post of the flashing orange headed Belisha Beacon. Passing motorists couldn't resist tooting their horns which turned our kiss into a lip biting chuckle. We parted and I could feel that familiar tingling in my loins, at the anticipation of us being together this evening.

Back to reality; Julie looked pensively towards Woolworths. Her mother Mabel, a short rotund lady in her sixties stood in the doorway arms crossed in her blue Woolworths smock. She tactfully diverted her gaze from us, but we were in no doubt about what she had witnessed. Julie smiled an embarrassed smile, shrugged her shoulders, gave me one more quick peck on the lips, then I watched her walking back to the entrance of Woolworths and her mother.

I turned to cross the crossing and looked across the road. I had completely forgotten Sue who was waiting outside the shop. She stood in her overcoat and miniskirt leaning cross legged against the window sill. Arms crossed not unlike Julie's mum and a wye smile on her face. Plainly our moment of early morning street passion had had another witness!

I couldn't help the smile on my face, I'm guessing by the way I felt, I was grinning from ear to ear!

"I take it, that was Julie?" Were Sue's only words.

That evening I drove to Julie's We decided to go to Sutton Park. It was still daylight, I parked the car at the Four Oaks entrance, and we linked hands and walked into the woods. This is one of my favourite spots. Holly bushes lined the hardened earth pathway and there was a sound of birds chirping and scurrying about out of site above us. Perhaps settling in for the night in their nests. We came across an old oak wood shelter called Mayors Arbor.

We entered the Arbor and sat on one of the benches together. Courting couples had scratched their initials all over the wood of this Arbour. We had done previously and we found Simon (HEART) Jules sure enough still there. It made me wonder how many of these couples were still together.

Julie told me that she had been out with this guy who owned a Gymnasium in Birmingham and a Karate Club. He was very focused in his business and after a while she no longer heard from him. She realised that she had thrown away so much, just because everyone was encouraging her to see other people.

"Oh well." I comforted her. "At least it all finished before she got more involved!" She looked at me then turned her head in shame. I saw her shoulders rise and fall she was sobbing. "Oh Si how can you ever forgive me?" I had to, but the churning in my stomach would return at the thought of what had happened. Julie had shared herself with another man. "It just happened." She said. This hurt terribly, but she was back with me. That was all I wanted.

We smoked and chatted for a while, cuddled and kissed then we walked a little further down the Holly bush lined path and eventually arrived at my childhoods enchanted wood and the Faraway Tree.

This place in Sutton Park held so many memories for me. I recalled my father being the only person I knew to climb the Faraway Tree, when he recovered my rocket. An Indian Head dressed John Chawner shooting rubber sucker tipped arrows at us cowboys. Now I was here with the girl I loved, who I thought a day ago I had lost forever.

I felt I needed a gesture to cement our reunion and dispose of this unfortunate episode. Where better for me to make such a gesture. "Jules, How would you feel about us getting engaged?" I asked "Oh Si, That would make me very very happy. Yes I love you."

That gesture; was followed by another. As twilight; set in over the enchanted wood. We made love under the Faraway Tree.

42 THE RING

I was very excited about having Julie back and I told Mum and Jim that we were to be engaged. They were glad there was going to be no more miserable Simon moping around the house. Miserable? I was ecstatically happy. Life had become a merry dance.

Julie came and looked at the engagement rings on the trays at RH Eames. The prices were pretty frightening for someone earning ten pounds a week. Even with the staff discount. The diamonds on the rings within our price range were barely visible. Mere specs. She tried one ring on and it looked gorgeous. I would be so proud of her to have that ring on when we next went to the jazz club. But it was way expensive.

That evening we went to visit Gangan to tell her the news. Gangan liked Julie. Julie liked Gangan despite the fact that Gangan could not refrain from correcting her pronunciation. True to say Julie did have a soft twang of a Birmingham accent that she tried to disguise with what I called her telephone voice when in the presence of Gangan. When she remembered. On this occasion, excitement got the better of her and she slipped into Brummie a bit.

It was a happy visit and it was nice for me to have the company of two of my favourite ladies in the world. "So Julie have you chosen the ring yet?" Gangan enquired. "We have looked at some at Si's work. There is a really nice one there, but they are so expensive in that shop." "Well Dear, I think we should be able to do better than that." Gangan pronounced lifting her self out of the armchair and walking towards the living room door. "After all I think you might have forgotten who you are talking to." Julie looked at me with her mouth twisted into a puzzled expression. I could hear Gangan dialling her telephone in the front room.

"Hello Leonard. It's Leonora here." We heard her say. "You remember my Grandson Simon? Yes Marie and Warwick's boy that it.......... Well the thing is Simon and his lovely girlfriend Julie have just got engaged." I looked at Julie, her eyes wide open as was her mouth now displaying an expression of wonder.

".............Yes I know Leonard. How time flies........Yes seems like only yesterday............Um just a minute" Gangan held the phone to her bosom and called "Simon how old are you now?" "Eighteen." I replied.

"He's Eighteen Leonard..........Any way I am calling to arrange when it would be convenient for them to come to Warstone Lane to choose a ring?"

Gangan came back into her living room holding a Samuel Hope Engagement and Wedding Ring Brochure and handed it to Julie. "That's all dealt with dear. I have just spoken with my managing director Mr Cooney, You can go to Samuel Hope any time they are open. He says he is looking forward to seeing you again Simon after so long and meeting you Julie. He will give you a tour of the new premises in Warstone lane, and you can choose your rings."

Julie's smiling eyes could not have looked happier, she stood up and hugged Gangan. Gangan smiled her kind smile and turned to me. "Well...... Doesn't your Gangan deserve a hug from you too?" "Always" I thought as I joined the hug. What a happy room that was.

I picked Julie up at lunchtime on a Thursday from the Estate Agent in Boldmere. It was half day closing at Eames so I was done for the day, Julie's sister said she needn't hurry back, she could take the afternoon off. Once again, I drove past the Unigate factory, feeling so grateful for my leap of faith leading to my escape from there. We drove up Vyse Street past the now derelict former premises of Samuel Hope, Turned down Warstone Lane and parked in the Parking Bay of Samuel Hope Manufacturing Jewellers. I opened the door for Julie and we entered a teak reception area. On the wall behind the desk was an old framed photograph of Samuel Hope Founder 1874. (I have that picture in my house now) A young receptionist came to greet us. "Hello it's Simon Edgington and Julie to see Mr Cooney." "Hello Simon." I heard from behind me. "Wow, it's been such a long time since I last saw you. How you have grown!" Leonard Cooney was an average sized man with a gentle but firm handshake. He wore thick glasses and a pleasant smile. I introduced him to Julie. Did she just curtsy as she shook his hand?

Mr Cooney led us into his office, which was of a modern teak finish similar to the reception area. So much nicer, than the former premises in Vyse

Street. I was amused to see hanging on the wall behind Mr Cooney's Desk a Manulife world map calendar presented by non other. Warwick Greatrex Edgington.

The young receptionist bought in a tray of tea and biscuits and after a catch up of small talk we showed him the rings in the brochure we liked the look of. Next a tray of rings were bought in. There was no decision to make. Julie saw the one like the one she was admiring in Eames. It was lovely with a tastefully sizable diamond that complimented her beautiful hand. I was allowed to choose a black onyx signet ring for myself. We decided that mine would have an engraving inside. "To Simon Love Jules" It would take a few days for sizing and engraving. "I will give Leonora the rings to bring back for you when they are ready." Mr Cooney said. Then we were taken on a tour of the factory. What a difference. A purpose built factory. We were shown the strong room and I was handed a gold bar. It was surprisingly heavy. "With what you are holding in your hand there. You could buy this factory." Mr Cooney let out a giggle at the irony of what he just said. "But why would you? Your family own it anyway." He must have thought. Julie and I were treated like royalty as we were introduced to all the crafts men working at their benches, I was beginning to get quite amused at the way Julie would curtsy whenever she shook someone's hand.

It was going to be a long wait for our rings. It wouldn't be this Friday's Jazz night that we would be able to show them off.

The next day was Friday, and Julie and I went to the Dog Inn for the jazz. We couldn't keep from telling everybody that we were now officially engaged, but there was something amiss with Julie. We know each other so well, we could not kid each other if something was wrong, and I was sensing something.

After the jazz we parked up in Worcester Lane for a bit of in car entertainment and I had to ask. "I've felt this evening that you have been bothered about something, is everything alright Jules." "Yes." She answered too quickly. Then she bit her bottom lip as she does and raised her big eyes under her lids. Took out a cigarette lit it, handed it to me then lit one for herself. "No…. Well Yes, look…. I didn't know whether I wanted to say anything because I didn't want you to get worried. If I tell you, promise me you wont be upset" "Well I don't know until you tell me do I? But now you are going to have to tell me."

I was beginning to feel anxious about what on earth I was about to hear.

"Ok. I was at work today and he came in to see me." My stomach started to churn instantly. "You see Si, I knew this would upset you, that is why I had decided not to mention it. It didn't mean anything to me, and I was happy about that. I love you."

She told me that he called. He apologised for not being in touch for a while, but he had been very busy moving his Karate Club to a new dojo. She said that she told him that we were back together and that we were now engaged. He said he wanted to invite her to the opening on Sunday morning.

"So why don't we go?" I heard my self say. I could not understand what urged me to suggest such a thing. I think I needed to face this situation in order to put it behind us. This had affected her, and it had affected me. I wanted to know as much as her about this episode in our journey. I wanted him to see that we were good together. I wanted him to know that he had no business trespassing between us. "What do you mean." Julie asked. "If we are really good together now. Let's go." I said. "I must admit, I don't think he really believed me when I told him I was engaged now." Julie continued. "He looked at my fingers and saw I had no ring. How I would love to go and flash it in his face!" "Well we wont have it by Sunday, but I think we should go."

And so it was decided we would visit a Dojo in Birmingham on Sunday.

43 THE DOJO

I had always been curious about Karate. I was a fan of Bruce Lee films. I suppose it was not dissimilar to the appeal of the Saturday Morning Matinee at the Empress cinema, where we enjoyed watching our super hero's in action. Maybe part of me still wanted to be a Super Hero. Karate Man Da Da Dar !

When I was in Jewellery college there was a lad from Manchester, David who had done some Karate. One weekend he came to stay and we all went to Streetly Youth Club. Dave was showing off some quite impressive moves whilst we waited at the bus stop to come home. He was perhaps even smaller than me, but non of the bigger kids were willing to come near him. He could deliver a round house kick snapping his foot a millimetre from your left ear, before you even finished saying the words "So go on Dave show us some of your Karate." He was lightening fast. We were sure if he actually made contact, you would be in for a headache, and a thick ear.

"I'd quite like to be able to do that" I had been quietly thinking for some time.

We arrived at the Karate Centre and walked down the stairs to the basement. There were photographs on the walls of body builders doing their Charles Atlas posses. Also photos of various Japanese Karate Instructors. There was an Emblem of a fist and a dove with the slogan Wada Ru which we were later told meant "The Way Of Peace." This was the style of Karate practiced here. There was a hatch were a large guy sat in a leather jacket, making him look even larger behind a counter. On the counter was a diary open to todays date and a telephone with a padlock devise on the dial, In coming calls only!

"Hi I'm Paul" The giant greeted us with a friendly smile. "Welcome to the Karate Centre." I recognised Paul as one of the Body Builders posing in the photographs on the wall, although perhaps he was a few years older now. He came from behind the hatch and led us to the doorway of the Dojo. This was a carpeted room with all the walls lined with mirrors. At the one end there were three wooden posts set into the floor about shoulder high, with a leather hood. On the far one, a Japanese black belt was punching and kicking the leather hood in quick succession. He looked very ferocious.

Two ranks of four or five students were advancing up the floor of the dojo on the command "Ish" Kick Out Punch Advance one step. "Ish" Repeat. When they got to the far end of the room on the last move, they would all yell and perform a turn and block.

You could only enter the Dojo bare footed and on entering one would face another Wada Ru Banner on the wall and bow respectfully. Paul showed us the locker room. Only one so ladies would change in Pauls Office after he closed the hatch. Julie had met Paul before. There was no sign of the guy she had dated yet. We signed up for the Sunday Morning Karate course at a pound an hour. We were told we could buy our Karate Kit there for five pounds, and collect it next Sunday. As we just about to leave, a couple came down the steps. The girl was wearing a leather mini skirt and knee high leather boots, she had long blond hair. The guy was well built, I recognised him as the other body builder in the old pictures on the wall. "This is Mick." Julie introduced me. I must admit, despite the history; I liked Mick instantly. He had a nice smile, I could see that he was one of these types who wont let the grass grow under his feet. I could also see that he was the kind of guy, girls would have difficulty saying no to. We shook hands and exchanged small talk about the business, and he said he was looking forward to seeing us again.

As we left the Karate Centre and walked past Mick's Blue E Type Jaguar Roadster parked next to my Blue Ford Anglia, I knew exactly what Julie was thinking by the way she ran an eye across her leather mini skirted replacement. "Well it didn't take him long to find someone else, since I saw him last, just two days ago!" Julie said.

The following Sunday we started our Karate training. There was one other girl training with us. It turned out she was the wife of our Japanese instructor. She had already attained a Brown Belt.

We entered the dojo and bowed to the Wada Ru banner. Then started a selection of warm up exercises which involved a lot of stretching. Then we were told to do twenty five press-ups on our knuckles. This was quite exhausting, and I began to realise how unfit I was. Barely able to stand without panting profusely, we then had to form ranks across the dojo and perform the same combinations of blocks punches and kicks progressing up the room as we had seen the previous Sunday.

I knew one of the other students. Steve, we were at Jewellery college together. He was quite a stocky tall guy, and his Karate looked quite awkward and gangly. Bigger is not necessarily better in Karate as he would find out!

Morning after the first lesson, I ached all over. I had muscles hurting that I didn't know I had. But over time I could feel the benefit of Karate. I grew stronger and fitter over the two years and I actually got my Green Belt quite quickly. Also it opened up a new circle of friends for Julie and I. Perhaps a slightly healthier one than the smoking, drinking fraternity which was the Jazz Club at the Dog Inn Friday and Sunday Night. We took Paul with us from the Karate Club to our Jazz night. He was a fish out of water. "I cannot believe that so many young people are smoking and drinking in here!" He exclaimed as he looked around the room.

Working on my roundhouse to the left ear!

44 MUM'S PIANO

Julie and I collected our rings from Gangan. They came in little Samuel Hope leather presentation cases. I handed Julie's to her. She opened it and beamed her lovely smile. She closed the box, handed it to me and held out her left hand. "Si, you have to put it on for me." I took the box and reopened it, removed the beautiful solitaire diamond ring and placed it on her finger. She lifted it up to her big brown eyes to admire it. Then our roles reversed and I looked at my Black Onyx ring which Julie had placed on my finger. "Oh I didn't look at the engraving" I said I removed the ring and read the engraving. "To Simon Love Dilly" DILLY! "Well we can't change it, that would be bad luck." Julie informed me with authority. "In that case perhaps I will just have to start calling you Dilly!"

It was about this time, that Julie had a change of employment. She was offered a job as a legal secretary to a lawyers office in Chester Road near Erdington. It was a better paid position for her and her parents were moving from the apartment on Lichfield Rd, to a Maisonette in a cul de sack just off Court Lane. This was great, she was going to be living nearer to me.

I drove from Eames the Jewellers one day and after calling in on Julie in her new home, so that she could show off her new room to me, I parked my car in our drive in court lane next to Jims.

When I got in the house Mum seemed very excited. She wore grin and said to me "Si John, I've got something to show you. Go take a look in the dining room. I opened the door to the dining room, and there against the wall next Jims Trombone case my Trumpet Case and Guitar Case, was a Piano.

"Wow Mum, a Piano!" I exclaimed. Why have we got a Piano." "Well" She replied, hardly able to contain her excitement. "One of my regular Taxi clients was trying to find a new home for it. So I said I'll have it! I told him my son played guitar and trumpet, my husband plays trombone. I can play piano! And he has just bought it round in his van."

"But you don't play piano Mum." I said. "That's alright, one of my other taxi clients a few doors down is a music teacher. I'm going to have lessons."

Well, Mum did have lessons for a while. I went too one time. I was taught a scale in C. I found the whole process tedious. I just wanted to play. The elderly gentleman who was teaching us, was not someone I wanted to be around. I found him extremely slow in his teachings, and for me he succeeded in making music, which after all was my passion, somehow boring. I remember telephoning him to tell him that I would not be coming anymore. I heard a disgruntled "Tut !"on the phone, and by the way he slammed the phone down on me, I suspected this was not the first time he had been told his services were no longer required.

I regret not having any formal music training at all. Had it been a different music teacher, who knows? Maybe I would have been encouraged more to take my musical journey down that road. So I set about teaching my self to play on a piano keyboard.

Mum's Piano. Notice my black onyx signet ring from "Dilly"

I had never really been alone with a piano. There was an old one I remember in the barn at the campsite in Devon where John Barton used to allow me to drive his tractor. I did raise the lid and stare at the array of

Black and White keys. I thought about our teachers at school playing so proficiently. It was a mystery to me how someone could possibly master this instrument.

I lifted the lid at the top and peaked in at the strings. When you played a note now on the keyboard, it became notably louder. I discovered that by moving a catch, you could completely remove the front panel of the instrument, revealing a sophisticated mechanism of strings, dampers, and hammers. I played a simple tune in C with one finger of my right hand. "Doe a deer a female deer, Ray a drop of midday sun." Was easy enough for me to pick out on the white notes. As I played I watched the hammers strike the strings, it was quite fascinating to me.

I contemplated the instrument. Every piece of music ever created was hiding inside it. The trick was to apply a little magic to bring those tunes out. Would I ever be able to? I related the piano to a blank canvas. For every blank canvas carried the potential depending only on the ability of it's painter to display any scene visualized by man. That put me in mind of my disastrous spotty painting effort back in infant's school. A painter I was not!

But as a musician, little did I know on that day I was taking the very first step in what would be a musical journey which would take me places I hadn't yet even began to dream about.

45 SELF TAUGHT

I knew about music from playing the guitar. I had knowledge of the basic chords, but what I found was as soon as I played the notes of the chords on piano, I started to see the logic of their structure. The chord of C Major was a shape that distorted your left hand fingers to hold down the guitar strings behind the correct frets to play the required note. I had learnt that chord on guitar, more by the shape you had to adopt with your fingers, than knowledge of what actual notes each string rang out.

Looking at your hands on the keyboard. You could see the route note the third fifth and octave right there before you. Like I learnt a chord shape on a guitar neck. I applied the same technique in holding my left hand in a claw playing every other white note in a chord triad. If my pinkie finger; started with a C note. I had taught my self C Major. Take the shape up to F, I had F Major, similarly with the G. I would later explore how I could create all the other Major chords. But for now; I was satisfied that I had mastered C, F and G. Now I could look at my right hand and play a song I thought. What song? I wondered would be a good starting point. One of my favourite songs that was played at the Jazz club was Saint Lewis Blues. Basically a Twelve Bar Blues using three chords. I learnt what I would later find out to be the route inversion of the chord, which meant that the lowest note would be C in a C chord and so on. So my right hand mimicked my left hand hovering over the chord. What I miraculously discovered was my fingers where actually above the notes required for St Lewis Blues. In my voyage of self-taught piano playing, my first discovery was, the chords of the song on a music chart, pretty much give you a hint of what the notes of the melody are going to be based around.

After all, this was pretty much how the song would have been written in the first place. The composer would sit at the piano, experiment with chord progressions and explore what melodies the piano would reveal beneath his hands. Did any body ever write a tune with the intention of making it difficult?

Learning a song was surely just a reversal of that process. That in essence is how one plays by ear once knowledge of chords and rhythm has been achieved.

So I adhered to my father's mantra written on the inside of my Burt Wheedon Guitar Tutor "Practice and Persevere Si John." Applied this advice to my attempts to play the piano, and pretty soon I was playing a not too shabby rendition of St Lewis Blues. My left hand was limited to a basic vamp, but nevertheless my performance arrived quite rapidly after I started practicing. Noticeably quickly enough, for my mother to exclaim. "That's not fair. I've been going to all these lessons, and here's Simon just playing the thing after just one!"

Using my left hand, playing every other white note, claw technique, I discovered I had more useful chords. D minor, E minor, A minor and B minor. Plenty of songs to play; with that arsenal of Chords.

I played David Hamber's Hit "I've found Carol" "I met a pretty little girl yesterday, such a pretty little girl yesterday.................." I sang. All the songs I knew on guitar, I could follow my chords on the piano and pick out the melody. Songs like Blue Moon, When the saints go marching in, Spanish Eyes, English Country Garden, Do ray me. These and many other simple tunes helped me build up a repertoire that was quite a party piece!

I enjoyed sitting at the piano, playing and singing. It was relaxing way to wind down, after a day, dealing with the pampered, rich and sometimes downright unpleasant customers of Eames The Jewellers.

I even had a go at composing at the piano. Again playing the chords and experimenting with the melodies as they spring up from the piano beneath your hands.

I had written songs on the guitar. "I've got a fever" "Anita" "Times" The one I wrote to turn Virginia Bumpstead into a household name. No doubt quite a few unmemorable ones too.

Lonely Shy Boy was the first song I penned on piano.

I had been a lonely shy boy once, but now I was engaged. I recalled the shy awkwardness I felt and fear of rejection. Many times it would prevent me from saying anything. As long as I said nothing, the fantasy could remain intact. Many guys would just come on out and cast their trusty pick up lines time and time again, until they eventually got a bite. Not me. Rejection leaves me dejected, feeling unlovable. So why would I want to do that to myself? In fact had Julie not come to Holly Lodge that Sunday afternoon. Maybe I would still be a "Lonely Shy Boy"

Lonely Shy Boy

I long for the time to tell you that I love you.

I long for the time, to show you how I care.

I wait till stars, are shining high above you,

And even then, I don't know if I dare.

I'm a lonely shy boy, who needs some company,

I want someone to love, someone to care for me,

So won't you take me by the hand,

and love me tenderly,

For I'm a lonely, Lonely shy boy.

Who knew, back then in Court Lane, Erdington? I had written my first record. The B side would be "Times."

46 A SAD FAREWELL

I would often go straight into the dining room, and tinkle on the ivories a little, before Mum would eventually lay the table and we would all sit down to dinner. On one such occasion, we were just finishing. Adam and David had asked "Please Mummy can I leave the table?" They were excused and ran into the lounge to watch TV. Mum Jim and I smoked a cigarette and were discussing together our day, as we always did. Sally had gone across the road to visit her boyfriend Billy, when the telephone began to ring.

Being the closest, sat with her back to the window, Mum picked up the receiver, which was a rare thing for her to do because of her stutter. "Hello" She said looking at us quite proudly, realising what she had done. It was Mums Sister, My Aunty Christine. Mum lost her nervousness, when she realised it was her, but she moved back and leant on the window sill. Her head bowed she bought a hand to her mouth. "Oh no! ....Yes of course........... We will come right away." With that, she put the phone down, remained

poised, leaning against the window sill. She bought her hands back up to cover her mouth, and started to shake uncontrollably. "Love, What on earth is the matter?" Jim asked as he left his chair to console his wife with a hug. "Mum put her arms around his shoulders, which seemed to make her shaking ease a little. "That was Christine. Mummy has had a heart attack, she is in hospital."

My Gangan has had a heart attack. This came as a huge shock to us all. She was, we had always believed, indestructible. The pillar of our family! God can't have her. She's ours!

Mum and Jim left immediately for Good Hope Hospital in Sutton Coldfield. I remained with Adam and David. I cleared the table in the dining room, washed all the dishes, and put them away. My head was spinning with worry. I had to be doing something. Gangan was the kindest person in my life. I could talk to her; we would have long meaningful conversations. She has always been there for me. The thought that one day, she would no longer be there, had just never occurred to me! It was getting late. Sally was still out. Adam and David had their orders as usual. Bed at seven thirty. School day tomorrow. I sat on the sofa alone and started to think about my Gangan

"Have I ever told you about my campaign Simon" She had asked me one afternoon in the apple orchard at the foot of the garden at Chadsway. It was a beautiful sunny day. For once the sun was warming my back, the smell of freshly cut grass was invading my nostrils as I held a cold wrought iron bucket for her to collect her apples. She applied a little pressure to each apple as it hung from the tree. If it resisted she would leave it to ripen some more. If it could be persuaded to come away, some how those green Granny Smiths seemed to be just right and always tasted best. Not too sweet with a glint of sourness. "When ever I am in my garden, I always talk to my neighbours over the fence." Gangan continued to select the apples good for harvesting. "I tell them. When your husband comes home tonight. Give him a hug; tell him that you love him. If it is the husband I am talking to, I tell them to go and buy their wife some pretty flowers, and tell her how proud you are of her for making such a beautiful home for you both." She bought an apple away from the tree. I could see her eyes warming and a smile come to her face, as she popped the apple into bucket I held. "Then the next time I see them, I ask them if they tried what I suggested." She continued "Many times they say that they had, and it was really nice how much more loving they felt towards each other thanks to her what I had said to them." She stopped attending to the apples and turned to me with a wry smile and glint in eye, magnified in the lenses of her horn rimmed spectacles. "I have even started spreading the word to people I get to talking to on the bus." Gangan had been widowed many years ago. She no doubt would have loved to be able to tell her Dennis how much she loved him. It would appear that by getting others to appreciate each other more. She was enjoying seeing people being as happy as they could be. "What is sad Simon. Is that my campaign has helped a lot of couples that I have met and got talking to. But I was unable to prevent my two daughters from breaking up with the fathers of their children. How did I manage to succeed with all these nice people, but fail with the two families I love the most? "

I was startled out of my reminisce by the sound of the front door squeaking on its hinges as Sally was silently attempting to enter without disturbing the household. When she saw the light was still on in the lounge, she came through. "Has Mum gone to bed?" she asked. "No." I replied "They have had go to the Hospital. I'm afraid Gangan has had a heart attack."

The next day, I was allowed to go with Mum to visit Gangan in hospital. It was a shock to see her under the white sheets. She looked so small, but more than that, for the first time ever. She looked so old. She always turned herself out immaculately. Even if she was not expecting visitors, she always wore makeup, lipstick and her eyes always looked big and bright through the lenses of her horn-rimmed glasses. Now with her glasses on the night table beside her, her eyes looked so small. She smiled at me and held her hand up for me to grasp it. I held her warm hand and kissed it giving it a loving squeeze.

Her voice sounded little and squeaky. I handed her a beaker of water so she could sip something to drink. That seemed to help her voice get a little stronger.

As we walked down the stairs from the ward, I said to Mum. "It was a shock to see her like that at first. But when I realised it was mainly because she was wearing no makeup I wasn't so worried. I really think that she is going to be okay." "Oh darling, I hope so. I really do." Mum replied as we made our way towards the car park.

She wasn't. The next phone call a short while later, told us she had passed away.

The Funeral was to be held at the Catholic Church to a packed congregation. All the family was present, including my father and Kate. My Dad always had a warm relationship with Leonora Ethel Hope as the engraved brass plate on the polished wooden coffin named my Gangan. I had never been to a funeral before. I had never had to face the loss of someone so significant in my life previously. There seemed to be a huge gap in my world and I could not see how it could possibly ever be filled.

As we filed out of the small church Julie and I climbed into my car. Julie had been overwhelmed by the service and the love shown to Leonora by the congregation. She started to sob; I found a box of tissues in the glove box. I handed her one so that she could wipe the black mascara running from her wet eyes. She pulled the sun visor down so that she could adjust her make up in the mirror.

We formed a long convoy as we followed the procession of funeral cars led by Gangan's hurse to Sutton Coldfield Crematorium. More people who I hadn't seen in church were waiting for the committal. Leonard Cooney and some of the crafts men at Samuel Hope were there all dressed in their Sunday best sporting black armbands. We entered the chapel. Gangan was placed on a plinth. The coffin sat on rollers. There was a pair of curtains in the wall, which the coffin would pass through during the committal.

I sat with Julie one side of me, Jim on the other next to Mum then Christine and her new husband Roger. All the ladies were tearful, it was just as well that Julie had the forethought to take more tissues out of the car and store them in her handbag. She was able to pass them down the line to Mum and Christine.

I looked at the coffin and anticipated its journey on the rollers behind the curtains. Was that the actual oven that would cremate her? My sense of humour that was known to me as a defence mechanism though dormant for this sad occasion did briefly speculate that surely it couldn't be. If it was it would surely set fire to the curtains! I didn't feel like laughing and decided it best not to share my thoughts. I didn't want to think of Gangan being burnt to ashes. I tried to avert my gaze and think of the happy times she had given me.

I reminded myself of Gangan day. When she would come and visit little Si John in 77 Park Road. How I would stand on the windowsill so I could see over the hedge. My patient wait would eventually be rewarded when I saw her coming down the pavement towards the house. She would wave and blow me a kiss, and I would do the same back to her. How I wanted to be back in those days then.

The committal began. The curtains parted revealing the hatch and the coffin slowly passed through. Like the curtains of the patio door of Chadsway, that had been my first theatre, they drew closed.

And she was gone.

47 SEEING A GHOST

We left the chapel of the crematorium and congregated in the memorial gardens. I was quite surprised to see Frank Titmus, my Superintendent from Saint John Ambulance. He was dressed in a religious robe as if he was some kind of minister. We acknowledged each other with a solemn nod. On any other occasion I would have loved to have spent time catching up with him but family were beckoning me.

As is the case on these occasions, there were many family members and friends who I had not seen in years. "Oh, Simon look at you, My how you have grown up into a handsome young feller!" became rather repetitive as I mingled with the crowd of long forgotten families and friends. "We must make an effort to keep in touch now." Was the other promise that everybody was making to one another. No doubt the crematorium attendants fall witness to such overtures of good intention from mourners on a daily basis.

I looked over the lawn to see Dad and Kate talking to Mum and Jim. Dad it appears was leaving. I saw him shake Jim warmly by the hand, then embrace Mum and kiss her softly on the cheek.

That was nice to see.

Then he approached Julie and Me. Hugged Julie and said his goodbyes. Dad and Kate walked off arm in arm towards the car park. Christine and Roger were next. Roger was nice man. Julie and I would often baby sit for them in their flat in Park Road, very close to number 77. Tamzin was close to Sally's age, and they had another daughter together nearer Adams age, Gemma. Christine was more tearful than ever. She had still been living with Gangan when I was small. They were very close. Then following the break up of her first marriage to Lloyd, she and Tamzin returned to Chadsway. Christine did try and spread her wings, living in London for a while but for me it was always nice when she would come home. Eventually she moved into the flat in Park Road. Roger was a neighbour. They found each other.

Isn't it nice when destiny works out like that for nice people you love?

The congregation was beginning to thin out, as people continued to say farewell and walk down the path to their respective cars. I looked over to see who Mum was now talking to.

It was Gangan.

What! How is this possible? Had she decided that she had enough of being dead already and just wanted to join the party? I began to shake with confusion. "Look who Mum is talking to Julie." Julie followed my gaze. "It can't be its Gangan. Are we looking at a ghost?" Julie exclaimed. We started to walk rapidly across the grass lawn towards the two ladies immersed in conversation. We watched them embrace. Mum looked over Gangan's shoulder and saw us approaching and exclaimed. "Simon, I want you to meet Aunty Margaret. Gangan's younger sister!"

Margaret turned towards us, she was clearly a lot younger than Gangan, in fact she was nearer Mums age. "I am sorry." I said as I hugged my new aunt. "I knew she had sisters Phyllis and May Hamber, but I had no idea she had a sister Margaret."

Margaret Minnis it turned out was Leonora's half sister. Gangan had never spoken of her. She introduced us to her husband George. Together they owned a book shop in a Mid Wales market town called Newtown in Montgomeryshire.

Despite being a half sister, Margaret bore an uncanny resemblance to Gangan to the extent that her presence amongst us was strangely comforting. We invited George and Margaret back to Court Lane so that we could reminisce some more and become better acquainted. As they entered the house Margaret said "Ooh I see you have a piano. I play too. Who is the musician of the house? "Every one but me!" Mum stuttered. "Simon plays guitar and trumpet, Jim plays Trombone. I bought the thing so I could join in, but now Simon plays that too!"

Margaret opened the bench and took out a piece of sheet music that had been siting in there idly ever since we acquired the piano from its previous owner. She immediately started to sight read and play. "I can only play from music." She explained. "Simon you are really clever if you can just play by ear. I have never been able to do that.

Eventually Margaret and George said their farewells. Leaving us with an invitation to visit them in Wales any time. We definitely wanted to do just that, and keep in touch.

48 A CHANGE OF FORTUNE

There was much to attend to with regard to Gangan's estate. The executors of the will had called a meeting with Barclays Trust Company and all the beneficiaries.

Mum and I entered the premises of Barclays at Colmore Row in Birmingham city centre. Christine and Roger were already sitting in the oak lined waiting room. I gazed out of the second floor window across Colmore Row.

Right across the road was the grounds containing Birmingham Cathedral. A low wall of no more than a foot high, surrounded the entire perimeter. Stubs of metal an inch in diameter protruded from the top of the wall at precise intervals of six inches or so. I was told they used to be an eight-foot high iron railings. During the Second World War, metal was in short supply, so any such source of this much-needed commodity was commandeered for the war effort. I speculated over what the metal railings surrounding Birmingham Cathedral may have been recycled to manufacture. A few tanks perhaps. I was familiar with this large place of worship. First I had sung in the school choir there and on one occasion I marched in there baring a huge flag staff with the flag of Saint John. It was a Memorial Day parade attended by Police, Fire, St John Ambulance, Army Cadets and Girl guides. A short audition one Sunday at the St John Birmingham Headquarters in Lionel Street opposite the Telecom Tower, was held. A number of kids attempted to read the lesson from the bible. Their reading was slow and delivery with varying degrees of Brummy accents, made the words and message unclear. I picked up the Bible and began to recite the passage loudly and clearly. I think I only uttered one or two sentences before the judge interrupted. "Okay, that's enough. You'll do!" I felt gratitude to my Gangan then for encouraging me to speak with clarity. So after I handed my flagstaff to another bearer on entering this historical cathedral. I made my way to the pulpit to read out the lesson on behalf of St John Ambulance.

My reminiscent mood fading, my attention came back to the oak panelled waiting room where I was in Colmore Row. Eventually we were ushered into a large similarly panelled room with an ornate ceiling with a chandelier gracing its centre. We were invited to take a seat around a large conference table.

The matter at hand was with a trust set up by my Grandfather Samuel Dennis Hope with regard to Samuel Hope Ltd Manufacturing Jewellers. And; the reading of the will of Leonora Ethel Hope.

Samuel Dennis Hope created a trust to protect the interests of his work force and his wife and two daughters. On his Death his wife Leonora would become beneficiary of this trust. It would provide her with an income for her lifetime and a position of director within the company. On her death, the new beneficiaries of the trust and it's income would be my mother and my Aunt Christine. As beneficiaries of unearned income were taxed heavily by the Labour Government of the day, Marie and Christine would become Directors of Samuel Hope and each enjoy a salary. On their deaths the capital from the trust would be released to their estate.

Regarding Leonora's assets, including Chadsway. Her will stated that with the exception of a number of personally specified possessions she chose to bequeath to people, and a number of modest charitable donations, her estate should be divided as follows.

Half of the estate was to be bequeathed between her two daughters. The remaining half; will be split into two quarters. Divided between each daughter's offspring. This was to be held in trust until their Eighteenth Birthday.

Mum was to inherit a large sum of money, along with an attractive monthly income, which she did not have to work for.

I was advised to open a bank account. As I was now eighteen, there was to be a sizable lump of money coming my way too. Thank you Gangan. How wonderful. I love you.

I opened a bank account at Barclays Bank in Erdington. The trust company gave me a letter of introduction, and I was immediately given a thousand pounds facility on the strength of my pending inheritance.

I consider a thousand pounds to be a lot of money today. Put into perspective. Back in the early seventies, for someone like me taking home now ten pounds a week, this was the equivalent of two years salary. This was a fortune!

Once the Estate was finally liquidated. My total inheritance was over two thousand pounds. A massive helping hand. Chadsway was sold at auction, for just eight thousand pounds. It must be worth many hundreds of thousands today.

Do you think a young eighteen-year-old Si John was about to handle his money wisely?

I think with the benefit of hindsight, perhaps twenty-one would have been a better age for me to come into a nest egg. Not to say I was reckless, but I did treat myself a little bit. I was able to do things that my Ten-pound a week salary could not support. And on my father's advice, I did invest five hundred pounds in a unit linked investment fund for the future.

49 NEW WHEELS

My Ford Anglia was coming up for its MOT. I had been dreading this. It had a few holes in the wheel arches. When it rained heavily, which it did a lot in Birmingham, water would spray from the wheels into the cabin and slowly fill the floor with water. If you ever had to stop suddenly, this water would create a wave and shoot forward soaking your shoes and socks. I drilled a number of holes in the floor to allow the water to drain out. Unfortunately before draining away completely, the floor was now being eaten away by rust. It was on it's final legs unless costly repairs were carried out.

I started scanning the motor pages of the Birmingham Evening mail for a replacement. I found an Austin Healey Sprite being advertised for Three Hundred and Twenty Five Pounds. O.N.O

Mum and Jim had decided to treat them selves to new car to. A Vauxhall Vectra. Quite a nice four door saloon with bench seats and a column gear change with just three gears. Julie and I had already tested it out one night after Jazz club. We parked up in Worcester Lane in our usual spot, and decided it was a much better passion wagon than the Ford Anglia with its own tidal system slopping about the floor.

So Jim and I set out in the Vauxhall to the other side of the city. We found the right street using the Birmingham A to Z road map. There parked outside our destination was a Blue Mk2 Austin Healey Sprite. I instantly fell in love with this car at first sight. I had to have it. I ripped the first cheque out of my chequebook, Three Hundred and Twenty Five pounds, a lot of money. I was given a written receipt and told I could collect the car as soon as the cheque cleared. That was a long week of waiting; I couldn't wait to take delivery of my new car. In the meantime I phoned around and managed to get some reasonably priced insurance organised. Although technically a sports car. The Sprite only had a one litre engine, which seemed to help someone as young as me get cover. I had looked into the prospect of an M.G.B. Roadster. But with a fifteen hundred CC engine, finding insurance would have been a problem.

My Austin Healey Sprite. Inset Front wheels of my first car.

The day finally arrived when I could take possession of my new, well new to me Sprite. It was a 1963 model so heading towards ten years old. As I sat in it, I recognised the familiar dashboard, identical in fact to my fathers M.G. Midget. I started the engine and heard the familiar sound of the exhaust. It had a large steering wheel, which I would soon exchange for a sporty small one, covered in black leather.

The seats were beginning to show their age too. So I went to Halfords and got some black sporty seat covers.

No more Ford Anglia with its Tidal waves. No more wet shoes and socks. I was travelling in style from now on!

Of course the first thing I wanted to do was show my car off to every one. I drove up Court Lane and pulled into the cu de sac where Julie's home now was. I beeped the horn as I stopped and saw a curtain move as Julie peered out of the window.

She ran out to inspect my purchase. "Oh my God Si it's brilliant. But there is only one thing wrong." She smiled a cheeky grin with her sexy smiley eyes. " What do you mean?" I queried. "Well. We are never going to be able to do it in that!" She pointed out.

I hadn't thought of that!

We drove together towards Four Oaks. Hood down; for the first time. It wasn't really warm enough for this but it had to be done. The heaters blew a constant supply of warm air on our legs; Julie's hair was waving in the wind as it formed a vortex over the top of the windshield. She was smiling and as we passed under the railway bridge in Little Sutton Lane the exhaust bellowed as the little car accelerated up the hill. John Chawner had a Vauxhall parked in his drive. No longer working at Sainsbury, now John was a Trainee Car Salesman for the 452 Vauxhall Dealership near Castle Bromwich. "Lets have a go then." John pleaded. I got out and he and Julie went for joyride down Clarendon Rd where we used to push our go-carts. Back round towards Worcester Lane. I could hear the exhaust sounding with a growl, as John changed down to turn back into Darnel Hurst Road. The two of them were sporting a big grin as they pulled up beside me.

Next. I had to go and show it off to my Dad. Didn't I?

Dad was very enthusiastic about my new wheels. "I had a lot of fun with my M.G. Midget," He said as he walked around to the drivers door." They are really good cars, I hope you get a lot of fun out of yours."

50 SEPARATE WAYS

It was about this time, that a number of people in my life and I went our separate ways. Little did I know that the gap left by their absence; would be quickly filled by new people, leading to new adventures.

Despite our attempt to cement our relationship together by getting engaged, the writing was on the wall. Julie and I were beginning to drift apart as our journeys were to take us in different directions. It was sad to think we had come so far, shared the same dreams of a future together. Even I was now beginning to see the inevitability of our romance cooling off.

I remember the first time, we had separated, I was devastated and alone. This time I was too exhausted to allow myself that kind of emotional turmoil. I recalled some words of wisdom from my Gangan one afternoon in the apple orchid of Chadsway. "Simon, if you love something, Set it free." She quoted to me some unknown poet. "If it comes back, it is yours to love forever. If it just flies away and you never see it again, then, maybe it was never yours to love in the first place!" I had decided to set Julie free. We would still see each other from time to time; I think we always would have a place in our hearts for each other. But our steamy romantic journey together had reached its destination.

One Saturday morning, Bill Thomas the manager of Eames the Jewellers gave me some instructions. "I've got to go home to South Wales now. Family emergency, you see." He explained. "The keys are on the hook as usual. I have arranged for a Policeman to be present when you lock up at one O clock. I can't leave the keys with you, under 21 see. So give the keys to him for safekeeping. I'll collect them from the Police Station, Monday." And off he went leaving Sue and me to mind the shop.

We had an uneventful Saturday mornings trade. A few people came in to collect their watch repairs. Sue had to use some stepladders to reach a piece of Capo De Monte from one of the top shelves. "Can I pass this down to you Si?" She called to me. Her mini skirted figure now at the top of the ladder, reminding me that she did have the most wonderful pair of legs. I took the porcelain figure from her and placed it on the glass counter. It had been on that shelf for sometime, and had gathered some dust. Sue liked to keep on top of this with the stock, especially when it was not particularly busy. A couple of cups of Nescafe Coffee and maybe some cigarettes later, it soon became time for us to start filling the safe with the valuables. One O Clock came; Sue and I were ready to shut up shop and leave. There was no sign of this policeman who we were supposed to hand these keys over to. "I suppose we better take them ourselves to the Police Station."

We walked to the Dog Inn Car park where I always parked. I would often give Sue a lift home. It was not out of my way much, and we had become good work mates. She wasn't so keen on my Ford Anglia which on a rainy day would wet her shoes and tights with its famous tidal wave action. Now I had the Sprite, she was happier to ride with me. I too was always quite happy, as she entertained me attempting to get those wonderful long legs in and out of a sports car that was merely inches off the ground, with a modicum of dignity.

We drove up to the Police Station. Sue remained in the car whilst I ran in to drop the keys off. I entered a long reception area scattered with leaflets about crime prevention. "Watch Out! There's a thief ab ut !" One poster on the wall shouted. With a picture of a thief running off with the missing "o" from "about."

There was a desk sergeant on the telephone. I waited patiently. Eventually his call ended and he turned to me. "Yes?" he greeted me boredly. I explained what Bill Thomas had told me had been arranged and he listened rolling his eyes at me. "So you are telling me that because you are only eighteen, you were expected to hand over the keys to the shop to a possibly also Eighteen year old Policeman? Sounds a bit silly to me!" The sergeant commented with more than a hint of sarcasm. Apparently he was unaware of any such arrangement, and refused to accept the keys for safe keeping unless I was handing them in as lost property. I decided either Sue or myself would hang on to them.

Monday came after a weekend of Jazz music and joyriding up to John Chawner's and I arrived at the shop early, in case Mr Thomas was concerned about his instructions. I didn't want to open up until he arrived. Eventually Sue joined me. We stood together in the early morning cold, by the time 9.15 arrived. "Sod this!" I said. "I'm opening up, so we can put the kettle on and get warm."

Ten O clock came and went, as did Eleven. Soon it would be approaching our lunch break. How could we have a break? There had to be two people manning the shop. In the end Sue quickly slipped out to the sandwich shop close by and bought us a sausage roll each. "What do you think we should do?" I asked Sue. "I don't know." She answered wiping a piece of pastry off her mouth, then noticing she had more crumbs collecting in her mini skirted. She brushed her skirt and looked up at me. "If he doesn't show up before Two, I think maybe we should telephone head office." "Good thinking Batman." I said.

Two came and went, and we were actually quite busy. Eventually I was able to leave Sue in the store and I went into the back to telephone head office in Stourbridge. I had been to the head office recently, and I was known to one of the bosses there. I asked to speak to him. "Hello it's Simon Edgington here from Sutton branch. We are a bit concerned that Mr Thomas has not come in today. He told me to leave the keys with the Police on Saturday because he was going to Wales. But they refused to accept them. I am just calling to ask you if you would like me to lock up tonight and take the keys home again"? The voice on the other end sounded panic stricken and told me he would arrange for someone from head office to come to us right away.

The director of Eames the Jewellers came through the door accompanied by the chime of the brass bell on its frame. The first thing he did was instructing us to close the shop, which meant putting all the stock in the safe. We retired to back office, and Sue put the kettle on, as I recited the chain of events leading up to my call.

"Right. We are going to put a sign on the door saying.. Closed for Annual Audit." He explained to us. "Then you two can go home. When you come in tomorrow, we are going to need you to assist us in taking an audit of all the stock." I explained that we had only recently performed such an audit. "I am aware of that, but under these circumstances, we need to do it again. This is quite serious Simon! If our insurers found out that the keys were held for an entire weekend by someone under twenty one, we would be in a lot of trouble!"

The next day we were introduced to Mark Hallet. A black framed bespectacled man with a nice smile and a shock of dark wavy hair. He was immaculately dressed in a dark suit, he reminded me somewhat of an eccentric orchestral conductor in his manner.

He was a bit wary of us to begin with. We had rolls of computer paper with stock, numbers, cost prices Etc. We had to check off every single stock item in the shop, which was going to be a long task.

I don't want to say that Bill Thomas helped himself to Watches and Jewellery to stock his own new shop in South Wales. I think the audit was pretty much in order. But there were some discrepancies in procedures, which head office, were unhappy about. Plainly things were about to change under Mark Hallet.

So now we had a new manager. His first task was going to whip his new work force into shape, show us his way of doing things. He was quite adamant about how stock had to be displayed. This was an art form to Mr Hallet.

It was also decided, that we should take on another member of staff. How on earth a forth person was going to fit in the small back office at coffee break I was not so sure. Interviews were held during the week and eventually both Sue and I were pleased when Mr Hallet offered the position to a young blonde girl with a gypsy smile, Jenny

I used to have lunch sometimes in the Dog Inn. Jenny's first week, she didn't know the ropes, so I invited her to join me. Whilst Sue could be quite aloof, Jenny was the opposite. Jenny was very natural and easy to talk to. I didn't feel that buzz of physical attraction towards her as I did with Sue and her sensational legs, but I really liked Jenny and we were soon to become firm friends.

It turned out she had a boyfriend in the Royal Engineers Regiment of the army, who we were eventually introduced to. He was a very dapper mixed race guy who was perhaps one of the few people who was smaller than me. Jenny was quite a buxom girl which made him look all the smaller when they stood close. What a strange fit Sue and I thought as we saw them walk out of the shop hand in hand accompanied by the chimes of the brass doorbell.

I started taking both Sue and Jenny to the Jazz club. It was quite hilarious fitting the two girls into the Sprite. There was a shelf behind the two seats that a child could sit on quite comfortably. Sue would climb in and have one leg on the drivers side and the other the passengers side of the gearstick. She would normally discard the mini skirt on those occasions in favour of a pair of tight black trousers. I didn't mind. It was then I discovered what a beautifully shaped bottom she had too!

One weekend Jenny called me and asked if we could go out. She sounded upset. I drove up to Little Hay to a semi-detached cottage and tooted the horn. She came out of the house, her blonde hair blowing in the wind and a low cut blouse, showing just a little too much cleavage for my taste.

We decided to take a walk in the park. I parked up inside Four Oaks entrance and we walked through the woods until we found Mayors Arbour. We sat on the wooden bench amongst all the carved graffiti declaring undying love for long forgotten liaisons. We smoked a cigarette and Jenny looked at me pensively biting her bottom lip. I knew that look. I thought to myself.

"My boyfriend has dumped me." Jenny told me matter of factly. "The trouble is, I think I might be pregnant." "Oh Jenny what a situation." I personally didn't think the boyfriend was a great loss. Although buxom blondes; have never been to my taste. Jenny was a very attractive young lady, and a lovely, lovely natured person. I knew that she could do better for herself. "Have you spoken with your mother?" I asked her. "Funnily enough." She giggled slightly and pushed her blonde hair back away from her face. She took a puff on her cigarette and continued. " She's actually quite excited at the prospect of becoming a grandmother."

Jenny was pregnant. She continued to work in the shop right up until she was due to give birth. We would all be sat in the small back office at coffee time with an ever increasing in size Jenny. And she did get enormous. She would sit in the wooden chair uncomfortably with a rosy complexion. It looked like quite an exhausting transition she was undergoing.

Mark Hallet was very supportive to his staff. Around Christmas, he had invited us all to his apartment for dinner. His wife was Dutch. A very pleasant lady, and they had an infant daughter. What a really nice family he had made for himself. I discovered something about him that we had in common. He had a piano. So the occasion turned into a sing song with Mark his wife and daughter, myself and the two shop girls around the piano.

Most nights I would drive Jenny home to Little Hay. Her mother was a nice lady with long dark fuzzy hair. A bit of a hippy. She liked me, and I am sure she thought it would be nice if Jenny and I were to become an item. I think Jenny may have been open to the idea too. We were good friends, but that sparkle of magic, that we all seek, just wasn't present for me.

Eventually Jenny left Eames to have her baby. Shortly after we were all sat in the back office of Eames eating our morning break sausage rolls. The brass doorbell chimed informing us we had a visitor. We all went out into the shop to greet Jenny and her mum as they struggled to lift the baby pram over the threshold. Jenny had lost all her bulk now and was looking just radiant. There was so much joy in the shop on that occasion as Jenny introduced us to her beautiful baby girl. Mother hood clearly suited Jenny and our old team was once again for a moment, complete.

I had no shortage of female company to go to the Jazz club. Jenny, Sue, sometimes both would accompany me to my favourite jazz nights at the Dog Inn.

I would bump into Julie from time to time. She was now working in a Birmingham City Centre Solicitors Office. I often called in for a coffee when I was in the area. There were two other girls typing franticly away. One of them I had met previously. She was the boss's secretary. The other was a young slim girl with long dark hair. "This is Debbie." Julie introduced us. "She has just started with us." Debbie smiled nicely at me and we shook hands. I carried on my conversation with Julie, finished my coffee, gave Julie a peck on the cheek and left.

As I walked across the tarmac to my sprite, I heard the click click sound of running hi heals. I turned and Julie was walking towards me. She had a shy smile on her face, eyes smiling in the way they always did. "Guess what Si?" She started to say as she approached me. "You've got an admirer. Debbie quite fancies you. You should ask her out!"

Apparently when I left the office. Debbie turned to Julie and said "So that is Simon that you have been telling me about? Are you insane? He's gorgeous!" Julie just couldn't wait to tell me. Julie handed me a piece of paper. I knew Julie's handwriting. It wasn't hers. Debbie wanted me to have her phone number.

Debbie and I dated for just a few weeks.

I discovered the most significant aspect of this liaison was intimacy with someone other than Julie provided me with that much needed closure.

We drove down to the West Country in the Sprite to meet Mum and Jim in Tynemouth Devon. They had driven down earlier and checked into a bed and breakfast. I had their spare keys. So when we arrived there in the early hours, we could park up the Sprite then cuddle up under a blanket on the back seat of the Vauxhall.

Mum and Jim had been considering using their newly found wealth to work for themselves. No plan had come into focus yet, but the purpose of their weekend jaunt to Tynemouth was to view a filling station and newsagents business that was up for sale.

Daylight came and we climbed out of the car, as Mum and Jim were leaving the Bed and Breakfast.

There is something about the Devon and Cornwall seaside that is so appealing. Seagulls sound their cries as they glide around the salty air. The crisp smell of ozone and the waves licking at the block stone jetty covered in a moss of seaweed.

Debbie and I walked hand in hand along the sea front admiring the scene of colourful quaint souvenir shops, selling seaside rock and postcards depicting scenes of picturesque West Country landscapes. She looked beautiful too in her black hot pants and tight red T-shirt revealing the shape of her narrow waist complimented by her small but perfectly proportioned breasts. My loins tingled in anticipation for the time we could once again lay naked together.

It was never to be.

When we got back from the West Country. Debbie made her excuses and asked me to take her home.

The next day she finished with me. The girl from West Bromwich who had never before been out of the Midlands, thought we were all just too posh for her.

51 PISTON BROKE

One of the few things I liked about the days when I was at Unigate Dairies. The shift rota worked in such a way you would occasionally get a long weekend off. Jim still working there still had these rotas. Those occasions would not be wasted.

The last time was their long weekend in Tynemouth investigating what possibilities life selling Newspapers and Petrol could bring. That fell on stony ground when the business loan they needed was dependent on how much bricks and mortar they would be buying as security. A phone call to the sellers revealed the answer was none. The purchase price was solely for Good Will.

So the next jaunt was going to be a long weekend at Mums caravan in Harlyn Bay.

John Chawner and I decided that we would share the driving and shoot down there in the Sprite and surprise them.

I pulled up outside Johns at about four in the afternoon. He came bounding out of his front door carrying his familiar gym bag that he had filled with a change of clothes. I had my karate kit bag in the trunk with some bits and pieces too.

We were excited about our road trip, and we were looking forward to the prospect that our adventure may include running into some Cornish Girls. With John as my wingman, what could possibly go wrong?

John took the wheel for the first leg of our journey. Spaghetti Junction was still under construction so it took us a while to join the start of the M5 motorway that would take us to Exeter. From there it was the A38 to Launceston then across the Bodmin Moor to Padstow and Harlyn Bar.

The roads were quite clear once we joined the M5. We planned to stop for fuel and then find a pub once we got near Bristol for a steak dinner and maybe a pint.

This is going to be so much fun! John and I hadn't spent a lot of one on one time together since we had both got involved with the fairer sex.

The Michael Wood service station came into view and John pointed the car towards the motorway exit. We filled up with petrol three pounds and three pence worth bought us nine gallons of two star at thirty-seven and a half pence a gallon, topping up the tank nicely. We figured on topping up again once we got to Exeter to make sure we had enough to complete our journey.

I took over the wheel and we taxied out to the motorway entrance ramp. I began to accelerate through the gears. Just as we left the ramp and re-joined the motorway, there was a judder and a noticeable loss in power, the Sprite felt like it was now only firing on three cylinders. Well we continued on a little in the hope that it would suddenly spring back to life. By now we were committed to remain in this southbound lane at least until the next exit. I began to get concerned when I noticed the Oil Pressure gauge was indicating no pressure. I pointed it out to John. We decided that we should attempt to get back as close to home as possible.

We exited the South Bound Carriageway at the next junction and found a pub. Our Cornish Adventure would have to be another day, but there was no way we were going to be done out of the steak meal we had promised ourselves.

It was a typical country pub. Oak beams, red flock wallpaper that seemed to be favoured by most breweries of the day. There was a large log furnace burning in the fireplace, and the locals were warming themselves by it as they drunk their beers.

We sat at a table by the window a jovial waitress came to serve us. We hadn't travelled far towards the South West, but far enough to be greeted by that lovely West Country drawl. "Welcome my lovelies, and what can we get for you tonight?" Our host asked in a farmyard accent.

We both started with a Prawn Cocktail followed by a most delicious T bone steak. Mindful of our journey back we only drank a half of beer each.

We climbed back into the Sprite. I was hoping by turning the key all would have cured its self. Sadly this was not the case. This was a very poorly engine under the hood.

At first it fooled us into thinking it sounded good enough to get us home if we were gentle. Gingerly I turned onto the North Bound ramp of the M5. Staying in the left hand lane, I coaxed the little car Northward. The Michael Woods Services was approaching, we had to decide whether to pull in there and discuss our rescue options or continue to limp home. We had both limped home in the past with poorly scooters and cars and the Gods had always been good to us and delivered us back safely. Our little engine was trying to convince us that she would be all right.

We passed the Michael Wood Service entrance ramp. Now we were committed. It was about two miles further on; the sick engine began to protest some more. I had been able to maintain a speed of around forty-five miles per hour, which would have got us home for bedtime. "Oh no she's really starting to worry me now." I said to John. Power was fading and just then there was an almighty Crash Bang! Sound, all power had gone and the cabin immediately began to fill with black smoke and a putrid smell of burnt oil and petrol. I depressed the clutch and the Sprite rolled to a silent stop on the hard shoulder. Silent; but for the hissing sound, emerging from a now overheated radiator.

We both quickly jumped out of the car for fear that it was about to catch fire and ran up the motorway embankment. We returned gingerly; when it became evident that we need not have worried. The smoke seemed to have cleared from the cockpit now so sat in the drivers seat and cautiously turned the key, in the hope that now it had cooled a little, we might be able to coax the little car into getting us a bit closer to home. My answer was a very painful clanking sound that I had never heard a healthy engine make.

Meanwhile John ran north along the hard shoulder to find an Emergency Telephone. The first question they asked was are we members of the AA or RAC. Neither of us was. So the only option was to call out the tow truck from Michael Wood Services. We sat on the bonnet smoking and waited.

Eventually a mechanic arrived. "Hello my lovelies, what seems to be the problem?" His West Country farmer accent greeted us." I wondered if he was related to the waitress in the pub who had just served us. Did they all talk like that?

He shone a torch under the bonnet at the oil stained engine. The smell of acrid burnt oil still in the air. "Just turn her over for me my Lovely will you?" He instructed me. The clanking sound repeated its self as before. "Lets see now." As he pointed the torch illuminating different parts of the engine compartment. "Everything seems alright around here, mmm nothing to see there." Just then he exclaimed "Fucking Hell! Come and take a look at this !" There was a gaping hole in the side of the engine block. A piston rod had shed its piston and eventually pushed its self through the block. The clanking sound was this dancing around inside the hole. This Engine was dead.

It cost us eight pounds (Nearly a weeks wages!) to be towed up the motorway to the next junction then back South to the Southbound Michael Wood Service. The first thing I was going to do on Monday was join the AA.

We gingerly climbed the barrier of the motorway, and crossed to the North Bound Service station. John, using his best telephone voice convinced a family travelling in a mini bus to give us a ride. We got as far as Perry Bar and walked the rest of the way to Johns house. It was four am when we arrived. Hazel, John's mother was very surprised to see the beds in John's room occupied in the morning.

Paul Stanway, Marks brother who played drums for us that time when Mark was grounded; helped me recover my car from the Michael Wood Service station. He was one of the regulars at the Jazz club. He owned an Austin Healey 3000. He would tease me about my Sprite, because his car was a classic monster. He offered to tow it back to Court Lane for me. I was not trusted to be at the wheel of the Sprite. No engine meant no servo for the breaks. A friend of his and him were used to these capers. So I sat next to Paul in the 3000. They had a long towrope and walkie-talkie radios so they could communicate. Paul Stanway was a mad man that day. He got the two cars heading north touching 100 miles per hour. I was glad I was not the one being towed by a rope at a ton!

The great thing about Austin Healey Sprites is a plentiful source of engine parts. The one litre engine block was used in any number of BMC models. I managed to buy an almost scrap Austin A30 van MOT failure for ten pounds. I drove it up Court Lane nearly passing out from the Carbon Monoxide. That the broken exhaust was blowing into the cabin.

John Chawner and Jim assisted me with the transplant. We removed the engine from the Sprite and the A30 van. We removed the cylinder head from both engines, modernised the replacement engine with the undamaged Sprite cylinder head, twin carbs and exhaust. Bolted the engine to the clutch and gearbox assembly. Put it all back together again, turned the key and wonder of wonders! It worked! Just like that!

The only thing left to do was to put the broken parts into the back of the A30 van. Hitch up the towrope and deliver the van to the local scrap yard.

That Sunday Night Jazz at The Dog Inn, Eddie Reed was in the line up for the final blast of When the Saints Go Marching In. You remember Eddie Reed taught me some moves on the Trumpet. "Hey Man how you doing." His big black jovial smile greeted me with his wide blood shot eyes. " I was here on Friday. Eddie told me that you never missed a night. We missed you man, you weren't here!" "Couldn't make it." I answered referring to my car. "Piston broke."

"Pissed and Broke! Tell me about it Brother." Eddie replied. "Why that's the God damn story of my Life!"

52 A CHANGE OF SCENE

We had remained in touch with Gangan's half sister. Aunty Margaret. She had written to us saying how much George and her would like us to visit them in Newtown. So it was decided that we would go there the next weekend that Jim was free.

As we got cheated out of our Cornish Adventure, John and I decided to test out the Sprite and it's newly revitalised engine. We would follow up on Sunday morning.

Once again I stayed at John's home, so that we could make an early start. We left a misty Darnel Hurst Road, just as the sun was beginning to come up. The roads were clear, as was our plan to leave at this hour. We headed North up the Lichfield road until we could turn left at Mutley Corner Roundabout on to the A5 to Shrewsbury. Mutley Corner Hotel actually at that junction, was another venue that Julie and I had discovered for Live Music. Friday Night hosted by "Maz" on the Piano and Derrick on Drums. The two of them were coal miners from the Rugely Pit. It was mostly instrumental, but Derrick was known for his rendition of "I left my heart in San Francisco."

(Who would thought it reader. As I write this chapter it is March 2015 and I am on the cruise ship "Star Princess" on my way to Hawaii having just sailed from San Francisco. That song is a popular request on this cruise too.)

They made a fun evening, but we moved on once we discovered Jazz night at the Dog Inn.

Arriving at Shrewsbury we turned and headed for Church Stretton past Dorrington Grove where my Dads sister lived with my cousins, Miles and Bizzy (Liz) I hadn't seen them since my adventure on my Vespa not long after my sixteenth birthday. Just before Craven arms, we took the sign for Churchstoke and Newtown. The further we got along this wood lined road, the more into the country side we thought we were travelling. Forest areas would pass us by exchanging them selves with a view of beautiful undulating green fields, scattered with dairy cattle, horses and sheep. Lots and lots of sheep; in fact.

As a very welcome sun; burnt away the remains of the early morning mist, we were treated to a stunning blue sky hosting an array of mackerel clouds. It was turning out to be a beautiful day to explore Mid Wales.

We needed petrol, and we stopped at a hotel on a corner just past Churchstoke. The Blue Bell Inn. There in front of the building was the oldest looking petrol pump I had ever seen under the shade of a large oak tree. A sign on the door next to a large bell button said "Ring For Fuel." So we did.

We decided now it was warm and sunny, we would take the roof down on the Sprite for the rest of the journey towards Newtown. We passed through the hedge lined country lanes, the exhaust growl of the little car momentarily interrupting the peace of the quaint little village of Kerry and up the hill, revealing the beautiful River Seven Valley hosting Newtown below.

Two boys from Birmingham pulled into a layby by a telephone box, to admire the stunning view. Our retina's; over whelmed by the feast of green wherever one looked. We had Sutton Park back in our town, and we considered ourselves very lucky compared to other midland towns. But this was just mind numbingly beautiful countryside.

We continued our journey down Kerry Road into Newtown past a large Victorian building displaying a sign on its roof PRYCE-JONES. We arrived at a junction with a white washed pub sporting the name. The Queens Head on the right. Across the road was a cenotaph on traffic Island surrounded by low railings. Behind that; was yet another Pub. The Cambrian Vaults. We were later to discover from George, Aunty Margaret's husband that in the small area that was Newtown town centre, there were a lot of pubs. Twenty-three in fact.

Newtown people; Liked a drink.

We arrived at Trehafren housing estate and followed the instructions to find number 178 Lon Gwern. Which was close to a small community hall and shop. We knew we were in the right place by seeing Mum and Jims Vauxhall in the car park.

As we opened the gate leading to the back garden, Margaret's Red Setter came bounding out of the back door to greet us, followed by Lady and Bess our family dogs.

I haven't mentioned that our house in Court Lane had two other residents. First we had Lady as a puppy. I remember getting home from work one day, walking into the kitchen and seeing for the first time this adorable black Labrador puppy. She was so excited to see me, her little tail was wagging so profoundly that her whole back end was shaking. I knelt down to say hello and she put her front paws on my knee and attempted to kiss my face with her tongue. It was love at first sight with Lady for the family and me. Bess came along later. She was a rescue dog that Mum and Jim felt deserved a lucky break. A beautiful Afghan Hound. Which would leave blonde hairs lying around wherever she went.

The dogs were in their element in Newtown. We took them down to the backfield, which led to the undulating river seven. Bess had to discouraged from chasing after sheep in the field. When she took off, there was no catching her. Eventually John got her and we decided it best to keep her on a lead. Lady was no trouble at all. Margaret's Irish Red Setter. What can I say? I think it was the dumbest animal I ever met! As soon as we got close to the river, she found a spot where a couple of fishermen were enjoying the peace and tranquillity of the day and launched herself into the water with a mighty splash! Ruining any chance of a fish being anywhere near the end of their lines. Margaret's daughter Gail, a petit spectacled girl about Sally's age; called the setter to coax it out of the water. If the two fishermen were not completely woken from the peaceful trance by then, they soon were when the dog exited the river took a look at one of them, turned an eye on the other then began to shake itself dry, drenching them both with a dog full of river water.

John said that he must tell brother Steve about this location for fishing. I was aware that they would often fish in the lakes of Sutton Park. It had never really appealed to me.

We carried on along the riverbank towards the town. After a large car parking area we arrived beside the Regent Cinema next to a bridge spanning the river Severn. Gail told us that sometimes the river would flood and some of the shops in Broad Street had marks on them signifying up to what level they had been underwater.

Opposite the Regent Cinema was the Elephant and Castle Hotel. This was a large Victorian Inn, which would host commercial travellers. At the rear of the hotel was a banqueting suite. Next door to the Elephant was Margaret and George's bookshop. Turn right into Broad Street and you were in the main shopping area. It housed many pubs, a Woolworths and at the end of the street a Town Clock tower soaring above the local branch of Barclays Bank.

I felt it was all here. In fact we all did. We fell in love with Newtown. Mum and Jim were not sure what kind of business they were going to go into yet but they knew they had found their new home away from the rat race that was Birmingham.

But how was this going to ever be possible?

53 BARNABY RUDGE

One of the couples that I noticed as regulars at the Jazz club was Roger and Jenny. Roger would occasionally join the line up at the end of the night and blow a clarinet solo. He was a striking figure, sporting the look of Jason King, a TV character played by Peter Wyngard. Curly haired sporting a moustache, I noticed he finished the look off by driving a British Racing Green E Type Jaguar. His wife Jenny was quite striking too. A slim figure, most often dressed in very complementary hot pants. He told me he was into antiques and had a shop in Erdington called Barnaby Rudge. He had invited me to visit, but up to now the opportunity had not presented it' self. Until; I had to be given some sick leave from work.

I sustained an injury at Karate. By now I had been really getting on with Karate. I was a Green Belt and soon to take my Brown. In order to qualify for my Brown Belt I had to attend a demonstration at Digbeth Civic Hall Birmingham. There were several other Karate clubs present too. It had been noticed that I was very good at performing a Kata. This is choreography of moves combining punches kicks and blocks against imaginary opponents.

Brother Adam and his friend Timmy Mannox; would watch me practicing on the lawn in the back garden. Eagerly waiting for the inevitable cursing from me when I realised I had landed from a well-performed roundhouse kick in yet another pile of dog poo!

So the day of the demonstration arrived. I performed my Kata spectacularly, even if I do say so myself. Then, I was called upon for semi free fighting. This is where you punch kick block your opponent but not with full force. I had not really bargained for this.

My opponent was a ginger haired lad who would have looked quite ferocious even without Karate skills. Whenever I was in this situation, my favoured move was to sweep away the opponents front leg just as they were about to step their weight on to it. This was very effective. I floored John Chawner once with this move so that he went down so fast, I was afraid that I'd hurt him. In order to prevent you from falling victim to this move Karate practitioners try to keep their weight on their back leg, leaving the front leg free to kick, sweep and block.

My ginger haired opponent knew all about the move I was trying to deliver. I swept his front shin away, but it just swung round and delivered a slap from nowhere with a sweaty freckled foot to the side of my head. I wasn't hurt but my ear was ringing. I moved to retaliate with a kick to the chest. As I raised my thigh before whipping my foot forward in a leg-straightening deathblow, he must have decided to perform the very same move on me. The result was the back of my foot colliding with his bent knee. The pain, was excruciating, the fight was over. I bowed to my opponent and limped painfully off the floor.

I had a lot of difficulty driving home that night. Every time I moved my foot from the accelerator to the break pedal, pain seared up my leg. I limped home. This time it wasn't the car that was poorly.

My foot had swollen up considerably the next morning. Mum drove me to the casualty department of Good Hope Hospital. X rays showed no fracture, so I was prescribed painkillers and a weeks sick leave.

After a couple of days, although still limping, my foot began to feel a little better. I could have gone back to work but I was under doctor's orders. So now I was getting bored.

I know! I'll go and visit Roger and Jenny at Barnaby Rudge.

I parked the Sprite behind Roger's E type, I noticed Jenny dusting some pottery that was sitting on one of the oak dressers on display outside under a canvas canopy. Still dressed in the familiar and pleasing to the eye hot pants. She looked up and gave me a friendly wave. "Well Simon, you have timed that well." She greeted me. "The boys just called they are on the way back. How do you fancy joining us for Beans on Toast and a cup of tea?"

I followed Jenny into the veritable Aladdin's cave of bric a brac that was Barnaby Rudge. There was a framed canvas pencil drawing with the signature Picasso on it. "Really!" I exclaimed as I held the frame to the light admiring the artwork. "You have a Picasso in the shop?" "Oh yes." Jenny answered with a grin. "We sell a lot of those. But really they are drawn by Roger." In the yard at the back of the shop there lay an Old English Sheepdog, curled up on an old sofa, quite oblivious to the world. I was starting to become quite curious about this couple that I had met at the jazz club.

Eventually a Volkswagen camper van drew up outside the shop. Roger and another guy dressed in overalls with the initials T.P.L. emblazoned on them opened the side door, and between them carried a large television into the shop next door. That task complete they came into the back of Barnaby Rudge where Jenny was just putting the finishing touches to our pan of baked beans.

"Look who has come to see us Roger." She greeted her husband, with a nice kiss. "Simon!" He exclaimed. "Nice to see you. Welcome to Barnaby Rudge." Barnaby Rudge it appears is the name of a Charles Dickens character. To say Roger appeared to be a bit of a wheeler-dealer was an understatement. The other guy was Nick Wellman. He remained in the background as Roger lorded all that was around him.

I noticed an invoice pad sporting the company name. Telemetric Productions Limited. (T.P.L.) Roger Hart; Managing Director. Company Secretary; Barnaby Rudge. "Oh so there is actually a Barnaby Rudge working here?" I queried. "Yes, would you like to meet him?" Roger answered. "Barney Barney here boy." With that the old English Sheepdog looked up from his sofa, stretched and with his stumpy tail wagging came indoors for a fuss and some toast. "We gave him beans once." Jenny said. "That was a mistake."

"It's quite handy having him here." Roger explained. If any body official comes in the shop asking to see Barnaby Rudge, I just tell them he is in the back chewing a bone!"

In conversation. I must have mentioned that the family had recently inherited some money. Roger was interested in that and asked me if I was looking for something to invest in. He had a project that he was just about to get up and running. Wow I thought, this guy is amazing maybe my next car could be an E Type Jag.

I don't know what Jenny did to the pan of beans on toast, maybe it was the addition of lashings of butter, but that was the most delicious beans on toast I have ever experienced. This was to become a regular stop off point from now on whenever I was running chores to the Jewellery quarter.

As I was leaving, still with a limp. Nick Wellman came out to me. "I'm having a housewarming party tonight at the new flat. Would you like to come? Roger and Jenny will be there."

Nick lived in an apartment at the top of Hill Village Road. Very close to where I used to live in Four Oaks. I climbed to the top of the stairs and knocked on the door. As the door opened a nice looking girl was leaving. "Okay Nick I will see you later." She said with a hint of a Scottish accent. "And once again, welcome to the building." With that she walked across the hallway and entered the other apartment on the landing. "That's Handy." I said to Nick with a grin.

Nick was originally from Bristol. Soon to be married to Sue, who was about to take up a position in the area of a kindergarten Teacher. She was still in Bristol. Nick had come on ahead to set up the home. I don't recall how he came to be working with Roger but he had some advice for me.

"Roger is not what he seems." Nick warned me. "He is a great guy, and Jenny is fantastic, but he lives in a bit of a fantasy world. Whatever you do, don't make the mistake I made. He has had money off me and I now doubt, I am going to ever get it back. Sue would kill be if she found out"

Telemetric Productions Ltd. Started its life as a Television Repair business. Then Roger diversified into second hand furniture and antiques. He was currently re-launching the TV side of the enterprise. They had one engineer working above the Glaziers shop next door. They advertised TV repairs in the Birmingham Evening Mail. They would be called out, looking very knowledgeable, although they themselves knew little about TV's. The TV would never be repaired in the home. They would tell the customer the TV needed servicing so they could charge five pounds every time. Most times the problem was a valve needing replacement at a cost of pennies. The engineer would repair the set, spray some switch cleaner in the back and then Roger and Nick would return the TV to the customer none the wiser! "Cooshty!" As Dell Boy would say, many years later.

So on Nick's advice, it became prudent to enjoy the Friendship of Roger and Jenny from afar.

I liked Nick and Sue. I told him about my dramas with Julie one night. "What star signs are you both?" Nick asked. "She's Gemini, I'm Cancer." I told him. "Well there you have it right there. Doomed from the start!" Nick explained with authority. Apparently he was a Gemini, and his ex wife had been a Cancer. He really believed in this stuff.

54 DESTINY

Once again we were sat at our dining table enjoying a post dinner chat. Jim was beginning to get itchy feet at work. "Have I told you the story of my new boots, Simon?" No he hadn't. "It's just that, I do this job every day. Nothing changes and then one day I ordered a pair of new boots from the catalogue. Now all week I have something to look forward to. The arrival of my new pair of boots." He put down his mug of tea, and proceeded to light another cigarette. "The point is. I'm very happy at home. I have your mother who is great, But, when the only thing I can get excited about at work is a new pair of boots arriving. I can't help but feel that there must be something more satisfying than driving milk bottles around the Midlands."

At this moment the telephone rang. It was Gail, Aunty Margaret's daughter. She was in a panic. George, her father had passed away suddenly and her Mother was beside herself with grief. Gail was afraid she might do something silly.

We travelled to Newtown that weekend. Margaret was very depressed over the loss of her husband. It was decided that we bring her back to Erdington after the weekend.

We did our best to cheer her up, but she was very tearful. I became quite close to Margaret during that time. I seemed to manage to be able to cheer her up. We related the conversation that we had had about Jims Boots. Margaret responded. "Well, if you want a change of scene. Why don't you just move to Newtown. You can stay with me, until you get a Newtown development house. I can introduce you Jim, to David Powell at Eagle Brewery. He is always looking for drivers."

Destiny had leant a helping hand. Jim was spared the need for the leap of faith. The prospect of delivering beer around the Welsh country was a no brainer for Jim. So much better than delivering milk on clogged up Birmingham Roads. Margaret had provided the much-needed stepping-stone for them to follow their dream of moving to Newtown.

Things were changing for me too. Nick Wellman acquired an Esso Garage in Erdington. His idea was to set up a tyre and exhaust centre. Sell petrol and also a car repair workshop. The premises were enormous. Nick had finally got his money back from Roger who was moving forward in strides too. Nick wanted to offer a late night service for petrol, so I started a side job manning the petrol pumps.

Meanwhile Roger and another partner used his powers of persuasion and charm to acquire a warehouse on a years lease with the first three months rent-free. He stocked it with new furniture that he managed to get on thirty days credit direct from the manufacturer and even persuaded A.T.V Birmingham to run advertisements on the local TV. It was a balancing act. He could do well or could crash and burn horribly. If ever there was a master of the leap of faith. It was Roger.

The E Type was gone. Repossessed by the finance company. No wonder Roger had once offered to swap it for my Sprite! He even let me borrow it for a weekend. It was magnificent to drive, but it's thirst for petrol soon proved to me that it was out of my league. He showed up at the filling station with a brand new Granada. He was living the high life. Although the petrol forecourt and general repair workshop was doing well for Nick. The tyre and exhaust centre was a bit ahead of its time. The days of Quick Fit Fitters in every town were yet to arrive.

So when Roger suggested he use that space for another furniture outlet supplied by him. Nick jumped at the chance. Nick required a manager. He offered me the job.

I said my farewells to Mark Hallet, Sue and Jenny who had recently returned and Eames the Jewellers. Nick had formed a limited company appointing himself as Managing Director. Company Secretary Simon Edgington. It appeared I could call myself a company director. I was now earning twenty pounds a week!

Rogers Warehouse T.P.L. as it was called was booming. Roger had a talent for making things happen. In spite all his bluff, his courage to leap into the unknown paid off. Within a short space of time, he was arriving at the filling station in a Ferrari Dino.

My poor Sprite was in need of expensive repair to get through the M.O.T. It had been becoming increasingly difficult to close the doors because a crack in the sill was breaking the whole car in two. "Two much sex down

Worcester Lane with Julie caused that!" John Chawner teased me. "What do you expect? You two. Bouncing up and down inside it. Something was bound to give!"

I was thinking I would like to get something a bit newer. Nick offered me a hundred pounds for my Sprite one night in the pub. He said he would get the lads in the garage to weld it up and put it through the M.O.T. So I went to see what deals John could offer me at the 452 Motor Company. He showed me a Vauxhall Viva SL90 in white. It was in pristine condition. John managed to organise finance for me with Nick's hundred pounds as a deposit.

Things were now moving fast for Mum and Jim. They had put the house on the market and had received an offer. They had a change of car too. Jim now drove an Austin Maxi. I realised that soon I was going to be homeless. Nick came to the rescue, saying I could stay with Him and Sue.

55 OASIS AND THE THREE DAY WEEK

Eventually Jim made the move. He worked his notice at Unigate. He was committed now. House sold, Nick allowed me to store the bulk of their furniture in a corner of the furniture store, until the time that they had somewhere to move it to. I was happy about that because it meant that I had mum's piano to play when it was quiet at The Oasis Garage and Furniture Centre.

As promised Margaret had spoken with David Powell at Eagle Brewery. Jim was immediately offered a job delivering beer around Mid Wales. Adam and David were enrolled into School. Sally was looking for work.

I would drive up to visit most weeks. It was a lovely journey to Newtown; the pace of life seemed so much more relaxing.

I was happy with my new job selling furniture. I recalled Mark Hallet's philosophy of shop window display design. To him it was an art form. His idea was always about the flow of the eye. Place the items in such a way that the eye will follow and see everything on display. Instead of putting all tables together, I created a display area with room settings. The back part of the large showroom was used for storage.

Business was good; money was being earned at Oasis. Until I had a glimpse into the future of what was about to occur. One day I was overseeing delivery of petrol from the large Esso tanker. There was a shortfall in the delivery. I asked the driver why we were not getting our full order. "Petrol shortage I'm afraid." Was his answer? "You wait and see by December petrol is going to cost 50p per gallon!" Not a chance I thought. It could never be that expensive!

It was around about this time that our Conservative Prime Minister Edward Heath was having a squabble with Joe Gormley, President of the Coal Miners Union. With a Labour government in power, the unions had become quite used to getting their own way. Ted Heath was having none of it. He was not going to have the nation held to ransom by a bunch of coal miners. He would fight them.

This was going to be the very crisis that would topple our world at Oasis. The result of which would then send me along my true path.

Both businesses Roger's T.P.L. and Nick's Oasis were in their infancy. There was no start up capital to speak of. The businesses were able to survive on cash flow. As long as there was cash flow. Up until now, the British economy was booming, people had money to spend on cars and furniture, and both businesses encouraged people to spend that money with them.

Then Edwards Heath's squabble with the miners started to bite the British economy. The miners went out on strike. Soon a number of other unions downed tools in sympathy. This caused the country to spiral into recession. All of a sudden luxury items like a new three piece suite would have to be put off until better times.

Both of the businesses descended into a cash flow crisis. Roger at T.P.L. was hit the quickest and the hardest. Mainly because his lifestyle had grown to reflect his new found prosperity. He and Jenny had bought a beautiful new house, and furnished it with stock from T.P.L.

Nick had chosen a number of items to improve his apartment, but he tended to keep his feet firmly on the ground. Nick was mindful of the responsibility he had towards his workforce in the garage. These were family men with their own responsibilities. The garage foreman Pete was beginning to show concern for our future.

There was talk of petrol rationing, and now our forecourt was running out of fuel between deliveries. When we had fuel to sell, people would fill their tanks to the brim for fear of not knowing where or when they will be able to get more.

Next was a coal shortage due to the miners strike. The consequences of this led to an electricity crisis, which led Eduard Heath to introduce a three-day working week.

Like many other businesses lacking; the financial latitude that a large hunk of capital provides. Without cash flow our businesses would be starved to death. Eduard Heath decided to call an election. Harold Wilson and the Labour government returned to number 10 Downing Street and the Unions returned to work.

We were hearing stories of failing business owners loosing every thing. Houses, cars. Nick advised me to leave my car in Newtown as a precaution. I could still use the Sprite that now belonged to him.

I had been seeing a girl. I was invited to a party at a neighbour of John Chawner's. The daughter Lynne took a shine to me, and we spent the whole time kissing in the living room whilst I held squeezed and stroked her quite delectable bottom. I was quite puzzled that her parents didn't intervene and stop such goings on. They did not seem to mind at all. I was staying at John's that night and when we climbed into bed he said. "Well you seemed to be enjoying yourself tonight." No one was more surprised than me about what had occurred with Lynne in the presence of her parents. "Well I must admit, I never saw that coming." I replied. "You want to be careful with her." John said. "She's only fifteen!" "What?" I exclaimed with shock! "She had me fooled. She seemed to know exactly what she was doing. I had her down for our age"

She had invited me to go to a school friend's party. We arrived in the Sprite at a semi detached home in Worcester Lane. It was full of teenagers. The Mum and Dad of the house had gone out for the evening. I felt very old in this company. Girls and boys were snogging groping adolescently in every corner of the house. Giggling. Boys who hadn't hooked up with girls were downing the content of party pack beer cans, and making a mess. "I really love you." Lynne had said to me. "I've got your name on my pencil case." I began to feel very uncomfortable in this situation. At this time in our journeys, she was plainly too young for me.

Eventually the parents came home and the mother went hysterical over the mess that the kids had caused in the house. Quite rightly! She ran some kids out of an upstairs bedroom and once again yelled to her husband. "Condoms! I've found used condoms in my bedroom!" My embarrassment was increased when she noticed the obviously older me sitting with Lynne in the living room. "And you? You should know better!" I agreed.

After that, I had decided to leave this situation well alone.

One weekend alone at Nick's flat; there was a knock on the door. It was Lynne. She wore a light dress, the first time I saw her not in her tight jeans. This made her look her younger age "How did you find me." I asked "Telephone Directory." She replied shyly brushing her hair from her cheek. "I knew the name was Wellman that you stayed with. Have you any idea how many Wellman's there are in Birmingham? Loads!" I watched her skip down the hallway into the living room. We sat on the couch and she immediately started to kiss me. "Do you mind if we talk a little?" I said breaking off the kiss. "Okay" She said with a giggly smile. "What shall we talk about?" She really was very pretty but it was obvious that our journeys were not on the same path at this time. I was more mature and felt wrong about taking advantage of her. "Can I get you a Coke or something?" I offered. "Yes please, do you have ice?" I went to the Globe cocktail cabinet and took out two Coke bottles, placing them on the coffee table. I took two crystal goblets and walked to the door. "I'm just going to see if there is ice in the fridge." I opened the fridge and found a plastic tray full of ice cubes. I placed two ice cubes in each goblet and returned to the lounge.

I must of only been out of the living room for thirty seconds, but in that time Lynne had removed her dress bra and panties and there she was lying seductively on the sofa completely naked. "Surprise!" She said.

Surprise indeed! I placed the two Goblets on the coffee table and sat on the edge of the sofa, looking in wonder at this beautiful creature that lay before me. I lay beside her with my hands on her shoulders and kissed her gently on the forehead. "Lynne. This can't happen. I'm twenty and you are a fifteen year old schoolgirl." "Today is my birthday." She replied "I hope you have got something to give me for my sixteenth birthday." For a moment I thought it was my birthday too. I kissed her brushed the back of my hand across her breast. I could feel her nipple rubbing on my skin. I squeezed her warm now naked bottom.

I looked into her eyes. Normally at this stage I would expect a look of steamy anticipation over what was about to be shared. Instead I sensed apprehension. "Lynne is this the first time you have ever done this?" I asked. She looked like she was about to get something over with that she was supposed to do. "Yes, but its Okay. I don't mind. You can do it to me." She replied. I sensed her nervously bracing herself.

This just felt wrong. I had enjoyed kissing her and touching her lovely bottom at her parent's party. I had fantasised about how it would be to go further. Now she was offering her body to me. Allowing me to be the first to explore its delights.

Julie and I had enjoyed discovering the wonders of intimacy together over a period of time. Lynne should share that journey with someone. "I can't take this from you Lynne." I said. "It's too precious." We lay together for a while just kissing. I ran my hand down her back and lovingly squeezed the cheek of her warm bottom. Then I helped her get dressed and she was gone.

Christmas 1973 was approaching. Mum and Jim had bought an end terrace house in Newtown. They were using some of their capital to renovate it and add some extra rooms. We arranged for their furniture and bits and pieces to be transported to Newtown.

I spent Christmas with the family in Wales. I was beginning to see the appeal of relocating there myself. It was likely my job was soon to go. There was nothing to hold me to Sutton Coldfield any more.

New Years Eve came. Nick and Sue were still in Bristol with family for the festivities. John was doing some thing with his girlfriend Val so I was facing the prospect of New Years Eve alone. Television was traditionally always crap on New Years Eve, so I decided to go to the pub.

The White Lion was heaving! Christmas Decorations still adorned the brass lamp fittings on the wall and ceiling. Loud music was blaring from the sound system, interrupted by the sound of party horns and laughter. A huge 1973-1974 banner hung from the ceiling above the bar. I got myself a pint of M and B Bitter and stepped away.

I noticed her stood by one of the shelves, which ran around the pillars. Jet black and short wavy hair. Tight black trousers and a waistcoat to match. She had mascara staining her cheek where she had been crying. I walked up to the mysterious girl in black and tried to make myself heard above the din.

"Why so sad? It's New Years Eve!" "He's done it again. My bloody boyfriend." She protested. "I don't know why I came here, I knew he wouldn't show up." "Well I guess that is two of us now who have got no one to share a New Years Kiss with." I answered. "Tell you what, I'll make a deal with you. If Twelve O Clock arrives and he hasn't shown, I'll kiss you if you like."

Where did that come from? I thought. My shyness would normally prevent me from saying such a thing! She looked at the time on her watch, pointed her finger sky ward beckoning me to look at the sprig of mistletoe directly above us. "It's a deal, but I tell you what. Why wait?"

The time was 10-30. By Midnight; Nick's couch was once again hosting a naked lady. This time two revellers seeking the same celebrated the New Years Eve with no holds bared. As we saw 1974 in, in the best way ever to the flickering light of the television screen. Somehow the awful TV show featuring Scotsman Andy Stewart didn't seem to matter.

I drove her home in the Sprite and she invited me in for a coffee. Her parents had gone to bed. The living room had a large fireplace with a gas fire. We kissed some more and before we knew it, we were once more lying naked together this time on the sheepskin rug, in front of the warm gas fire.

As I pointed the Sprite towards the flat, I realised I didn't even know her name. Or she mine.

56 A JOURNEY WEST

I gazed out of the grubby window at a sea of darkness, interrupted by the occasional shaft of sunlight, illuminating the tunnels grimy brickwork. My train was on a different track out of New Street Station to the norm. The time had come for my journey to take me in a different direction.

Eventually the carriage became bathed in the mid day sunlight filtered through a sheet of dreary cloud cover that was so often the case in Birmingham. Rain began to drizzle down the pane of glass and form swirling eddies in its corners in the wind.

I passed through a scene of industrial midlands. Large factory buildings with smoke billowing out of the chimneys that formed the Birmingham skyline. Evidence of the canal network still existed as a reminder of how communication had first been in earlier days of the industrial revolution.

As the train gathered speed the scenery outside became a motion blur. Accompanied by the clickity clack of the metal wheels as they passed over the joins in the track. My focus began to turn inwards. I thought back over the previous year. So much had changed. Julie and I had finally set each other free, letting go of our childhood daydreams of a life together forever. I now felt a huge sense of gratitude towards our destiny, which allowed us to share our precious journeys for a little time together.

Moving westwards the view outside became less of a blur as the murky brick walls gave way to hedgerows and then fields. I felt a little apprehensive about life without the Dog Inn Jazz club. This had been the sound track of my life for a long time. I wondered about how my musical journey was to continue. Could this be the end of my musical journey after all? I wasn't quite as willing to discard that childhood daydream. I felt troubled about letting that one go.

Nick and Sue had come back from their Christmas break in Bristol. Over the holidays they had been discussing their future. Oasis was going to have to go into receivership. They had decided to return to Bristol and Nick was going to study law. This did not come as a huge surprise to me. We more or less saw the writing on the wall before Christmas. We didn't want to spoil Christmas for the garage lads and their families. But now it was time to look the reality straight in the eye.

There would be a creditors meeting at some point, when the company would go into liquidation. As a limited company; we would be protected from bankruptcy. But from now on it was important that we were seen to follow the right procedure.

We held a meeting with the lads in the garage. They were not stupid; they were expecting something like this. Some of them had already sounded out other contacts should they need them. So to our relief, everyone parted on good terms. Pete, the garage Forman came back into the office to speak with us. "I could see where this was going. It's been a struggle. Who could have expected the three day week and petrol shortage?" He said. "It's been a great privilege to work with you lads. Thanks for letting us have our Christmas."

My Newtown bound train continued its journey through Shropshire and into Mid Wales countryside.

The sun was starting to break through the cloudy sky now and I could feel its warmth on my face. I looked at a patchwork of undulating green fields, divided by dry stonewalls. The same scenery that John Chawner and I had been in awe of as we arrived in Newtown for the first time.

I began to wonder about what this new adventure had in store for me. Last year had been a year of wonder that I could never have predicted. I briefly caught my reflection in the train window. I noticed that I wore a wry smile, as I thought about my anonymous companion in black. Unlike that inappropriate episode with the adolescent Lynne. This was a case of two ships passing in the night. Nonetheless; together we rescued each other from a lonely New Year Eve. 1974 started well thanks to that chance liaison.

I doubted that the rest of the year could be any kind of match for that beginning. I was job less, gig less, girl less, home less as I travelled surrendering my fate blindly to destiny.

Little did I know as the train started to brake to a halt at Newtown Station; that 1974 was to see all of this change.

It would become the start of the most significant changes in my journey ever!

But, reader. That is another book!

ABOUT THE AUTHOR

A full time Professional Entertainer since the Mid 1970's Simon John G Edgington. Stage name "SIMON JOHN" has enjoyed a musical career that has taken him to all corners of the world.

A career initially inspired by a love of Show Business, particularly the spectacle that is Live Music. Simon began his professional career in Wales, playing organ in local bars. This was soon augmented by his renowned vocal talent, progressing to synthesisers, keyboards and eventually Piano. Simon honed his craft in UK Working Men's Clubs and Holiday Parks.

He was engaged as an Entertainments Manager for Haven Holidays through the eighties during Summer Seasons. Off season Simon would entertain in Hotel Piano Bars Worldwide.

In the early Nineteen Nineties, Simon moved residence to Torrevieja Spain, and continued to entertain on the Costa Blanca.

Today. Simon is mostly found at sea as a much loved Cruise Ship Guest Entertainer. His First Book "Tinkle Tinkle Little Star" Is an Autobiography covering a childhood and adolescence inspired by music of the Sixties.

41849845R00161

Made in the USA
Charleston, SC
13 May 2015